THE CONSTANT SEARCH

COLLECTING MOTORING & MOTORCYCLING BOOKS

Charles Mortimer

ISBN 0 85429 260 8

© Charles Mortimer

First published March 1982

A FOULIS book

Printed in England by the publishers
Haynes Publishing Group
Sparkford, Yeovil, Somerset BA22 7JJ, England

Distributed in North America by
Haynes Publications Inc.
861 Lawrence Drive, Newbury Park,
California 91320, USA

Editor: **Jeff Clew**
Cover design: **Phill Jennings**
Layout design: **Tim Rose**

Contents

An Introduction to Motor Literature Collecting (Chapters and Sub-Headings)

The Constant Search

Foreword

The number of books about motor-cars and motoring is quite prodigious. I should know, because I seem to have reviewed most of them during the past thirty-five years! Add to that the increasing quantity of titles covering motorcycles, commercial vehicles and aviation, and anyone dealing with such books, setting up a transport-library, or just wondering what to search for as stimulating reading about cars and periods of personal appeal, must be, to say the least, often confused. Even knowledgeable motor-book folk need an overall picture, in order to be able quickly to sort out the vast array of material available.

This is what Charles Mortimer, whom I associate as much with the nostalgic pleasure of pre-war Brooklands motor-racing as with the quieter pursuit of knowledge and enjoyment in the library, seeks to provide, in this comprehensive survey of appropriate books and periodicals. Armed with it, you can set forth to the autojumbles, the auction-sales, the secondhand book vendors, well able to get what you seek and save time in so doing.

The Hall,   BILL BODDY
Nantmel, Powys.   Editor: *Motor Sport*

Acknowledgements

With the Classification of Titles completed to the extent that details were known, it was found that details of some two hundred titles were lacking having, over the years, slipped through the net. In many cases it amounted to just one piece of information such as the name of the author or publisher, or even the year of publication but, in others, only the title was known. To track down the missing information involved quite considerable research and requests for help from a number of people, all of whom were generous in the help and time that they gave.

Lt.Col.Barrass was most kind in helping me not only with information concerning the Rolls-Royce Enthusiasts' Club of which he is Secretary but also with other aspects of Rolls-Royce, and my friend David King not only helped me with Rolls-Royce information but also sought out details of a number of very early titles, which he mailed me from the States.

Wilson McComb, whom many think of as purely MG orientated, but whom I know to be enormously knowledgeable on a wide vista of motoring, gave me great assistance and encouragement. On the motorcycle side, Bruce Main-Smith was good enough to give me the run of his well stocked shop in Dorking, which enabled me to halve the gaps in this area.

Peter Brockes, Reference Librarian of the National Motor Museum at Beaulieu, inherited from me some real 'stumours' and I am grateful not only to him but also to the Museum, which has done so much not only for authors but for motoring and motoring enthusiasts generally.

My friend Cyril Posthumus has never once failed me in any situation, no matter how busy he may be at the time, and I must also thank another good friend, Richard Poulter, for clearing up one or two points regarding *Autocourse* and *Motocourse*, even though he was moving at the time and had to unpack his records of these and also *Automobile Year*.

Peter Richley, who has been collecting for longer than anyone I know, has the most comprehensive collection I have ever seen, the greatest knowledge of the subject and should, therefore, really have been the author of this book. He leant over backwards to help me, and no words I can say, or write, can express my thanks sufficiently. I first saw Peter's library some ten years ago and, though it amazed me even then, it made me feel very small indeed when I saw it again a short time ago. I have never cherished the thought that 'The Constant Search' would do more than help motor literature collectors and, after spending a full day with Peter, my feeling is that it does go further than scratching the surface of the subject to the extent that it makes a fairly substantial dent. What I did wish, at the end of that day, was that I had developed and kept such superb records of everything and even trumped his ace on some things. But knowing his application and dedication, that could never have been possible!

Even though he had moved since we last corresponded and had become involved with new interests, John Schroder, whose knowledge of every aspect of Rolls-Royce and particularly its literature must be at least as great as anyone's, was good enough to unravel some intricacies for me, and without his help there could still have been gaps. After speaking to him on the 'phone, I wrote, sending a copy of the standard form we used for classifications and his letter replying said 'I am sending you photocopies as your form is not big enough for all the information. I think I have found the lot. If you have any more queries, do not hesitate to come back to me. I love research work'!

Stanley Sedgewick kindly helped me with one or two Bentley mysteries and so did my friend Geoff Goddard in several directions. And Frank Stroud who, with his son Clive, runs that old established firm, Chater and Scott. I don't recall how many visits I paid to Isleworth or how many gaps Frank and Clive filled for me, but to put it mildly there were so many that, in the end, I began to wonder whether I dared call again. The help and information they gave me was so great and spread over such a long period that I can never thank them enough.

Mr Tee gave me helpful information concerning

Motorcycle Sport and I must also thank many old friends and customers of my business who have kept in touch, sometimes coming up with items that they thought I might not know about and, more than once, they were right!

My friend, motor racing photographer Geoff Goddard, went to great trouble in solving the problem of illustrations for the book and, as I breathed a sigh of relief on that front, another headache arose in the discovery that we still had no suitable colour photograph for the dust jacket. By then time was the factor and, unable to contact Geoff, I unloaded the problem onto anyone who would listen, including my family. My daughter, Pippa, had a friend, Tim Walder, who in turn had a friend, Graeme Scaife, who they both thought may be the very man.

Graeme's work, the dust jacket, is the result of three hours work on a Saturday afternoon and shows Tim, the 'poseur', seated in a very small corner of a very small cottage loaned for the occasion by other good motorist friends to whom I am as grateful as I am to Graeme, Tim and Philippa.

Perhaps, most of all, I must express sincere thanks to Mrs Barbara Haine who, for many years, looked after the secretarial and administrative side of my bookselling business. It was Barbara who, for countless years, operated the foolproof system she had devised to ensure that when books were sold, none left the premises with details unrecorded and it was I who, time and time again, somehow contrived to beat the system at times when we were under pressure. Her patience was limitless and, in the end, she devised a 'long stop' back up system which even I couldn't beat!

I am grateful to my publishers for having given me the opportunity to write the book and, particularly, to Jeff Clew, their Executive Editorial Director, the most patient of men, who inherited the problem of editing it. I hope that, from their point of view, it goes well.

I sincerely hope that I have forgotten no one, but the writing and setting out has taken so long that this is possible. If this should be the case, let me say that I am more than grateful for help I have had from all sources, clarifying problems, some of which may even have cropped up five, or more, years ago.

Author's Note

The thought that there should be a book written concerning the literature of motoring first occurred to me back in the mid-1950s. I had begun to collect books and magazines long before then, around 1925 in fact, and continued until 1930 when the need to finance my own first powered transport caused the sale of my entire collection. From 1930, almost to the start of World War Two, I was so busily involved in motoring, motorcycle and car racing that I hardly gave a thought to literature although, in the early part of 1939, I did start again to build up another collection.

In the late 1940s and early fifties, new motoring titles began to emerge by the score and I added what seemed to be the best of these until, by 1955, I again had a good, but not very big, collection. By then, I had become an avid reader of *Motor Sport* and an irresistible urge to acquire the complete run, back to 1924, caused, once again, the sale of my book collection. Though, at the time, I didn't realise it, that decision was, in the end, to make quite big changes in my life because, in order to get all the early copies I needed, I found that time and time again I had to buy many that I already had. These I sold off and, in almost no time, I found that without knowing it I had become the proud proprietor of a brokerage business in back copies of *Motor Sport*.

Sometimes, in order to get copies that I needed, I had to buy complete libraries, keeping the better books and selling off the 'dross', so that for the third and last time I became a collector, and have been ever since. By 1959 I was both collector and part-time dealer and a year later a full-time dealer. I wished then that there was a book concerning the literature of motoring and, feeling that sooner or later one must be written, I started to gather up and record details of titles, just in case it didn't happen. This is how the idea of this book came to be born more than twenty years ago.

Throughout the fifties, sixties and seventies my business grew, and I was fortunate in buying many fine motoring libraries and in building up an equally good collection of my own. In 1979 I was paid the compliment of being asked to value the contents of the library of the National Motor Museum at Beaulieu, which I did over a period of many weeks. Though interesting and enjoyable, it left me with the feeling that where bookdealing was concerned, I had come to the end of the road. Almost all the time spent in dealing had been good fun but, over the years, the business had become increasingly demanding in terms of time, and I now wanted to write. So I disposed of the business and sat down to write this book — a book that I never, for one moment, had expected to write or, earlier on, would have felt able to write. I thought long and hard before starting.

I hope that this book will provide not only good references but also make interesting reading. It is in no sense an encyclopaedia but rather a guide to what is currently thought of as 'collectable' where books are concerned, with certain other aspects added.

Interest in motor literature collecting really began after World War Two, but it has increased ever since and still shows no sign of abating. In this context, thirty years is a long time and a motor car manufactured in 1950 will appear to a thirty year old as antique as one turned out in 1883 would to me.

1883? Were there any motor cars in 1883? Not really, so it's a sobering thought to reflect that, at the ripe old age of sixty eight, I was born only twenty years after the first motor cars appeared on the roads of Britain. The point is that with so many younger collectors entering the field, there is a vast band of motor literature collectors who, through their own efforts, enthusiasm and research, have learned a lot but still want to know more about what has been written. I therefore hope that at least some of the answers will be found here.

There are, of course, specialist collectors in every sphere. Maybe they will find less that is new to them — it depends on how long they have been specialising. Even so, there may well be something because, over the years I have maintained contact with many specialists, apart from titles I have come across myself.

Chapter 1

The Eras of Motoring

When one looks at today's wide and congested roads and motorways and compares the scene with that at the turn of the century, it is hard at times to understand how such a transformation could have happened in so short a time span of eighty years.

Though I was born in 1913, my first clear recollections of motoring occur some four or five years later, towards the end of World War One. We lived in Surrey where, even in wartime, motoring seemed to be on the increase but the fuel shortage was noticeable with many large and even small saloon cars running on coal gas, supplied from vast and billowing gas bags firmly fixed to their roofs. I can recall many of today's fine macadam roads in the county as little more than dusty tracks, potholed and repaired with barrow loads of flint, and for every one car spotted at that time there must be a hundred or more now.

Surprisingly, the design of cars seemed to progress rapidly in those years for I never recall seeing what would now be termed a 'veteran' in daily use, though there were steam traction engines galore and steam wagons too. At the time, some cars on the roads certainly looked older than others but it wasn't until after the war that, to me, nearly all cars looked 'modern'. As far as I was concerned our family motoring really began at that point, for my parents invested in a new car, the first of the post-war Austin 'Twenty' tourers. I still recall clearly our whole span of ownership of that car, from the day it arrived from the agents till the day it was sold. By the ratings of today, that car was either Edwardian or vintage, for the first to emerge from the factory came out in 1918. So what are the Eras of Motoring? They are

1 **Veteran**   Cars manufactured prior to 1905
2 **Edwardian**   Cars manufactured from 1905 to 1918
3 **Vintage**   Cars manufactured from 1919 to 1930
4 **Post-Vintage Thoroughbred**   Certain cars manufactured from 1931 onwards.

These are the Eras set out by the Veteran Car Club of Great Britain, and by the Vintage Sports Car Club, after much discussion and thought. Even though later designations such as 'Historic' seem to have crept in from time to time, these four remain. When one thinks about it, dating and classifying must always be a headache to the various Committees concerned, with outstandingly good and beautiful cars continuing to emerge year by year, thus changing the picture constantly.

I have never known where my absorbing interest in cars came from. It was there as far back as I can remember and still is, even though, later in life, other interests emerged without taking its place. Not only cars, but motorcycles as well, although that was inevitable — it meant getting power propelled sooner!

The period in my life that involved waiting to start motoring seemed to be eternal and throughout the whole of it I did the next best thing — I read. I could never understand why, at a time when everyone seemed to be turning to motoring, there were almost no books on the subject so that today one can see the scarcity of good books during that era more clearly than ever. But throughout the 1920s and 1930s, I never ceased to take both *The Autocar* and *The Motor Cycle,* those wonderful weeklies that kept one in touch with all that was going on. How I wish, now, that I had kept them.

So, from the point of view of motoring, I grew up in the vintage era, and I still think that that was the best period of all. At the time, motor and motorcycle racing was my passion but, of course, as one gets older, one's tastes change and though one seldom loses completely the interests of youth, other aspects creep in.

For many, but not for all young people, it was a wonderful period. Unlike today, money was scarce, but if one had £1 in one's pocket it really bought something and that applied to motoring and motorcycling as well as to everything else.

The roads were nowhere near as good as they are today though they carried the traffic far more comfortably. What bottlenecks there were occurred mainly at week ends on routes between London and the coast for, to many, the small car and motorcycle combination were starting to open up the countryside for thousands who had never seen it.

In every respect it was a boom time for motoring except, possibly, for the literature of motoring. To me, it has always seemed that the real shortage lay in the scarcity of good books on motor racing, for the personalities were there to write them and there was much to write about.

Charles Jarrott with his *Ten Years of Motors and Motor Racing* first published in 1907, and S.F.Edge with his *My Motoring Reminiscences,* were two early exceptions, and Sir Malcolm Campbell, Sir Henry Segrave and Capt.G.E.T.Eyston joined in during the 1930s, supported by George Monkhouse with his beautifully illustrated *Motoraces* and *Motor Racing with Mercedes Benz* and Barre Lyndon with *Combat, Circuit Dust,* and *Grand Prix.* Books on motor racing by drivers less well known must surely have found a market because the famous were already established and, at the time, there were so many who longed to get into motor racing but found difficulty in knowing how to start, and what the problems were.

Still the shortage continued and it wasn't until after the war that motoring books written by all and sundry began to emerge, first in a trickle, then in a flood and, finally, in a torrent. It was this that caused me to write my own first book, *Racing a Sports Car,* published by Foulis way back in 1951, for it seemed to me that then, more than ever, countless young drivers yearned to get into racing but were deterred largely by lack of knowledge and by the possible cost. Good sports cars were emerging from Jaguar, Frazer Nash, MG, Healey and many other factories, all either suitable for sports car racing or, at least, easily adaptable. It seemed to me that if one raced such a car, and described not only the racing but also the preparation and the cost, there could well be a market — and there was. It may not have been the greatest of literary gems but it sold because it came out at the right time, told young aspirants what they wanted to know and, most important of all, told them the cost. With hindsight, it did a little more, for it is still the only book to have been written concerning the Silverstone Healey and, years later, Tony Brooks told me that it was through buying and reading *Racing a Sports Car* that he bought and raced a Silverstone and went on to reach Grand Prix stardom. So it does seem to me that if, in the 1920s and '30s, books of that sort written by less well-known names had appeared on the shelves of book dealers, some of the races at Brooklands, for instance, could well have been far better supported.

Each decade had its highlights of course. Like most others, I only know what I have read of motoring and motor racing in the early 1900s, but I would dearly love to have motored to Paris and on through France to see some of those great early classics such as the Paris-Madrid or, for that matter, any of the Grands Prix that took place up to 1914. Virtually all the competitors were giants, and so were their cars, and the records of those races will never die. And, racing apart, that first decade was an era of enormous progress and development for, in it, the motor car emerged from an appallingly primitive conveyance, unreliable, limited in range and hard to control, to something which did resemble most of the cars manufactured in the decade following.

Apart from the higher priced cars, the 1930s seemed to me to be a period of decline caused, largely, by the policy of mass production which, though obviously progressive, had the effect of making the run of the mill models appear not only shoddy by comparison with those of the 'twenties' but also completely lacking in individuality and character. Reliability had, by then, long since been accepted but, in many cases, character had disappeared without being compensated for by increased efficiency and performance. But throughout that period the high price range continued to improve and few could be denied the title of 'Classic'. Take Rolls-Royce alone, for example — 20/25, 25/30hp and Wraith, and in the larger range Phantoms II and III, many of them elegantly styled by leading coachbuilders such as H.J. Mulliner, Barker, Freestone and Webb, Thrupp and Maberley and others.

It was a good period for motor racing too, made even better by the entry into Grand Prix racing of Mercedes and Auto Union in 1936 culminating, for us, in the appearance of both teams at Donington in 1937 and 1938. What a lift that was. They say 'See Naples and die'. The same could be said of the Mercs and Auto Unions — once seen, never forgotten. But it all came to a sad, sad end in 1939.

Nothing lasts for ever, though, and in the late 1940s racing restarted after a couple of years of hill climbs and sprints only. It had to be that way because not only was there a dearth of usable circuits but virtually everything was scarce in the 'recovery' period — cars, spares, fuel, tyres — everything. But Shelsley, Prescott and the odd airfield did at least enable one to recapture the sound and the smell of racing cars which, after all those years, was so good as to enable us — almost — to forget circuit racing. In the end it fell to a small British automobile club, the Cambridge University, to put on the first full scale motor race meeting held in Great Britain for six years. I still recall every detail of the events that ran up to that because members of the club were, at the time, customers of mine and I even recall my feeling that they must be suffering from a severe dose of over-optimism in their idea of such a project. Months before it happened, I went up to Gransden airfield in the passenger seat of my old friend George Abecassis' two litre supercharged Alta, meeting Earl Howe who was representing the RAC and the committee of the club. I watched George take the noble Earl round the circuit and recall even now the latter's words when they pulled in at the end of the run 'Splendid George, nothing wrong with that, we'll do it'. And that was the restart of motor racing in Great Britain after World War Two. The Club was

given help in organising by the Vintage Sports Car Club and the event was run with a programme of short races and one fifty mile Formula Libre race on June 15th, 1946.

Heaven known how much midnight oil was burned in efforts to get cars to the line on the day, but what a day it was. For me, the highlight was the fall of the starter's flag for the fifty mile race in which I was running my single-seater Maserati Type 4C and the surprise at finding that, as I looked down the long straight at the end of the first lap, there were only six cars ahead and that whereas I had only 1½ litres, nearly all were bigger capacity and led by Poore's big 3.8 litre Grand Prix Alfa Romeo. A lap later I had passed one and found myself on the tail of Ken Hutchinson's 2.9 Alfa, which soon began to puff out smoke on the over-run and retired at about half distance. The Maserati was a joy to drive — far more like a sports car than a racer and, even after its long wartime sleep it was running as happily as it had in pre-war years. I began to wonder what had happened to all the ERAs and to think that I might not only finish in the first six but also be the first 1½ litre home, but soon I saw, in my mirror, another shape looming up astern, the big Darracq of Leslie Johnson and after a short scrap, found there was nothing I could do about that. So the finishing order turned out to be Poore (3.8 Alfa Romeo), Abecassis (3.3 Bugatti), Salvadori (2.9 Alfa Romeo), Johnson (4.0 Darracq) with my game little 'Maser' fifth. The mystery of the ERAs was solved, for all had proved difficult to extract from 'mothballs', unlike my willing little car.

In fact, though this was certainly the first post-war motor race in UK, it wasn't the first public appearance of racing cars for, on July 14th, 1945, that great motoring enthusiast Rivers Fletcher had staged a 'demonstration' at a building site at Cockfosters, North of London and this, too, had been well attended. Though only a 'demonstration', the event became quite competitive on the day and the course was packed with spectators totally unprotected either from the elements or the 'demonstrators' and I have always since admired 'Rivers' for his confidence in the latter, and felt glad that it wasn't misplaced.

Initially, and for some time, car styling in the late 1940s was generally pretty dreadful, seeming to be, in many cases, nothing more than a flamboyant re-hash of the worst of the late 1930s though, mercifully, there were notable exceptions. Rolls-Royce, with its radiator mounted further forward was, to the purist, a little hard to accept at first but soon looked right even to him. In any case, little or nothing had been lost in the styling of the coachwork or the quality and excellence of the product, and the same applied to Bentley, of course.

The new Morris Minor, initially with its side valve engine from the Series 'E', and later to become the Morris 1000, was a gem right from the start. In its day, it was the classic among all small cars and, even today, is fast becoming a collector's item. But it fell to William Lyons of Jaguar to really 'ring the bell'. Lyons, who had always been a genius for both style and value for money right back from the days of the Swallow sidecar, the 'SS', and later the SS-Jaguar, not only rang the bell but sent it right off the clock with a range of modestly priced and superbly styled cars which received the same acclamation as does each new model announced by the firm today. New makes came into the field, notably Healey and, later, Austin Healey. At the time, the Healey Elliott sports saloon was considered by many to be one of the most attractively-styled cars of its period and the Silverstone sports two-seater one of the best value for money. The pre-war Frazer Nash-BMW became the Frazer Nash and, though expensive when compared to the Healey range, was both faster and lighter despite its smaller engine capacity. Many new makes entered the fray but not so many survived and some pre-war, notably Bugatti, sadly left. As a great enthusiast for Bugatti, having raced a 2.3 litre Type 35 at Brooklands in the years immediately preceding the war, this has always seemed the greatest tragedy of all.

From time to time one hears a gathering of enthusiasts discussing which were the classic decades. Though not everyone can agree, partly because not everyone looks at a decade from the same viewpoint, very few will dispute the claim that, in most respects, the 1950s were 'golden' years both from the viewpoint of road car development and from racing. This isn't the place at which to go into the claim in detail, but there can be little doubt that production and development in design of both road and racing cars did forge ahead fast during those years even though, while efficiency increased, as the positioning of the engines of racing cars changed from front to rear, something was lost in individuality. But that is progress and no one can deny it, so in the 1960s and '70s progress in racing car design continued on those lines even though, today, different manufacturers of road cars have their own particular ideas on the subject.

No essayist of a general motoring tome of this nature could possibly overlook the Mini. Nor will I because, even though its strange shape and unorthodox layout took me time to accept, I haven't been without a Mini for the past ten years now. It is said that when one enquirer asked Alec Issigonis whether it would be possible to design a smaller car to take four passengers and their luggage, he replied 'Certainly — no problem at all — but they'd have to travel standing up, of course.' A wonderful man who, besides advancing the design of the motor car in one big leap ahead, gave pleasure and a new type of motoring to millions. As a great admirer of Henry Ford, who actually gave motoring to millions, I would hesitate to claim that Issigonis gave more, although he did provide a car that was not only a resounding success for every day motoring but also for racing, rallying and even hill climbing. You name it and the Mini has done it.

And while talking of small cars, what of the Coopers, father and son? Their first 500cc single seater racing cars looked right and were, from the start. They were developed and developed, adapted to take 1000cc and 1100cc engines and later became a basis from which, finally, a highly successful Grand Prix car emerged. The rise of 500cc racing was just as exciting and inspiring as its demise was depressing and, of all types of motor racing, it has turned out to be the one worst chronicled from the point of view of literature. Even today, with 500cc racing long since dead and buried, enormous interest is maintained among collectors of motor racing of anything readable relating to the five hundred era.

Nor must one forget the design and development of the motorcycle, whose manufacturers provided the power units for so many of the 500cc cars. JAP, Norton, Vincent and others all played a part. But in this book, the motorcycle has its own section in which its ups and downs form part.

Chapter 2

The Techniques of Collecting

While I would hate the thought of the reader thinking of the following notes as a list of 'do's' and 'don'ts', it would surely be wrong to leave out any reference to collecting technique because so many people, myself included, have at one time or another embarked on the task with no clear plan in mind. Sooner or later, one finds either that one has run out of money or shelf space or even that, while collecting, one's tastes have changed.

In the first place, it pays, in today's conditions, not only to have as clear an idea as possible of what one wants to collect but also to buy it as soon as possible because, next year, it will be dearer and the year after that, dearer still. And if one does know, right at the start, what it is that one wants to collect, and assuming that it is something that is already in fairly short supply, it is probably right to close one's eyes and buy it whenever or wherever it is offered. By this I mean that nearly every collector, myself included, thinks that the item or items he is offered are too dear — no matter how much he wants them, with the result that, very often, he fails to take the offer up — and subsequently pays a higher price later on.

What it really boils down to is deciding, before you start, exactly what it is that you want and, in saying that, I realise, of course, that almost everyone who reads this will already have started! Even so, it may not be too late to change course if indeed there are thoughts of doing so anyway. Most established collectors would not only agree with this but would probably agree also that if one has

gone a long way down the 'collecting' road, changing is expensive but better than continuing down the wrong or even poorly defined road.

To me, then, Rule Number One is

collect what you like

Whether you regard your collection of motoring literature purely as a source of enjoyment and pleasure, or whether you regard it as an investment, or both, collect what you, yourself like, because doing it that way, you will always get pleasure. If you like the collection yourself, the day may come when you decide to sell it and you will almost certainly find that someone else will like it also.

Specialising

Sooner or later you may find that almost without being aware of it you are specialising, that is to say collecting a particular type of item such as marque or even something of a more general nature like sales literature, programmes and photographs,

The Constant Search

and my own feeling is that specialising is always good. Wherever one goes, such as markets, sales, auctions and autojumbles, one hears collectors saying how scarce everything is and to some extent this is true. But there's no doubt that if one becomes known and established as a specialist collector, one does get offered things that one would never know about if one's particular interest was unknown to vendors.

In this connection, one has to bear the obvious in mind — that as a specialist one will, from time to time, be offered things at inflated prices. But this is no problem — the answer is a polite 'No thanks' — and get a friend to buy it from the chap, a few days later, at its proper price.

How does one decide the proper price? Only by experience which, if one is specialising, does come much more quickly than one would think and this, I think, is another good reason to become a specialist. And there's another point here — that by specialising one quickly learns all about that particular sphere so that once one has 'got with it' one can widen and take in something else — and become a specialist in that as well.

On the price aspect, it is good to mix with and talk with not only other collectors, but dealers as well — and where possible listen rather than talk yourself. Collectors of all things are tremendous gossipers and one can learn no end, not only about collectable things but also about personalities — and this can be useful. I recall a sale where I heard one book dealer ask another is he had a particular book that I badly wanted myself. The reply was 'Yes' and the price £50. The buyer replied that he would call in next day, and maybe he did. I knew the vendor and went at once, not waiting for the sale, to his shop where I found the book marked up at £22 and bought it. At the time, I would have given £50 for it even though the price was high. But I could never decide why he had it originally marked up at £22.

The collector who is starting

The newcomer is better placed than anyone, even though he may not be sure where and how to start for, not actually having started, he has had no opportunity to make mistakes which can later prove expensive. If he starts on the basis of having a policy, being conscious of outlaying finance and of using his storage space to its best advantage, he is winning as from the moment he makes his first purchase. He should not be deterred by being told what a pity it is that he came into the thing so late in the day, or how much less expensive everything was a year or two ago, even though that may be true. He is in — he has started to collect and, like everyone else, he will have his failures and his successes but, unlike his advisers, he will be 'on course' right from the outset and, through making less mistakes, will be on a winning horse at once.

The established collector

Collectors exist in many different forms: private, trade, general, specialist and many others. Most have, at one time or another, made mistakes or at least changed course, become short of finance at the wrong moment, or run out of space through collecting the wrong type of thing. Certainly most will have recovered and got back on the road and some may even have forgotten. But it is a measure of the attraction of collecting that nearly all are still doing it and, if one talks to a group, few can recall anyone who has dropped out unless they specialised and ended up by acquiring all that they sought.

Hoarders

There's a big difference between a well laid-out collection and a hoard. There are 'collectors' and there are 'hoarders' and the basic difference between them is that while the true collector knows what things make up his collection, the hoarder has no idea. Some years ago, when I was trading, I had a 'phone call from a nice man who had a large collection of books for sale. No, he hadn't got a list of them but they were all good and mostly early books. Could he tell me just a few of the titles? He did this and the ones he mentioned were certainly good, but he lived some distance away and I would still have liked a list of them all. Though this couldn't be done because there were so many, there was one book he had always wanted and if I had that and would bring it with me he promised that I wouldn't go away empty handed. This book was Lyndon's *Combat* which he had never been able to find so, in the end, I took it with me. He was delighted and showed me his collection, all in one room and piled in great heaps around the floor. He left me to look through them while he went to make coffee and one of the first to come up was *Combat*! Looking through them all took the best part of an hour, in the course of which I found two more copies of *Combat*! I bought his collection and still have the memory of meeting a delightful 'hoarder'.

Keeping an inventory

The moral of this is to keep an inventory, bringing it up to date whenever additions are made and deleting books which have been sold. My own way of doing this has been to keep two typed copies of the inventory, showing not only the titles but also the date of purchase and the price paid.

Insurance

In these days, with inflation leading to price escalation in the case of almost every commodity, insurance is obviously a must and is made so much easier with an inventory. The rate is low for the cover that is given and though it is a good idea to keep touch with book prices, it isn't necessary to go through the whole thing, book by book, when the policy comes up for renewal — the value of the whole can be increased by a percentage each year.

Collecting Policy

My own policy, which may not be the policy of others, has been to concentrate and specialise in certain areas.

Books

I prefer books to other forms of motoring literature, partly because there is a wide variety, partly because I find them more enjoyable to own and read, and partly because they are easier to store. My way of collecting books has been to build up a library of books that I like, of as good a quality as possible both from the aspect of content and of condition, with as high a percentage of early books as possible. In other words, they must not only be readable and enjoyable but also in the finest condition possible. My years spent in trading helped me very much in getting together a collection of books in fine condition and, to me, that's important because, nowadays, though one does see some early books come up at auction and in the markets, nearly all are in poor, or at least mediocre, condition. Though many of my own books have dust jackets I am not too particular on this point. If I am offered a book with its dust jacket, I always remove it to look at the book itself because, in the past I have known vendors to offer a 'tatty' copy camouflaged in a 'mint' dust wrapper.

Though this hasn't happened in many cases, it's sad to reflect that, on each occasion that it happened to me, the vendor was private — not trade.

Content — that is to say the subject of a book — is purely a matter of personal preference. My own favourites are motoring autobiographies and biographies, the best of the marque histories, particularly Bugatti and Rolls-Royce, and the best of travel, both early and contemporary. I have found that, over the years, my tastes have changed to some extent and that while I have quite a high percentage of motor racing books, my interest in racing began to wane when I ceased racing and has waned even more from the end of the 1960s onwards. Though I realise that, to some extent, this is a result of old age, it doesn't apply, in my case, to books other than racing and I really do think that where marque books are concerned the 1970s have proved to be a 'golden' era. More lovely marque books have been published, I think, in the last ten years than at any other period and, here again, I have added to my own collection those that seem to me to be the best.

The Constant Search

Magazines

Though I still subscribe to *Motor Sport, Thoroughbred and Classic Car* and *Old Motor* and keep and bind them year by year, I confess to not being a great lover of magazines. But, here again, there are certain guidelines and I think they are —

Storing magazines. If you have magazines in your collection, **keep them carefully in the house so that they remain dry and bind them at the end of each volume or year.** Don't lend single copies to anyone, no matter how badly that person may need to scan the road test of a car that he owns because, more often than not, that is the last you will see of it. Where magazines are concerned, the value of a run depends largely on its **completeness** and so often one finds that, for some inexplicable reason, the copy one has lent is hard to find again.

Easibinders. Though they meet a need, I confess to disliking them. The types with string or elastic inserts don't hold the copies squarely and firmly and though the types with metal rods do, I have seen more valuable magazines wrecked through the rods rusting so that it is impossible to remove copies without tearing them, than by any other way. If one must keep magazines in Easibinders, then keep them in the house in the dryest place possible and **never in the garage** no matter how dry you believe the garage to be. **Few literature items relegated to the garage ever return if left there for long.**

Binding magazines (monthlies). The binding of monthlies presents no problem but here again there are 'ways and ways'. In the first place, not all magazines run from January each year to December. *Motor Sport,* for instance, has run volume by volume from January to December only since 1938, although before that, right from its start in June 1924, volumes didn't match years. *Thoroughbred and Classic Car,* to take one instance, started in October 1973 with the first volume ending at September 1974, and has continued ever since from October of each year to September of the next. So bind by volume and not by year and bind immediately the last copy of the current volume comes out, because £7 or £8 to bind one volume is less of a financial stumour than £70 or £80 to bind a decade. **But at all costs, if you have magazines, try to keep them bound** and not loose. They look better, command an infinitely better price if you decide to sell them, appreciate more quickly pricewise, and eliminate the need to lend single copies. And, of course, when bound they are far less likely to end up in the garage, which is certainly a bigger mortuary for literature of any kind, even than the loft.

Binding magazines (weeklies). Always a headache, with 52 copies amounting to two, three or even four volumes a year. The problem, of course, is twofold: bulk and cost or, put another way, storage space and cost. If neither of these are a problem then some weeklies are lovely things to have, particularly titles like *Motor, The Autocar, The Motor Cycle* or *Motor Cycling* in the 1920s — the most popular period of all for many magazines. *Autosport,* which began in 1950, is another, for it gives a lovely record not only of big time racing but also a high percentage of National and Club racing. *Autosport* in its early days bound neatly into two volumes a year, changing later as its size increased.

If you do decide to collect a weekly, particularly a pre-war one, bind it complete with covers and advertisements, no matter how big a volume it amounts to, because with this type of presentation, covers and advertisements form a great part of the interest. If I really felt my own library to be incomplete without a run of a bound weekly I would go for *The Autocar* and *The Motor Cycle,* bound 1925 to 1930 — all 'golden' years to many collectors. If space and finance were still no problem I would extend back to 1920 and then on to 1939, and be a very happy man.

Condition of magazines

The condition of magazines to be bound is not only important but also hard to check, particularly if the quantity being bought at any one time is large. Many vendors of magazines of all eras, and particularly elderly vendors, seem to have the habit of cutting out illustrations or even pages that were, for some reason, of particular interest to them. The mutilation of copies in this, or any other way, reduces their value drastically. The problem is that to check thoroughly, say a copy of *The Autocar* of the 1920s takes up to half a minute which, in the case of 300 copies, adds up to more than two hours during which the vendor will classify one as pernickety and will become restive. It's even more important to check, say, early *Motor Sport* which currently commands a price of £25 or more per copy. But there's no way round it. It either has to be done or waived and, if not done, the lot priced to allow for finding imperfections later. The method I adopted during my dealing days was to check every fifth copy and, if I found one cut, go back to the start and check the lot. Doing it that way is fairly safe — in a big lot, a cut copy always turns up sooner or later and if there's one, there will certainly be more. Copies should always be clean and complete with covers and advertisements even if, in the case of early copies, there is the occasional slight tear to a cover. The dealer's method of marking a cut copy of a magazine is to snip off the top right hand corner of the cover and one does see, from time to time, copies like this at sales and autojumbles even though the vendors may themselves have no idea of what it denotes. It goes without saying that no dealer, and very few collectors, would sell a cut copy without disclosing its faults.

Collating

While on the subject of imperfections, this may be the moment to revert to books. Early books in particular tend to shed illustrations and even sometimes pages. More often illustrations which, in the case of an early book, were usually glued in. A missing illustration from a book which may have

cost between £20 and £70 is serious, and even one missing page a disaster. Collating is the answer and if substantial money is changing hands, the time spent in collating is well worth the effort. If you find such a book or any other faulty or incomplete item in your collection, note its faults in the inventory because if you have no note, it's easy to forget. Better still, keep it in a place apart from the others. Contemporary books, partly because of their comparative youth and partly because production methods have improved, tend to be less of a headache.

'Ex Lib' Books

Books acquired from Public Libraries, and there are many in circulation, must always be regarded with suspicion, even though some can be found in good condition. There are many collectors to whom the thought of owning an 'Ex Lib' book is abhorrent but provided one is selective and collates such a book with care, exceptions can be made, even though I have only two in my collection. In the first place some rare and extremely good titles emerge from Public Libraries, books which would command high prices in the normal way. Prices of 'Ex Lib' books are always way below market value and some have fared better at the hands of their numerous readers than others. A deciding point can often be the degree of stamping in the book itself. Some libraries stamp only the title page or the blank page opposite the frontispiece, others stamp here and at the back and, occasionally, every illustration. Don't let anyone tell you that such stamp marking can be erased by placing an adhesive label over the marking and heating it with an iron. Occasionally it can, but far more often not. If it could, there would be far more 'Ex Lib' books on the market. The 'Ex Lib' area is one where the rule 'Caveat Emptor' prevails.

Scrapbooks

Many items cut from both magazines and even books go to make scrapbooks and, make no mistake, a really well-made and well laid-out scrapbook, particularly on a single aspect of motoring, such as marque interest or motor racing, will almost certainly become valuable one day. There has always been a strong interest in well laid-out scrapbooks on the right subjects and, in recent years, it has escalated enormously. A friend of mine who is elderly, retired and knowledgeable on motoring, spends countless hours scouring auto-jumbles in search of cut or otherwise mutilated books and magazines from which to make scrap-books. He doesn't make a fortune or even a living doing it, but he makes a useful profit, has a lot of fun, and supplements his pension.

Sales literature

The collection of sales literature, both car, motor-cycle and even cycle, has always been popular and is certainly absorbing. A good collection of early motor car sales literature, even if small, can be equal in value to the best of book collections. It can also occupy less shelf space, provided it is laid out with care. I know of no better way to lay out and store sales catalogues than slotting them into binders containing 'Clearview' plastic wallet holders, where they can be laid-out make by make and year by year. When one gets back to the 1910s and 1920s the format size of catalogues and broch-ures tends to vary from the miniature to the over-size, but this way is, I think, the best. Here again, it is a specialist field and not all that easy to learn if one is starting from scratch but, in any era, it would be true to say that with a few exceptions such as Austin Seven, it is the sporting or luxury type of make that commands the highest price.

Service literature

Though there is a constant demand for early ser-vice literature, I don't recall a single customer gathering it together as a collectable item of inter-est, during all the time I was in business. I don't say there are none, but I never met one.

Club magazines and journals

There are so many of these that we will leave quoting particular titles until reaching that section. Interest in them is vast, but there are snags. In the first place it is extremely difficult to find copies of club journals in the pre-war area and, even if one is successful, prices are becoming prohibitive. Sec-ondly, and for no known reason, so many clubs have, over the years, changed the format of their journal or bulletin. The Brooklands Society and the Veteran Car Club are cases in point, whereas the Bugatti Owner's Club and Vintage Sports Car Club have remained the same. But, either way, I wouldn't be without my run of Brooklands Society Bulletins or Bugantics, even though the latter looks nicer on the shelf. Where two wheels (pow-ered) are concerned, I like the Vintage Motor Cycle Club's Official Journal best, and when it comes to pedal power my favourite is the Cyclist's Touring Club Gazette.

Programmes

The programmes of Grands Prix and other motor races are popular among many many collectors and there are some specialists in the field. The interest lies mainly in pre-war and in Grand Prix and other important races post-war. Some others covering veteran events and one make functions such as Rolls-Royce also have a following. Many programmes of big pre-war motor races and meet-ings virtually amount to art items.

Commemorative brochures

Brochures can take many forms from motor racing and marque histories through to commercial and industrial. Nearly all are absorbingly interesting and the best of the pre-war are valuable. Again, easy to store and display, history in the making and always good browsing. Some of the most interesting and least expensive are those compiled and published in the early 1940s concerning the wartime contributions to the National effort made by leading motor manufacturers and allied firms. Probably the most expensive of all are those put out by manufacturers such as Bentley and MG, describing pre-war motor racing successes.

Photographs

Though not included within the confines of this book there is no denying that, in the literal sense, a fine collection of photographs, well laid out, can amount to a continuing record of history either of a specialised or general nature. Of all things, they are probably the easiest to display and, at the same time, take up the least space. Sources of supply are probably better than is the case with other items of motoring literature and, although I have only a few, there must be the best possible case for collecting them.

Letters and manuscripts

Usually of the famous and of personalities in the motoring and motor trade movement, they find their way to dealers so seldom that little can be said about them here. I can recall having bought only one during all the time I was in business — a letter from Rudyard Kipling to his Vauxhall dealer, strongly critical of the Vauxhall car he owned at the time. I had no difficulty in finding a loving home for it but I always thought that marque items of this nature tended to go straight from the auction room into the collections of the experts and enthusiasts concerned — and perhaps that is the way it should be.

Buying and buying sources

Broadly speaking, they amount to:

Private sources

These are the best if one is well in touch with prices. If not, and it is unlikely that the vendor will be better informed, the problem is obvious — you don't know what to offer and the vendor doesn't know what to accept. Even with knowledge, buying privately can be difficult because the workings of some vendors' minds are hard to fathom. Writing as a past dealer I would say that almost invariably the initial reaction of many private vendors is that they haven't an idea of the value of the item or items that they are selling. My own counter to that was always that if he had no idea of the value, how could he either accept or refuse whatever price I offered, and invariably this produced some idea of value — usually high — which was, at least, a point at which to start talking. I am thinking now about the purchase of a complete collection from which one wanted some books more than others, so that one would first try to buy the lot or, if that failed, to buy only those that one wanted. The latter was often easier because, having started from the point of the vendor's idea of value, one would divide the complete collection into two piles — wanted and not wanted, the latter pile always being at least twice the size of the former. On finding the price of the former much nearer one's own idea, instant acceptance of the offer sometimes follows. Even if not, one could often pull off the deal. The easiest vendor as far as I was concerned was the one who said to me 'You are the expert. I will accept what you offer'. I met quite a lot in this category and they always fared best because one was able to offer them, right away, the highest price to which one could go, whereas the 'haggler' would often accept a higher price than the original offer but one that was still well below that to which one would have gone in the end. But 'hagglers' are 'hagglers' and, to be truthful, I always rather enjoyed it myself!

When paying by cash, I always made a point of getting a receipt and, as the years went by, I found it increasingly necessary to look more carefully at what I was buying, always depending on the type of vendor with whom I was doing business. Strangely, quite a high percentage of those from whom I bought books returned to me years later, again as buyers, not of the type of book they had sold me but always on a totally different aspect of motoring. A far smaller number than one would expect seemed to lose interest completely in the subject.

In many cases, wives have a strong influence in the sale of a husband's collection for not only are they often thankful to have the space taken up by the books, but they will sometimes insist that in order to clinch a deal on the motoring books one had to take also a mass of books on other subjects. In this connection I once recall having to take a vast collection on a variety of subjects which, in an effort to avoid, I priced so low that I could hardly bring myself to name the figure. My offer was instantly accepted and that particular wife must have had her head screwed on because, though I came out quite well on the motoring, I not only made a loss on the others but also consumed a lot of time and petrol in unloading them.

Rebinding books

Increasingly, nowadays, one comes across copies of good early titles in tired condition or worse, and it is often difficult to decide whether or not something of this nature is beyond rescue. Any good book should preferably be in a good, or at least acceptable, condition from the aspect of desirability, and is always better left with its original binding, if possible.

But even so, rebinding is sometimes worthwhile and what has to be taken into account is (a) The popularity of the title were it in good and original condition, (b) Its value when rebound (c) Whether to rebind in leather, cloth or rexine and (d) The condition and completeness of the text and illustrations.

Where (a) is concerned, my own feeling is that to merit rebinding any title must be worth at least £20 in good and original condition, bearing in mind that even if expensively rebound it is unlikely to be worth more than if it were original. When considering (c) I really wouldn't consider rebinding any good title other than in leather and (d) The contents must be reasonably clean and complete and not lacking any illustrations.

Author interest

Fewer collectors in the motoring field are author orientated than in most other areas of literature and, here again, it is purely a matter of personal preference. In his day and in the area of motor racing particularly, the late Laurence Pomeroy was certainly one of the most revered and few would deny that, where motor racing history is concerned, Bill Boddy stands out today.

I confess that I have a few strong personal preferences, among them A.F.C.Hillstead for his *Those Bentley Days* and *Fifty Years with Motor Cars* both of which epitomise the low and highlights of motoring and motor trading in the 1920s and early 1930s. For the same reason, I have enjoyed most of W.O.Bentley's books.

Having in a modest way written one or two books myself, I know both the importance of accuracy and the problems of research and for these reasons I am a great admirer of authors like Cyril Posthumus and Doug Nye, both of whom seem to make almost no mistakes on whatever subjects they write. I also admire anyone possessing specialist technical knowledge and for that reason I love all of Hugh Conway's books concerning Bugatti which is, I think, the most under-written marque of any.

Marque histories, two or four-wheeled, are favourites of mine and where motorcycles are concerned I think that Jeff Clew's books are great, particularly the Velocette *Always in the Picture,* the Douglas *The Best Twin* and Scott *The Yowling Two Stroke,* and I wish Dr Joe Bayley would do a follow up to his *Vintage Years at Brooklands.*

Ghosting

Ghost writing, that is to say the writing of a book by someone other than the name on the spine and title page, is something that has probably happened for as long as books have been in existence. It is a major part of the business of some professional authors and a valuable service provided to many of the famous who, over the years, have perhaps not had the time, the inclination or even the ability to write their own books.

S.F.Edge's *My Motoring Reminiscences* was ghosted by St John Nixon. Sir Henry Segrave's *Lure of Speed* and many of Sir Malcolm Campbell's books were ghosted by Wentworth Day while Cyril Posthumus was the ghost writer of Ken Gregory's *Behind the Scenes of Motor Racing.*

Though there have been countless others, I have purposely not gone too deeply into the question of ghost writing because, for some, it undoubtedly does destroy an illusion and, to do this, seems a pity. There can be no doubt that it requires the touch and skill of a professional to make the best use of the material available. What could have been a great book by a personality who is, or has been, famous in his sphere, has sometimes been spoiled, if not ruined, by his own inability to write.

Dealers

Every collector has his own ideas when it comes to buying, some preferring to buy privately while others build up a good relationship with a dealer or dealers they know. Again, it is a matter of personal preference but I think that the advantages of buying from an established and reputable dealer far outweigh all others.

Obviously, the dealer in motoring literature has to make his profit and the profit margin must take into account not only his knowledge and skill acquired over many years but also the overheads of his business. Rent, rates, wages and advertising apart, there are other overheads: among them travel for, above all, the dealer in secondhand books is primarily a 'finder'. Finding what one wants is an expensive business and though, obviously, one must concede the dealer his profit, the chances are that in the end one saves because few people are as well placed as the professional dealer who can, and does, spend a great part of his time in searching and opening up fresh sources of supply.

Though no longer a dealer myself, I have a great respect for all those who are currently dealing professionally, nearly all of whom issue lists so that the price of any particular book can be compared, one list against another.

When I was dealing, even though my book stock was always available for inspection by clients, my business over the years changed its character in that whereas at the start my clientele consisted of roughly half UK and half overseas trade, it had changed towards the end to 70% or more overseas and 30% UK. The effect of this was that, since the majority of my customers were buying books unseen, one had to be specially careful to keep the standard of condition of the stock right up to the mark. This meant that whereas in the early days I was buying quite a lot from private sources unseen, and selling to customers who called, it then became necessary to exercise more care and to journey round the country in order to buy. In fact, the changed conditions worked out well for me and for my customers because, realising that I would need to travel more, I made it a feature of my advertising that I would travel to buy from vendors at their homes. Although this became time consuming, it did increase the supply enormously and, in one period, almost balanced supply with demand.

If I was a private collector now, possessing no more than average knowledge, I think that my method of buying would be to get as many dealers' lists as possible, compare their prices and, having done so, visit them all to see whether there was much difference in the condition and quality of their stocks. Having done that, I would then trade with those of my choice. At the same time, I would spend what spare time I had in visiting autojumbles and sales and, in this way, form my own view of the best method of acquisition.

Bearing in mind that we are talking in terms of secondhand books, it may be helpful to list names of a few reputable dealers here together with details of their specialities and methods.

Chater & Scott 8, South Street, Isleworth, Middlesex. Tel: 01-568 9750

Frank Stroud, Managing Director, must rate as the most knowledgeable and oldest established in UK and, although the firm's activities are divided between the supply of both new and secondhand motoring literature, it is the most easily reached from central London. The stock of new books is enormous and the firm also has its own publishing operation, Transport Bookman Ltd. After a lapse of some years, on the secondhand side, the firm returned to this aspect of the business several years ago and now has a very large secondhand stock which includes many good titles. Frank's son, Clive, came into the business a year or two ago and rapidly acquired all his father's drive and keenness and much of his knowledge. Every aspect of motoring literature is now covered, including new and secondhand books, magazines bound and unbound, club journals and gazettes, sales literature, programmes and ephemera.

Automobilia Queens Park Villa, West Drive, Brighton, Sussex. Tel: 0273-690333

There can be no doubting the fact that dealing in secondhand motoring literature has its own special appeal for, although Automobilia is a comparatively new venture, its proprietor could hardly be more knowledgeable. Kenneth Ball, who has recently re-entered the field together with his son Adam, was deeply involved in the business more than thirty years ago, later turning to publishing during which his firm Autobooks put out many handbooks and manuals covering a wide range of cars. Knowing Kenneth's drive and business acumen, it was no surprise to receive his first catalogue and there is no doubt at all that Automobilia will quickly build up momentum and gather round it a strong clientele.

G. Roberts 41 Glengall Road, Bexleyheath, Kent. Tel: 01-304 1817

A small personal business run by Geoffrey Roberts, who is himself a collector. Lists are available and contain a variety of interesting items, which is not surprising since the proprietor spends much time in autojumbles and markets up and down the country.

Ray Roberts (Booksellers) of Whiston Whiston Hall, Whiston, Near Penkridge, Staffs. Tel: Penkridge (07851) 2232

Trading under the slogan 'By Wheels, Wings and Water' Ray Roberts, who was for years a good customer of my business, embarked on the business himself at the start of 1981. Enthusiastic and extremely knowledgeable, particularly in the field of Rolls-Royce and Bentley, Ray's activities cover aviation, nautical and railways, in addition to motoring, motorcycling and cycling. His stock is substantial and lists are available.

Eric Thompson Long Common House, Shamley Green, Guildford, Surrey. Tel: 0483 89219

At the time that Eric acquired my bookselling business at the end of 1979, the stock was generally acknowledged among collectors all over the world to be the most comprehensive and best of its kind.

A well-known and extremely successful racing driver in the 1950s and 1960s and a collector of long standing in his own right, Eric has put his knowledge to the best possible use by building up the stock even further, together with the business clientele, and comprehensive lists are available.

Terry Wills Highways, Thornbury Rd, Alveston, Bristol, BS12 2LJ

During the time that I was in business, I did regular 'two way' trade with Terry Wills, whose bookselling interest has widened a lot in the past two years. His lists have become far more comprehensive during that time and every book is accurately described from the point of view of condition. Perhaps because of the area in which he lives, Terry's prices are among the most competitive of all and the selection is good and constantly improving.

Eric Thompson, well-known racing driver of the 1950s and 1960s, and former works driver of Aston Martin. He acquired and enlarged the motor book-selling business run for many years by the Author.

Eoin Young Motormedia, PO Box 3, East Horsley, Surrey

Eoin, perhaps better known to many as a motor racing author and journalist, claims to have the world's finest selection of rare old motor books and certainly issues the most elaborate catalogue of all. He, too, was a customer of mine, a contributor and subscriber to my *Collector's Review* and, since we live only a few miles apart, we meet constantly. Though his listed prices are generally higher than most others, the quality of his stock is unrivalled and his knowledge of books is considerable.

Vintage Motorshop 500, Bradford Rd, Batley, Yorks. Tel: 0924-470773

A tremendous worker, Richard Hunt entered the arena full time with his Vintage Motorshop two

years ago, since when a fine stock of books, sensibly priced and generally in excellent condition, has been built up. Prices of most tend to be lower in the north than further down and although no lists are issued the Vintage Motorshop, which is open on Thursdays, Fridays and Saturdays only, is well worth a visit.

Though there are others in the field I have listed only these because I know and have, at one time or another, done regular business with them all.

Auctions

Whether buying or selling, there is a great deal to be said for doing business with one or more of the leading auction houses and, if time permits, even more to be said in attending auctions purely in the capacity of an observer, because there is no quicker way of learning the value of items in which one is interested than seeing them sold under the hammer. Several of the big London auctioneers put on motor literature and ephemera sales from time to time and, since more material passes through these than any others, it is here that I would start if I were embarking on collecting. My own way of doing it would be first to subscribe for a year's supply of catalogues, because by doing this one sees not only the expected prices listed but also the prices obtained and can then compare the two afterwards.

Although, in my view, this is certainly the quickest and best way to learn, there are reservations which have to be made. To some extent, auction prices are unpredictable for the results depend on many factors. Of these, money supply is the most important and, when the supply of money is short, prices realised are generally lower. For an item to make a really good price there must be at least two people in the room, both of whom want it badly. One will bring it up to, or fractionally above, reserve but for it to go higher than that there must also be another. The circumstances necessary for it to go even higher than that, demand two wealthy and not very knowledgeable buyers, both of whom want it badly even though neither really know the true limit of its value. From time to time recently there have been indications that a new class of buyer sometimes attends auctions, not as a true collector who loves that for which he is bidding, but one who is buying more as an investment in which to put 'spare' money which he rightly thinks will later show a capital profit. Conversely, it can work the other way and, from time to time one does see 'flat' sales at which no amount of hard work on the part of the auctioneer will bring good prices, purely because not enough 'strong' buyers are in the room. But there's no doubt that the more sales one attends, the more 'with it' one becomes.

Auctions (selling)

Nowadays, selling one's own goods at auction presents almost no problems, for all the leading auctioneers have experts on their staff well qualified to give some idea of what price any particular item may be expected to raise. Over the years Christies, Phillips and Sothebys, in London, have all specialised in sales of this sort and all three are well qualified to advise. Over the years I did quite substantial 'two way' business with Christies, had

almost no disappointments and was always happy with their methods.

In what way could one be unhappy, in this context? Well, there are several. In the first place all auctioneers need to have entries well in advance of sales, which means that they will be storing them till the day of the sale, during which time they will be handled not only while 'lotting up' but also at the sale preview. If, at the end of the day an item is unsold, it's nice to get it back in the same condition as when it went in. In all the years I dealt with Christies, nothing was ever lost or damaged, and though I have never done business with any of the other big auction houses, I have no reason whatever to doubt that their standards are as high. So it adds up to the fact that you are safe if you go to the top.

Auctions (buying)

Again, if you go to the top, the same applies and, as a rule it does wherever you go, though not always. Now and again there have been sales out

An auction of motoring and motorcycling literature in progress at Christies, South Kensington. The auctioneer is Robert Brooks.

in the backwoods where buyers, believing that they were bidding against other buyers, have in fact been bidding against no one except the auctioneer himself who, sensing their keenness, was from time to time throwing in the odd bid to keep the pot boiling. Even though 'nodding on' is a risky and dying art, it does still happen occasionally.

A worse hazard, where inexperienced buyers are concerned, is 'auction fever' which usually takes the form of wild and usually fast bidding, ending in the discovery that not only has one bought the lot but that one has paid over the odds for it. Here again the cure is experience, together with firm resolve not to go above the limit decided on before the sale starts.

On a purely personal note I would say that though I never, at any time, grudged any auctioneer his commission, or even the Government its VAT, I never did much like the idea of buyer's commission. As a seller I expected to pay commission not only for the care taken in handling, cataloguing and keeping an eye on my treasures during sale previews but also for the auctioneer's skill in selling them and for the many other overheads to be covered. But I never much liked paying, not only for the item I wanted to buy, but also for the privilege of buying it, and that was one more reason why I placed almost all my business in the same hands.

So much for the big London auctioneers — a good point at which to start. Though there are a number of provincial auctioneers, their sales are rather less frequent, usually well advertised and almost always well attended by buyers and sellers alike. I always found provincial sales rather more enjoyable because they always seemed to be held in an atmosphere of informality and also in such very nice parts of the country. To be truthful I must say that if I aimed to get the very top price for something I was selling, I would put it into one of the London houses but that line of thought works two ways and was a principal reason why I always went to the country sales purely to buy, and in the hope that my competitors wouldn't have heard about them. Needless to say, they always had, so the result was an enjoyable session at the best pub in the town followed by the usual in-fighting at the sale itself. Very occasionally one would get news through the grapevine of a general sale of furniture and effects in which a few nice motor literature

items were to be sold and, although this does happen from time to time, the grapevine usually seems to fall down in passing on the news to everyone who could possibly be interested.

Postal auctions

Motor literature postal auctions, though common in the States, are rare in UK. I know of only one, Motor Book Postal Auctions at Pulborough, run for more years than I can recall by Peter Moore, son of the late Oscar Moore who was well known as a racing driver in the 1940s and 1950s. The essentials of any postal auction are that the organiser, or organisers, shall be of the highest integrity for, if this is not the case, the clients inevitably suffer. I have done business with this organisation almost from the time it first started and have never, at any time, found the service other than first class. Customers of my business who also dealt with it always said the same. From time to time, when I was trading, an item or items that I had bought would for some reason fail to sell and, over the years, I formed a policy of holding such things no longer than a year, after which they usually went to Pulborough. Almost invariably they sold through MBPA at prices higher than I had been asking — something I could never understand since they were priced just as competitively as the rest of my stock. One of the interesting things about MBPA is that, right from the start, it has never once advertised, and the clientele has built up over the years purely by word of mouth. But running it must amount to near slavery, with six catalogues per year, each with 1000 or more lots, to send out to subscribers, hundreds of parcels to pack and send out at the closure, unsolds to be returned to vendors and then back to work to compile and draft the next. Each catalogue shows the prices obtained in the previous sale, so one can see at a glance what sold and what didn't, together with the prices obtained.

Autojumbles

Beaulieu must surely have been one of the first, and gradually over the years the number of autojumbles has increased to the point at which, in the height of the summer, there are sometimes as many as three or more within range on the same day. Call them what you will, Autojumbles, Flea Markets or Swapmeets, they are not only good fun and sometimes social occasions, but are valuable to many collectors as a source of collectable material. There is something about them that compels you to be there. Maybe it is the thought of missing out if you don't go, maybe the enjoyment of meeting and talking with fellow collectors, but go you must and you will nearly always come home with something. They vary a lot and, in recent years, some Victoriana such as furniture, china and bric-a-brac has crept in so that despite the prefix 'auto' there is sometimes not much about motoring. Others have more secondhand motoring parts and accessory stalls than literature but, in the end, one gets to know the good ones and it's as well to be around on the day if you can.

Where autojumbles are concerned there are certain guidelines to follow, whether buying, bargain hunting or exhibiting and selling. If there are shortages in your collection and things that you want, they can often be found reasonably priced at autojumbles — if you can give up the time and have the patience to sort through mountains of dross. Now and again you will be lucky enough to spot the very thing you want lying on a table but, more often, it will amount to digging. The most important thing of all is always to have with you a list of wants, preferably in a small notebook, loose leaf and with an alphabetical index. If you don't have that you will be certain to see things that you think you want and either buy, feeling fairly sure, or leave it till next time. If you stick your neck out and buy without knowing, you may be sure that when you get home you'll find you already had the thing you've bought. If you exercise caution and wait to make sure, there's a long wait till next time. Never, at any time, be put off by other seekers telling you that there's nothing worth buying, even though it may look as though they're right. Note also that nearly all of them have well filled briefcases or carrier bags or, at least, bulging pockets to give the lie. Never give up, always press on in your search and, in the end, you will be amazed at what you find over the whole season.

The rules change when exhibiting or selling and the whole thing becomes more a test of wits than stamina. You have a chair on which to sit so you'll no longer be footsore and the first thing to remember is to take with you plenty of small change because very few autojumble stallholders have any with them when they arrive on the assumption that they will accumulate some as the day wears on. One of the most likely moments to make sales is when you are in process of unloading your stock from your transport onto your stand. This happens, of course, before the buying public have been admitted and the sight of it is like a magnet to small traders who feel that they are first in to spot the bargains. They are, of course, but no matter how they flutter their tenners and fivers no business can follow if you've no change, because nobody else will have any either. You can take this as gospel. Certain it is that they won't have the right money and, if you've no change, it's stalemate.

The usual size of an autojumble table is six feet by two, so take as much as this space will hold. Don't worry about setting it up to look neat and tidy because even though it will look nice to you, it won't mean much to the average buyer. Autojumble addicts love nothing better than to pore through masses of junk, so throw everything on that the space will hold. Put price tags on items where you feel you know the value or, if not the value, the price you would be happy to accept — plus a bit to allow for haggling — and sit back and wait.

Several types will start to hover round, flocking once they know that you're friendly. The commonest will be the browser. It's surprisingly easy to spot the browser and not always wise to discourage him because, in a quiet and lazy market with not much money changing hands, it's better to have a few browsers poring through your goods than no one at all and all types are attracted to a stall where there appears to be activity. In that sense the browser acts as a decoy and can be useful, even though he is the last person you want to have around when things are swinging. Browsers come in different forms and the most time consuming is the one who, while poring, gives you a running commentary on every item in his totally uninspired collection of junk. They are almost impossible to hook. The only way is to watch every move and strike hard and mercilessly at the slightest sign of real interest, then reel in quickly before he realises what's happened.

Real buyers know exactly what they want and nearly always ask if you've got it, often not stopping but asking the question as they pass by. They are the ones you need for the day to be successful and you, in turn, need to give a quick and definite answer. You'll also get many embryo offerers, and these can sometimes be landed. The embryo picks up an item, clearly marked with a price tag of, say, ten pounds and he may or may not have some degree of interest, unlike the browser who never has. He always starts the same way — either 'How much for this?' or even 'How much?' and the first rule is to resist the temptation to reply 'ten pounds' because, to him, that's offensive.

Take it from him, turn it over appearing to revel in all its finer points, then hand it back to him slowly and carefully to give him the impression that you really don't want to part with it. Say 'nine fifty' and you've lost him. Say 'nine' and he'll either say 'seven' or walk away saying nothing. Far better say 'Well, it's a market. What will you give?' Always use the word 'give'. Never say 'What do you think?' because what he thinks and what he will give are two totally different things. 'What will you give?' is the first move to get him into a corner, even though he is still not nearly hooked and, if he is a wily embryo, he may counter with 'Well, you're selling it. It's up to you to put a price on it'. If he should come up with 'eight', accept instantly because you should have at least a twenty per cent margin on everything when trading in a market. If 'seven' and, deep in your heart you feel that, at a pinch, you would let it go for that but are tempted to try for more — don't, because he will be so terror struck at having been so nearly 'hooked' that a try for another fifty pence will send him flying. Take his money and congratulate yourself.

Forgive me if I have written too lightly about autojumbles but, when doing them, the day can seem long and can be lightened by the variety of the clientele. When we used to do them, we used to spend the quieter spells classifying the customers — and were seldom wrong in our assessment.

There are more serious aspects of autojumble trading and one of them is that it isn't hard to lose items of stock unless one guards against it. The first thing to bear in mind, in this context, is that this is most likely to happen when unloading or loading your transport at the beginning or end of the day. Really, one needs three people: one to stay with the transporter, one to carry, and one at the stall. Done this way, there is no risk. With some sites it is easier than others because you can sometimes get the vehicle right up to the stall. With others it can be a hundred yards or more away and if you have only two people it must be locked and unlocked again for each run. As far as the stall itself is concerned, it's best to have the valuable things near the exhibitor's side of the table, rather than on the further side, because when one is busy, one notices an arm stretched across the table more easily than a hand. It's a shame that one has to think like this but it's worth it. At one market we lost a valuable book. Everyone on our side of the table thought they knew the chap but, at the time, there was little we could do. The next year, at the same mart, we all spotted him and, that time, caught him in the act. Quick as he was to replace the item, he was quicker to depart into the crowd and, though we were on the watch for him the year after that, we never saw him again. The interesting thing was that he knew quite a lot about motoring books and didn't even need to look at the price of the book he selected on the second occasion. I'd like to have seen his library.

Storage

The first essential is dryness, for more valuable motor literature has been lost by damp than through any other cause. Lofts are bad places in which to store valuable literature items but not as bad as garages which, over a long period, prove to be tombs. Even if one is seeing the stuff regularly it isn't until you pick it up to move it that you discover damp is working its way in, and by then it can be too late. There are really no other risks, bar fire or theft.

Shelving

In my business we used prefabricated ladder rack shelving of the type used in the stores of motor factors. The advantages of this are cheapness, ease of construction and the fact that with it one can get different spacing between shelves in order to store differing items like books, small, medium sized, large and outsize, magazines, models or even boxes. The principal disadvantage is that it doesn't look too attractive in the house and that, now and then, the metal uprights can chafe or tear the odd dust wrapper of the book at the end of the shelf if the shelf gets too full.

My own collection, or at least the best part of it, is in Minty bookcases, mahogany with glass doors at the front of each shelf. Apart from the fact that the modern format of books has tended to increase in height and width of page so that the spacing of the shelves is too close, I know of nothing better. The height of each shelf in my own bookcases in 9½ inches which is, I would say, the absolute minimum necessary today. With the ladder rack we had 10½ inches for all banks except one for books of the largest size that we set up to 12 inches, which would take almost anything. The important thing is to go as high as possible with shelving even though, initially, you may have far more shelf space than you need. The chances are that no matter how high you go, you'll run out of shelf space sooner or later. And, with ladder racking, it's important to attach the shelving firmly to the wall because, without this, it can spiral and collapse. We had this happen once with a bank seven feet high by ten long — filled with unbound copies of *Motor Sport.* The result — a wrecked shelf and a whole day wasted in sorting the spillage.

From all this, three factors emerge:

1 To have a policy in collecting
2 The problem of finding what one wants
3 Acquiring a knowledge of values

The collecting of almost anything that is in short supply does, in the end, amount to searching constantly in both likely and unlikely places and, in searching, one does, in the end, become familiar with values. But that aspect of collecting is complicated by the fact that in today's conditions values can change not year by year but, at times, almost month by month. To be really with it one needs to be in the centre of the picture all the time: at auctions, sales and autojumbles, meeting and talking with private collectors and the trade.

Mulling over this, way back in the 1970s, it seemed to me that some sort of guide was needed for private collectors, and particularly overseas collectors who were even more remote from the centre of things, to give an idea not only of current prices but also to advise on items hitherto not sought but which were moving into the sphere of being collectable. It was in 1975 that I got down to writing a three times yearly guide that, for want of a better title, I called *Collector's Review,* sending it out initially, on subscription to my overseas customers, whose enthusiasm for it was so overwhelming that it was soon expanded to take in UK collectors as well. The basis of it was to draw attention and focus on not only currently collectable material but also things that seemed likely to move into the collectable area and to report, Lot by Lot, the results of both the London motor literature sales and many provincial ones as well. At the time, it was easy for me to do as I was always on the spot and, by the time I retired from dealing, the *Review* had grown to the point where it had become a full time interest, together with my other writing. It has never ceased to expand its circulation from the day it first went out and, so long as interest in collecting is maintained, it probably never will.

I hope that the guidelines set out in this Chapter will be helpful, not only to those who contemplate starting to collect but also to some who have already taken the plunge.

Chapter 3

Guide to Layout

Motoring Literature is rather a loose term so first it is necessary to make a division between books and other forms of literature. To define a book should be easy, but it isn't. Twelve magazines, whether bound or unbound, are still twelve magazines, even though they appear to be a book after a visit to the binder. Nor can one define by minimum number of pages so, in the end, one just has to survey the marginals and assess their content. but in doing it that way one ends up with some books which, despite their obvious merit, consist of only ten or a dozen pages — something that must be made clear to the reader when one gets down to classification.

From there one goes on to accept that, in order to classify subject area correctly, one must first divide titles into categories, making a start by dividing the subject of motoring into two halves as far as books are concerned, into motor racing and other than motor racing, and follow that by further sub-divisions. Then it is necessary to arrange the titles in alphabetical order in each of their categories and finally to give as much information as possible on each title, that is to say the author and publisher, date of publication, number of pages and whether or not illustrated and with index. A rather daunting prospect about which to think carefully before starting. One felt fairly sure that throughout those twenty years the collection of data had been thorough but inevitably, over so many years, it wasn't co-ordinated and was contained in many files, lists and even at times on odd scraps of paper, for a book had never been allowed to leave the premises without making sure that its details were on record, or if in doubt, to record them. So when the great day dawned to pull out and study all this data, it was found that details of some titles had been recorded, not once, but many times. In consequence, one began to wonder not only where to start, but if.

A far better job of collection and collation could have been done if one had known twenty years earlier that one was going to undertake this task. But it wasn't realised at the time and, now, here it all was — piles and piles of it.

The answer, of course, was to go ahead and make a start. At first it was easy, but later it became more and more difficult, eventually to become a nightmare! One thing alone made progress possible, the conviction that if it wasn't done this time, it almost certainly never would be, so in the end it all came together.

The first stage was to divide and subdivide the whole spectrum of motoring, motorcycling and cycling into some fifty different categories, each of them numbered. Then followed stage two, to make an Alphabetical List of Titles, at the same time labelling each title with its appropriate slot. Stage three, the hardest, was to drop each title into its slot and, from the vast pile of data, seek out its details. Stage four demanded drafting a linking text, chapter by chapter, to enlarge on and to pinpoint particular items generally considered to be classic or, at least, desirable.

The Constant Search

Throughout 'The Constant Search' the aims have been to keep the layout as simple and as clear as possible so that:

(a) The reader who is interested in a particular **type** of book (**i.e. marque history**) can find the section quickly by referring to the **Classification Index**.

(b) The reader who seeks details of **a particular title, the name of which he knows,** can find in **which section** it lies by referring to the **Alphabetical Index of Titles**.

(c) The reader whose **knowledge of motoring literature is comparatively elementary** and who **aims to widen it as quickly and simply as possibly** can do so by first referring to both the **Alphabetical** and **Classification Indices**.

(d) The information sought is easily found.

The Alphabetical Index of Titles

This covers everything, including motoring, motorcycling and cycling book titles, magazines, club magazines and journals, commemorative brochures, etc. Not all club journals are included since details of some are not available, but a list of clubs and their secretaries is included at the start of that Section. Since most collectors usually know the title of a particular book in which they are interested, it was thought best to arrange the Index of Titles in alphabetical order. The classification of each title is quoted against it in the Alphabetical Index so, having located it there, it can be found immediately in its particular Section. Titles in each Section are also listed in alphabetical order.

Classification Index

The breakdown of Classifications is self-explanatory. Though great care has been taken to ensure that each title has gone into its correct 'slot', the location of many items is a matter of opinion since some could fit equally well into two or more Sections. No one is able to read every book and summarise its subject, particularly as some titles are misleading. But here again much checking has been done and great care taken.

Classification (Titles)

It is hoped that no errors will come to light as regards the titles themselves. The last to be found was 'Cornwall *and* a Light Car', previously thought to be 'Cornwall *in* a Light Car'.

Classification (Authors)

Though the initials of many authors are not known, it is hoped there are no errors regarding surnames.

Classification (Publishers)

Though there is a possibility of error in a few cases because certain titles were, on different occasions, put out by two or more publishers, this column should prove correct.

Classification (Editions)

This has proved to be the most difficult column of all, particularly in the case of early books. Both columns (1st Editions and later editions), have been completed with information that is known and can be taken as correct with regard to the information given. But there is still more information to be found ultimately. If, for example, one has in one's hand a 10th edition of a book dated 1910, the dates of the previous editions may or may not be shown in it, but at least one knows that nine preceded it even though one may not know how many followed. The important factor is that the existence of rare titles shall be known. Some works show no date of publication and, where this is the case, a title is entered as ND to indicate 'Not Dated'. In some of these cases it is not difficult to date within a decade, from the wording of the text or even from the style of print and, in such cases, this has been done, i.e. '1930s'. Editions of some titles have been quoted with brief details of later editions, if known, and where only a later edition has been seen, the '1st edition' column has been left blank.

A '1st edition reprint' can be taken to be identical to the 1st edition, even though the year of publication may be later. A '1st edition revised', even though the number of pages may be the same as in the 1st edition itself, will have at least minor revisions. 2nd and subsequent editions usually contain more pages and high numbered later editions many more.

Opinions, among collectors, vary as to the value and/or desirability between 1st and later editions, many having a strong preference for 'firsts'. Where my own collection is concerned, the condition of an early book is, to me, more important than its edition and I would much prefer to own a later edition in fine condition than a 'tired' 1st. Later editions of early books, particularly, contain much additional and valuable information.

Classification (Content)

Where the content, that is to say the subject matter of a book, is divided, it has been placed in the section for which it has the greatest content. Barrie Lyndon's *Grand Prix*, for instance, has a predominantly Grand Prix content even though other races, including sports car events, are interwoven. Some titles are harder to classify than others. Lord Montagu's *Jaguar — a Biography,* for example. Biography it may be but it would be preferable to classify it as a marque history.

Classification (Page numbers)

The number of pages of each title are as shown in the book itself, sometimes including the Index, if there is one. In the case of a few early books, instances have been found of two of the same numbered editions, one with fewer pages than the other.

Classification (Illustrations)

It can be taken that where a book is said to be illustrated that is the case, even if there is only one illustration, probably opposite the Frontispiece. Sketches, line drawings, diagrams, charts and even maps are regarded as illustrations.

Classification (Index)

The column shows whether or not there is an Index.

Classification (scarcity rating)

For obvious reasons it is not practical to indicate the scarcity of individual books on a price basis. Certain books, even in the middle and lower price brackets tend, for some reason, to suddenly become scarce. Typical of these are *The Racing Coopers* by Owen, for a long time easily found and not of great value and then almost overnight hard to find. Slightly up the price range is *The Enzo Ferrari Memoirs*. A book that has sold well and then gone out of print will often go to two or three times its new price on the secondhand market within a year of going out of print. This can work two ways and such a title, if reprinted, will drop in price overnight to a figure identical to the price of the reprint, or slightly higher as an earlier edition. A recent such case was *Those Elegant Rolls-Royce* by Lawrence Dalton, published by Dalton Watson. From time to time the value of a particular 'out of print' book will fall drastically overnight, should a cache of them be unearthed in the stockroom of a publisher or retailer. Two examples of this are

The Constant Search

Grand Prix Racing 1906-1914 by Mathieson where a cache of French text copies were unearthed and, later, a larger block in English, and the run of *Monza Yearbooks 1960-1966.* In both these cases the value plummetted down to the new price but, again in both cases, it started to rise again once supplies at the new price ran out.

Other points worth bearing in mind, when referring to the ratings, are that when compiling the book they were left to the last so that they are as up to date as possible. Even so, a year may have elapsed from the time they were inserted until the time that this book is published and, inevitably, some titles will have moved up a category, say from scarce to rare. Even so, over the years, almost every title will remain relative in relation to the others over any period of time.

Again, when referring, the reader should bear in mind the degree of his experience in collecting. What may to a dealer be a fairly commonplace title, could rate as a scarcity to a collector who is just starting. Some of the more recent titles, no matter how good, have a lower rating than they might appear to merit and the reason for this is that some are still available as new books at their published prices in the shops and premises of dealers. In this connection it should be borne in mind that the assessment has been made on scarcity and not on price.

The ratings are, therefore:

Rating

A. Titles or items almost impossible to find
B. Extremely rare
C. Rare
D. Scarce
E. Fairly easy to find
F. Easy

Condition

The condition of a secondhand book has to be taken into account. It is obviously harder to find an early book in exceptionally good condition than a later one. The rating is set out on the basis of books being in good condition, bearing in mind their age. Some collectors attach importance to a book still having its dust wrapper and, in the case of post-war books, it is assumed that they will still have them.

Text

An asterisk opposite a title in the column headed 'Text' indicates that the title is referred to in the text accompanying that Chapter.

Abbreviations

Although, in most cases, the names of publishers have been quoted in full, a few are abbreviated. Motor Racing Publications, for instance, is shown as MRP and there are one or two shown by initials only where the full name is not known.

ND Though most titles and editions show a date, some do not and where there is doubt, the letters ND denote 'Not Dated'. Where the decade of a book can be established either by the print or by the illustrations, it is shown. i.e. 1920s, 1930s etc.

NN Some books do not have numbered pages and the letters NN denote this. In a few cases titles in this category have had page counts and numbers are shown.

App The letters 'App' in the index column of the Classification denote that there is an Appendix.

Chapter 4 Section A

Technical Books, other than those under specialist headings

The thought behind this section was, originally, that most of the very early books were technical and would require such a classification. To some extent this has been the case, but eventually a higher percentage seemed to be better placed in sections more clearly defined.

Obviously little was written on the subject of motoring in the very early days and what did appear was not too excitingly illustrated, with line sketches instead of photographs. Nor was there much to write about, for whereas today a run of four or five hundred miles may be commonplace, four or five miles would be nearer the mark at the turn of the century, and forty or fifty something to make headlines.

The era was one of experiment and the motorists themselves were far too preoccupied with the problems of motoring to spare time putting pen to paper in order to describe their efforts. But, make no mistake, their efforts were nevertheles praise-worthy and often superhuman. In this context it is interesting to watch the Veteran Car Run from London to Brighton, in order to see what brutes some of the early cars must have been, particularly when one reflects that today's Veteran events are supported by thousands of enthusiastic suppor-ters, unlike the hostile watchers at the turn of the century.

Very few books seem to have been written con-cerning the trials and tribulations of the early motorists themselves for, at the time, trials and tribulations were taken for granted and few of the early sufferers would admit to them. Almost all the early writings centred round the technicalities of the cars and the devastating effect they were likely to have on what, at the time, were termed roads. The poor motorist, apart from being rated a con-genital idiot or worse, had no friends. Hated by horse owners, frowned on by farmers and despi-sed by drivers of horse-drawn vehicles and gener-ally ostracised, he nevertheless plugged on relent-lessly and, in the end, triumphed. If one approves of motoring and the motor car as we know them today, we owe a debt of gratitude to the tenacity and singleness of purpose of the pioneers, even forgiving them for the sparseness of early litera-ture.

In those halcyon days almost all the parts of an early motor car requiring repair, except for the engine, were regarded as tasks either for the black-smith or for the carpenter. The engine remained a mystery to all but a few, so the engine and particu-larly its ignition system formed the content of many of the early books of the 'hints and tips' and 'questions and answers' variety. In this section, there are three of this type, *The A.B.C. of Motor-ing, Complete Hints and Tips for Automobilists* and *Modern Gas and Oil Engines.*

The Constant Search

By the arrival of the next decade, the 1910s, a number of authors and publishers had seen the need for better and more comprehensive versions of this type of book and, by the 1920s, three, four and even five volume sets were coming out in a stream. Though most of these fall into Chapter 21 and not in this Chapter, there are still one or two useful titles here, notably *Carburation* by Brewer and *Electricity and the Motor Car* by Hutton, both published in the 1910s.

Peter Brockes (left), the Reference Librarian of the National Motor Museum at Beaulieu, himself a collector.

Chapter 5 Section B

Books on touring and travel

More early books on motoring centred round travel than on the technical aspect of the motor car and, if one thinks about it, one can see how, with the improvements that were being made, the country, the Continent and even the World was being opened up to the early motorists in a way in which they had never dreamed. When the interest in collecting motor literature began, the demand for books about early travel was sluggish, until it suddenly dawned that almost all the early motoring travel books were not only recorded history but also a part of motoring literature that was fast disappearing. This had come about largely because in many cases editions had been small so that, taking into account the wastage of copies over the years, shortage must soon result.

To me, early motoring travel is not only the area of motoring literature most filled with romance but also one of the most impressive in terms of courage, determination and achievement. One of the first motoring travel books I read, a birthday present way back in 1924, was *Across the Sahara by Motor Car* by Haardt and Dubreuil. The fabulous account of the crossing of the Sahara by the Citroën Kegresse expedition of tracked vehicles, the perils and obstacles overcome, and stubborn determination of the men who overcame them, has always stayed with me, so that it is a title I would recommend to anyone. The same two authors followed *Across the Sahara* with another book, *The Black Journey,* four years later and this is another cast in the same mould.

Many are the devotees of John Prioleau's *Adventures of Imshi* and *Imshi in New Europe,* among his other works. Both are accounts of travel undertaken in 1922 and again in 1924, with two different 'bullnose' Morris' but, to me, these were tours rather than adventures, both slightly lacking the excitement of Haardt and Dubreuil. But John Prioleau certainly covered distance, knew the best places to visit and the best spots at which to stay when he got there and, moreover, pinned his faith to a well loved model among vintage car collectors.

Two more that one seems always to regard as a pair, perhaps because their titles are linked by the figure '8', are Jackson Budd's *Around France in an 8hp Car* and Horsley's *Round England in an £8 Car.* Budd's car was a 1950 Standard, and though I have read Horsley's book, I never did find what make of car it was that he used. Though both are nice little books, neither feat is outstanding because, by 1950, motoring round France and even much further afield in a car of 8hp was no great feat. Furthermore, way back in 1932 one could buy a very respectable car indeed for £8.

It is rare to find a travel book written in 1939 and without a single illustration but William Hatfield's *Australia Through the Windscreen* must be good because it was, and still is, always in demand. Francis Miltoun, who was a most descriptive writer and ever faithful to the Ford Model T, wrote *The Automobilist Abroad* in 1907 and *Italian Highways and Byways From a Motor Car* in 1909. The first was good and I have always regarded the second, not only for its text but for its standard of production and illustration, as not just superb but an art item by any standards.

The Constant Search

Though some collectors prefer to stick to the early titles, there were some good and very popular travel books produced as late as the 1950s, as evidenced by the McArthur-Cassell partnership in the *Auto Nomad* series. *Auto Nomad in Sweden* (1948) was the first, followed by Barbary's *Through Africa* and ending with *Auto Nomad in Spain* in 1953. All must have sold well at the time and are still in fair demand.

By Car to India by Forbes Leith, featuring a 1924 14hp Wolseley Colonial tourer, *China to Chelsea* by McCallum (1927 Buick), published 1930, *Cape to Cairo* by Court Treatt (1927 Crossley) and *Cape to Cowley via Cairo* by Belcher (1926 'bullnose' Morris), published 1932, are all good stories with a higher than average quota of illustrations of the cars. Although it is a much later book, published in 1962, the same applies to *Drive Round the World* by Baudot and Seguela who did their marathon in a Citröen 2CV.

Next on the list, *En Route*, by Roy Trevor in 1908 is, I think, generally acknowledged as a classic. Mr Trevor was not only an enthusiastic motorist fortunate enough to own and tour in his magnificent 70hp Mercedes but also conscious and proud not only of his knowledge of cars but also of his ability to undertake basic servicing, although it has to be admitted that on these occasions his expert 'man' seemed never to be far away. There are many illustrations of the car and its occupants and the book itself comes into the 'ornate' category, by which I mean that the front board has on it the profile of the car, embossed in gold. Not all books that have this are as good, but many collectors specialise in early 'ornate' works.

Express to Hindustan by M.H.Ellis, 1929, is less rare and featured a specially built car, 25hp and six cylinders, so hideous before it started its long journey from London to Delhi that one shudders to think what it must have looked like at the end. It was mainly suspension and bodywork that seemed to suffer on runs like this and even standard products which looked nice at the start of some of these early journeys, weren't recognisable at the end.

Again featuring a Ford Model 'T', *Four on a Tour* by Robert and Elizabeth Shackleton is a favourite of mine. The full title, which one doesn't see till one gets to the title page, is *Four on a Tour in England*. Next, *Grand Tour* by Patrick Balfour, not dated on the title page, subjects two 40/50hp Rolls-Royce, leading one to believe that it is a book of the 1920s and much sought by Rolls-Royce addicts. The journey is from London to the Malay States and Sumatra and the last words on the last page read Perry Green, 1934. Rare and hard to find.

Deserts attracted motorists of all eras, as witness *Desert Encounter* by Holmboe, 1934, *Desert Journey* by Rodger, 1944, and *Desert Watches* by McArthur, 1954, but I think that none compare with the early desert crossings and when you have read one crossing of the desert you feel you have read them all. There are no interesting towns in deserts and the problem of crossing deserts — sand — becomes less interesting the further one reads.

Escape from Peace by 'Bunty' Scott Moncrieff, published in 1949, is one I would never want to be without. The immediate post-war years of peace were frustrating but who, except 'Bunty', could hit on the idea of not only escaping but doing it in a 5 litre Bugatti. A 'must' for me because Bunty is a friend, the Bugatti my favourite car and I still haven't visited any of the Nordic countries. *An English Holiday* by J.J.Hissey, 1908, rings a bell because Hissey is my favourite author. Writer of fourteen books, the first ten on horse-drawn travel through England, and the last four by car, Hissey must have known every lane in the country and was, I believe, the only author to span the horse to petrol era. To read them all you have to be a confirmed addict but they are best at the end of a long, tiring and frustrating business day. Of all authors, Hissey has the ability to help you up the steps of his dog cart or early motor car and transport you to peace and beauty which he alone could find — but you mustn't be in a hurry for the pace is slow!

A Light Car Odyssey by Davies is good, particularly if you are an Alvis lover, and *Morocco from a Motor* was by courtesy of a Renault and has really lovely colour plates.

Motoring — so many titles start with this word that it's hard to know which to recommend — Abroad (two of them), in the Rhineland and Black Forest, in the Balkans, East Anglia, France, Italy, Sussex and Kent, the North of England, the West Country, the West of England, West Sussex, Irish Byways, Scottish Byways or the Continent. Where does one start? I think that, to sum up, one could say anywhere because any one of these will give you a good idea of what the countryside and roads were like at that particular time — in short, very much nicer than they are now.

The *Motor Routes* series by Home, put out by Black in the 1910s, covered England, France and Germany. They come into the 'ornate' class and all are good, with some nice colour illustrations.

Motor tours? The same comments apply, I think, as applied to the prefix 'motoring'. *Motor Tramp* is different — an account by John Heygate of motoring with an MG in Nazi Germany during 1935 and, as such, an item of interest to MG fanatics.

Nine Thousand Miles in Eight Weeks was no mean feat when accomplished by the Hon. Mrs Victor Bruce and her husband in 1927. Mrs Bruce was also an experienced aviator and wrote two other books, *Bluebird's Flight* on her flying experiences and, in 1977, *Nine Lives Plus,* all of which she was kind enough to sign for me when, after the last was published, I visited her at her home in the Cotswolds.

Round the World in a Baby Austin by McQuarrie and *Round the World in a Motor Car* by Scarfoglio are both rated classics in their class and, though I haven't read it, I believe that J.J.Mann's *Round the World in a Motor Car* is good as well. I liked *Rumania Through a Windscreen* by Forman, who did his trip in a different way: journeying to Rumania by train and hiring a car and driver when he got there.

There are two books with the title *Three Men in a Motor Car,* the first by Maxted in 1904, the second by Scarritt in 1906. In 1906 Maxted went on to write another book, Three Thousand Miles in a Motor Car. All three are good reading and give good accounts of the hazards but my favourite of this type is *The South Bound Car* by Llewellen and Raven Hill, published in 1907, which is not only interesting but filled with humour from time to time. In this case, the car was a Daimler, again with three occupants. Three in a four-seater car was the usual number for a long tour in those days, since the fourth space was used for luggage and, of course, tyres and spares since there were few, if any, service depots, apart from the odd blacksmith or ironmonger.

Through Brazilian Jungle Lands with The Book is something out of the ordinary. The car was

another Ford Model 'T', the passengers missionaries and 'The Book' the Bible, the idea of writing their travel adventures being to raise funds. *Through East Anglia in a Motor Car* by Vincent in 1907, is an interesting little book in which there are no photographs at all of cars but some nice colour illustrations and a wealth of information on East Anglia. That the car is so neglected may account for the fact that, while one doesn't see it every day, it isn't too difficult to find in nice condition. The other interesting thing about this book is that it is sought by Rolls-Royce collectors since the only reference to cars in it evolves round a meeting between the author and the Hon. C.S.Rolls.

Through the Alps to the Appennines by Konody is another 'ornate', with a picture of the car printed on the front board, looking like an early Daimler but, in fact, a White Steam Car, leading one to wonder how the crew managed for water in the Alps. *Through Europe and the Balkans* is another that I liked, written by Etherton and Allen in 1928, their transport being a 14/40 Vauxhall tourer of which there are plenty of good photographs.

My friend, author and collector Cyril Posthumus, had a motto that he told me to bear in mind when looking for books. It was 'look among the thin'uns' and he was right, for it was 'among the thin'uns that I found *Travel* by Brereton, a nice little book of the early thirties, interesting, well illustrated but so thin that, but for Cyril's advice, I would never have spotted it. Although I haven't read Fred Basnett's *Travels of a Capitalist Lackey* it is one I plan to read and I know that its Alvis content will appeal to the fans.

Another thin'un, *Turn Left for Tangiers,* is quite scarce and the thinnest of all. A nice little book and the car a Triumph Herald. *Two Roads to Africa* by Humphrey Symons describes two separate runs, one in a Wolseley and the other with a Rolls-Royce Phantom III. Of interest to Rolls-Royce collectors and to me because I was at school with his co-driver, H.F.Hamilton.

Finally, *Under My Bonnet* by C.R.N.Minchin, a delightful 'pot pourri' of the author's motoring life, the cars that he used and loved and famous people in the racing world he knew and met. Through finding himself a tenant of Lady Shelley Rolls, Mr Minchin became not only a friend of the Rolls family but also a Rolls-Royce and, later, Derby Bentley owner. Very enjoyable and well illustrated.

Chapter 6   Section C

Books on roads, Road maps and guides and Road transport

'Few ordinary men ever loved any personal thing as I loved and still love the never ending road'. The words are those of the late Charles Jarrott, one of the most famous of early racing motorists. John Bolster quoted them in his book, *Motoring is My Business'*, adding 'The Road, that is it. I might almost be persuaded that it is simply my mechanical bent that has made motoring a life obsession with me. I might more easily come to the conclusion that it is the very many friends, the absolutely grand people, that I have met and am always meeting, among motoring enthusiasts in all walks of life. It might even be the sense of artistic accomplishment, the sheer sensual thrill of tackling the myriad difficulties of a road circuit in a really fast car, with man and machine as one. Yes, partly it is all these things but, above all, it is the road that has made me its slave.'

Some will agree, others may not. But, to me a continental holiday or, for that matter, any holiday is one in which you get into the car at home and motor all the way to your destination, wherever it may be. If time is a factor, an aircraft and a hired car are the obvious answers but to me the journey by car, especially if not hurried all the time, is a great part of any holiday. If you feel the same, you will understand. If you don't, there will still be some titles in this chapter that will be of interest as

a motorist, for though many are early there are some a lot later.

Freeston's *Alps for the Motorist, Cream of Europe for the Motorist* and *France for the Motorist,* all published by Cassell in the 1920s, may not be much help to a motorist who is in a hurry today but are, with their good photographic illustrations, great to browse through and aren't expensive to buy either, even today. *The Dunlop Book* and its twin sister *Newnes Motorist's Touring Guide* both of the 1920s and both big format books, are not only filled with maps and good text but have really lovely illustrations.

Great Motor Highways of the Alps by Merrick, published by Hale in 1958 and reprinted in 1961, is sought not only by collectors but by motorists currently wanting it.

If you are prone to nostalgia and want to look back further, then cast your eye over *Harper's English Roads* the first of which, *The Brighton Road,* was published in 1892 and, to the best of my belief, the last, *The Manchester and Glasgow Road,* in 1907. Sixteen altogether because some, such as the London to Glasgow and London to Edinburgh, go into two volumes. If you have these in your library, you need nothing else as far as the roads of Great Britain are concerned. But don't think of them as guide books. They may be, in a sense, but the text is massive and readable, taking in every aspect: monuments, historic buildings, road development, railway influence, coaching and the arrival of the motor car. Nothing that I have seen is better.

If you must go further back than that, then keep an eye out for a copy of *Paterson's Roads.* My own copy, the 18th Edition published in 1822, is interesting but though one can identify many roads that one knows, now dual or three carriageway and then described as 'potholed', it is not readable in the same sense as Harper's and is information, pure and simple, on what hazards the unfortunate traveller of those times would have to face.

Charles Freeston's knowledge of Europe was as extensive as Harper's or Hissey's were of England and all his books were good, descriptive and readable. Two more are *The Passes of the Pyrenees* and *The Roads of Spain.* He had access to, or maybe owned, some nice cars too, and the latter book features a 40/50hp Rolls-Royce tourer. There have been some superbly colour illustrated books on road travel, among them Selway's *The Regency Road* and Cecil Aldin's *Romance of the Road.* Many of these delve deeply into the history of the inns along the road, tracing their history back, and all are good reading.

Conversely, there have been some appallingly dull and stodgy books on the subject which, it must be admitted, does need a light and interesting approach.

Chapter 7 Section D

Books on motor racing

Section D.1

Grand Prix Motor Racing

Though there was no doubt from the start of this book that the first division of the whole spectrum of motor literature should be between motoring generally and motor racing, it has been less easy to define the sub-divisions of motor racing itself and, in fact, the only easy subdivision was to segregate Grand Prix racing from the rest.

Though, for years, I was a close follower of Grand Prix Racing, I have to admit that there was a point at which my interest began to wane — the point at which the engine of the Grand Prix car moved from front to rear and although I did follow racing for a long time after that, I became increasingly out of touch to the point at which I confess that I find it hard to tell one Grand Prix car from another. It is better to admit this and, in doing so, I should like to make it clear that I realise that the change is progress and leads all the time to increased efficiency. I am not in the least anti-progress but not too well 'with it' in this context.

I know most of the 'Grand Prix' books and, starting at the beginning of the list, I would say as a devotee of both Hough and Doug Nye, and bearing in mind the demand that always exists for their books, I have always thought of both their *British Grand Prix* titles as high up on the list. Although I have never met Richard Hough, I know Doug well and have always thought of him as a painstaking and accurate writer.

Bearing in mind all that went into it, it always seemed to me that the BRM was not too well covered in writing, which may account for the popularity of both *'BRM'* by Mays and Roberts and Louis Stanley's *BRM Story*. No one could overlook the contribution made to racing by the Ford Grand Prix engine, so the story of it, by Blunsden and Phipps, is the next, as is *A Story of Formula One* by Denis Jenkinson, for who can possibly know more about the subject.

I could never understand why *The Formula One Record Book* by Thompson, Rabagliati and Sheldon came to be remaindered because surely no other book on the subject contains so much well laid out and easily found information. I read and enjoyed both *For Practice Only* by Klemantaski and Frostick and Cyril Posthumus' *German Grand Prix,* the latter one of a series put out by Temple Press and, perhaps not surprisingly, the most difficult of the series to find.

German Grand Prix Cars 1934-1939. Yes, I know that well enough for it is one on its own and highly prized by all collectors. Put out by His Majesty's Stationery Office and nothing in outward appearance, it gives more information on the pre-war Mercedes and Auto Unions than any other publication. Technical and reasonably well illustrated, it is a **'must'** for the Grand Prix follower of history and for many other collectors as well. But, for all its rather drab appearance, it is hard to find, not cheap, and becoming dearer every time it comes along.

The *Grand Prix* series of books by Stanley, which went out year by year covering the scene of the previous year, were large in format and always popular. Some years are harder to find than others and, strangely, as time went on it became not the same ones that were difficult. Even so, it is a collection which is not impossible to build up. I would make one observation while on this subject. If you had every one in that set except one or two, and saw a full set coming up for auction or even private sale, my own feeling is that it would be better, if you have been searching for a long time, to buy the full set if you can afford it than to go on trying, and then sell off your own part set privately or at auction. I say this because I have seen so many collectors wait for years to complete runs. If, some years back, they had done it this way, it would have proved not much dearer and would have eliminated endless searching. By waiting, they may well have reached the point at which they are not going to succeed anyway. One has to know enough about what it is that one is looking for, of course, but as a general rule I would try to do it that way. One can also bear in mind that some of the volumes in the redundant and incomplete set may be becoming scarcer, so that if one can wait to dispose of it, the change may not be too costly anyway.

What should one say regarding Laurence Pomeroy's *The Grand Prix Car?* Quite a lot, actually, apart from the fact that it is acknowledged as the finest of its kind and, as a result, has suffered a price escalation on the secondhand market unrivalled by almost any other work on the subject of motoring in any of its forms. The belief held generally is that there were just two volumes, the first covering from 1906 to 1939 and the second from 1947 to 1954, but this is only part of the story.

The first Volume, entitled 'The Grand Prix Car 1906-1939, was, in fact, published in 1949 but, shortly afterwards, it was decided to revise it and, at the same time, extend further to add another volume covering the period 1947 to 1954 and to bring these two Volumes out as a pair. There were also later impressions of both Volumes 1 and 2. So the effect of it is that there are two different versions covering the period 1906 to 1939, several

later impressions of the second version, and several later impressions of the volume covering 1947 to 1954. But it can certainly be taken that any one volume of this fine work is a valuable item to own, any two even more so, and all three very valuable indeed. Though the purist may not agree, my own feeling is that I would be very happy to have any impression of the second Volume 1947-1954, and any impression of either version covering 1906 to 1939, in order to feel that I had good coverage even though I do, in fact, have Volumes labelled 1 and 2.

One reason why Setright's *Grand Prix Car 1954-1966* took longer to enter the scarcity field seemed to be that it was initially longer on the shelves of booksellers in new form. But it is good, it is the same format as Pomeroy's and it follows on consecutively. Now, at last, it is being assessed for what it is.

It was difficult to decide into which category to place Hermann Lang's *The Grand Prix Driver* for it could have fitted equally well into Categories D7 or F. Even now one doesn't feel entirely happy about its presence here. It was the Mercedes influence that did it but, whatever the reason, it is one of the best and now seldom seen. *Grand Prix Mercedes Benz: Benz Type W 125* by Jenkinson is one of a small format series, all of which are good, and *Grand Prix Racing 1934-1939* by Walkerley and Fellows has always had a good following and was put out both as a hardback and, by Motor Racing Publications, in spirobound form. I am a bit of a diehard about this and much prefer hardback books, for I saw so many 'tired' softbacks, stiffbacks and spirobounds when I was trading that it left its mark.

I have always thought of 'Taso' Mathieson's *Grand Prix Racing 1906-1914* as way ahead of anything setting out to describe the Grands Prix of that era, and still think so. But good as it is, it is at the moment one to be wary about pricewise. Never in very free supply on the secondhand market, it increased in price over the years till, at one time, it was changing hands at close on three figures. Unexpectedly, a cache of new copies was found with French text, bringing the price down a bit, followed by an equally large number of English editions which caused it to plummet. It's a superb book but one to be conscious of when buying.

Grand Prix Racing, Facts and Figures by Monkhouse and King Farlow, was always a good reference work and is one for the historian and the 1st Editions of his *Motoraces* and *Motor Racing with Mercedes Benz* are books to make any collector's mouth water. I wouldn't personally put one above the other, as both are different, for whereas the latter is almost all Mercedes with inevitably some Auto Union, the former covers a wider aspect of pre-war motor racing. Both are predominantly 'photograph' books, of course. George Monkhouse was, in his day, king of them all, with the possible exception of Klemantaski. Though there have been later, hardback, editions of *Motor Racing with Mercedes Benz,* the only one I have seen of *Motoraces* was from the States, and softback at that. Court's *The Power and the Glory* is another one to think about and is extremely well produced with numerous good photographs, particularly if you like very large books.

Other good titles under this heading are *The Vanishing Litres* by Rex Hays, published in 1957 by Macmillan, *The Vanwall Story* by Klemantaski and Frostick, always a good partnership, and if you are technically minded, *V-16: The Story of the BRM Engine* by Rivers Fletcher, in which there is a superb cutaway drawing of the first engine produced by the company among many more interesting technicalities.

Section D 2

Formula Racing, other than Grand Prix

One of the surprises when originating the classification scheme used throughout this book was to find how very few books qualify for this heading, although to some extent that is compensated for by the fact that nearly all are known to be good. One can certainly say that all books of the Klemantaski and Frostick team are good and *British Racing Green 1946-1956* is no exception. Like several of their others it is one of a series of fairly thin medium format books which collectively cover a wide aspect of motor racing and make up a nice set.

There are four books under this heading that deal with 'half litre' racing. They are *The 500cc*

Motor Racing Yearbook 1952, 500cc Racing by Gregor Grant published by Foulis in 1950, *Formula 3: A Record of 500cc Racing* by Austin May, published by Foulis in 1951, and *The Formula 3 Yearbook 1953-1954,* by Pearl/Armstrong. Cheating, one can add one more which came out in 1980, *Iota 1947-1953. Edited Highlights of F.3 500cc.* from Transport Bookman.

Of all forms of racing, Formula 3 seems to have been the least well covered and, when I was in the book business, the demand for anything relating to Formula 3 exceeded supply by a greater margin than almost any other aspect of racing, except possibly classic books on very early motor racing written by those who had taken part. The 500cc Formula has, in this context, always been something of an enigma. Starting as a way of giving inexpensive racing to thousands of young drivers who longed to get into the sport, it flourished and, in the end, died. One could never see why because, although the cost had escalated by the time of its demise, the interest still seemed to be there and, even at the end, the class provided some of the closest racing and best 'cut and thrust' ever seen. Of the five, only Gregor Grant's, Austin May's and *Iota* are hardbacks. All three are good and, as yearbooks, so are the other two. *Iota,* of course, was the Journal of the 'Half Litre' Club and what Transport Bookman has done is to edit and extract from the run the best and most interesting copies to make into a book. This is a useful and valuable addition to a sector which now probably holds more interest for many people than some other, better publicised, forms of racing. Grant's *Formula 2,* again from Foulis in 1953, always did fill a gap and Kent Karslake's *Racing Voiturettes* is a title which was always sought and is now seldom seen.

Section D 3

Sports car racing & races

Here again, one would imagine that there would be more titles on this aspect alone of motor racing and the emphasis is on the word 'alone', since so many books have tended to take in all aspects of motor racing and included Grand Prix, other formulas, sports cars and many other forms of racing.

But, of the titles listed, I would suggest a close look at *Ford — The Dust and the Glory* by Levine and an even closer one at *Ford versus Ferrari,* particularly if you can find a copy of the latter which is now nearing entry of the 'rare' category. One would have expected there to be more on Jaguar who, at one time, contributed so much to racing. *Jaguar — Motor Racing and the Manufacturer* is an interesting little book but still only a stiffback and one feels the marque should merit something better.

Racing a Sports Car — my own first effort at authorship, came out in 1950 and set out to describe a season's racing, including the Tourist Trophy in Ireland, with the then new Healey Silverstone. It sold well, mainly because even then there was a dearth of books and, since it included details of the cost, it appealed to many young people who wanted to get into racing at that time. It still has a good secondhand value for a different reason — it seems to have been the only book written concerning that particular model, which has now become a collector's item. I haven't read *Racing Sports Cars* but, coming from the Klemantaski/Frostick 'stable', it is bound to be good.

Tourist Trophy by Hough is fast becoming a classic of its type and is also very good reference, and since everything that flows from the pen of Cyril Posthumus is enjoyable and accurate, *The World's Sports Car Championship* follows suit.

Section D 4

Long distance road and track races (sports and racing cars)

A point that I should make here is that books included in the classification but not mentioned in the accompanying text should not be thought of as not worth a mention. The vast majority are good but in the first place there just isn't space in which to mention them all. Those that are mentioned are included in the text either because they are titles I have read and liked or because, when I was in the bookselling business, the demand for them indicated their quality. Others came very close in demand and it is sometimes difficult to know which to include or leave out.

American Automobile Racing by Bochroch and *American Road Racing* by Rae were both always popular and in demand.

Blue and Yellow by Prince Chula is, of course, one of a number of books on motor racing written by him, others being *Road Racing 1936, Road Star Hat Trick* and *Wheels at Speed.* All set out to describe the White Mouse motor racing equipe that he financed and managed so successfully with his cousin, Prince Bira, as driver. They were a highly successful and well organised team and deserved all the acclaim that they had. All Chula's books on this subject are enormously popular but, to me, his style has often seemed stilted and, at times, humourless. In motor racing there is both sadness and humour and it has always seemed to me that humour should be brought out. Both he and Bira wrote other books, among them *Brought up in England* by Chula and *Blue Wings to Bangkok* by his cousin who, besides being an absolutely first class racing motorist, was also a competent pilot.

Besides *Grand Prix*, Barrie Lyndon's best known books were *Combat* and *Circuit Dust,* all written in the mid-thirties, all highly desirable and therefore not easy to find. Less well known and even more sought after is his only novel, *Speed Fever,* to be found in its slot I.2. He was also co-author with Eyston of *Motor Racing and Record Breaking.*

Great Auto Races by Helck, published in 1975, was one of my forecast failures. During the time I was buying and selling secondhand books, I always kept abreast of new titles and, from time to time, would come across one that I felt would sooner or later become a 'classic', usually buying half a dozen copies to put on one side to 'mature' till it went 'out of print'. Then, almost invariably, the second hand price would rise, at first slowly, and later steeply. Though *Great Auto Races* is a very large book which, personally, I don't like, I bought six or eight copies and put them away, only to find a few years later that it had been 'remaindered', that is to say much reduced in price since the edition hadn't sold to a finish. The worst aspect was that it was quite an expensive book, around £30 to £35, but I picked it for the superb colour illustrations and high standard of production, despite its size. Ah, well. I was rather badly wrong that time but, as they say nowadays, 'You can't win 'em all'.

Stirling Moss' *Le Mans '59* is another title that has gone 'under the counter' and is now really hard to find, mainly due to its Aston Martin content. Aston Martin is always popular.

Pekin to Paris in a Motor Car by Barzini hardly needs comment, being a first-hand account of the great Pekin to Paris race in 1907. What a race! I forget now the time lag between the arrival of the winner in Paris and the last to arrive. I'm sure it was weeks and may have been months as some competitors spent almost as long in train journeys in search of spares and repairs. A very expensive book to buy but there was a good and modestly priced reprint in 1977 which is well worth having. Writing about this one has reminded me that, since my own copy is in French, I really would like the reprint and Eric Thompson, who acquired my bookselling interest, has come up with one.

There are two *Targa Florio*s, one by Bradley in the 1950s and another by Owen, via Haynes, in 1979. I know the first to be good and the second, though I have only perused it, seems to follow suit. Yet probably this great race has still not been as fully documented as some others. While on the subject of great races, Bill Boddy's *200 Mile Race* is another that, due to its quality, is becoming harder and harder to find.

Wheels Take Wings by Burn and Bradley covers not only the motor racing and flying that took place at Brooklands but goes right back to the start, describing even the clearing of the site, the invasion of the Irish labour force, the opposition of local residents and the legal battles that the construction of the track brought about. Not at all easy to find but it is so good that it is worth the effort.

Section D 5

Veteran, Edwardian, Vintage and Historic Car Racing

First on the list is *The Batsford Colour Book of Historic Racing Cars.* There was a time when I used to look upon Batsfords as newcomers to the motor and motor racing field, but this isn't so at all for they were, in fact, among the earliest of publishers to assess the appeal of four wheels. So it isn't surprising that they should have come up with so many well-produced motor racing books in colour and also books on other aspects of motoring. This one is well up to their standard.

Full Throttle by Sir Henry Birkin, came out first in 1932 and later ran to many editions and reprints. It was one of the first motoring books I ever had and anyone having seen Birkin drive the big supercharged single seater Bentley at Brooklands would never part with it for among all the drivers of his time, he had charisma — and could also drive. Whether he actually wrote *Full Throttle* or whether it was 'ghosted' on his behalf, I don't know, but it's a great book.

The Mad Motorists is a re-hash of *Pekin to Paris,* and none the worse for that. The two *Motor Racing*s by Howe and by 'Sammy' Davis, though excellent, are entirely different types of book, the latter being an autobiography in reality. The former is one of the Lonsdale Library series, with Earl Howe's name shown as Editor. It is more a series of articles that form separate chapters, with subjects ranging from racing cars to circuits, hill climbs, suspension, braking and many other technical aspects. Like Davis' book, it is a nice one to have.

Motor Racing Memories by Bradley, a great motoring journalist and one time Motoring Correspondent of *The Times,* is one that all collectors of books on racing seek and never can find. *Racing an Historic Car,* in this case an ERA, is now almost as difficult and so is Berthon's *Racing History of the Bentley Car* and Rose's *A Record of Motor Racing 1894-1908.* It wouldn't be stressing it too much to say that if one aims to have a really fine collection of books on racing, all these four should be included.

I always find it difficult to comment on the books written by Sir Malcolm Campbell. Though I never knew him, I saw a lot of him during the years I was at Brooklands and, for a long time, was a devoted disciple. He was always pleasant to meet and talk to and obviously a good driver and a good business man who, through his Land Speed Record runs, did a great deal for this country. He was also a great showman and it has sometimes seemed to

A dealers get-together. Eoin Young (left) combs the stock of Frank Stroud of Chater and Scott (right), longest of all in the bookselling business.

'Up and coming' dealer Terry Wills (centre) in search of bargains at the 1981 Beaulieu *Museum at Home* Book Fair.

me that this aspect of his character came through too strongly in his writings. It seemed at times that as he wrote he felt he was writing for a reader who knew nothing of his achievements, whereas the reverse was true. His love for motor racing was obvious to all who saw him race, his cars were always the best that could be obtained and always meticulously prepared and tuned by his foreman mechanic Leo Villa. He needed no build up — it was there for all to see.

I have a feeling that I am not alone in thinking this, for Campbell's books, though really good books, have never, I think, been in quite such demand as books by some of his contemporaries even though, in the main, they were well written and illustrated.

I don't know why but for some reason Rex Hays' *Tribute by Trophy* was the only title of his that I never read. I don't like admitting that because Rex is a friend as well as being one of the finest constructors of scale model motor cars in the world. Examples of his work can be seen in the National Motor Museum at Beaulieu, examples so good that one feels that if one could shrink to the same scale, one could almost drive off in them. But I know *Tribute by Trophy* was good, because of the demand there has always been for it.

Section D 6

Racing Cars. Design, Construction (Inc. Specials), Development, Evolution, Tuning (For histories see Sect G).

To many interested in racing, the design, building and construction of the car sometimes takes greater priority than the running and racing of the car itself and it is to them that this Chapter will probably appeal most. *Austin '7' Specials* (Williams), *Building and Racing my '750'* (Stephens), *The Construction of Ford Specials* (Mills), *Design and Tuning of Competition Engines* (Smith), *Ford Specials* (Stephens), *The Ford Ten Competition Engine* (Smith), *One Off* (Havart), *Specials* (Bolster) and *Turbocharging and Supercharging*

for Maximum Power and Torque (Setright) are all for the designer/constructor who is almost as well provided as far as literature is concerned, as any other reader. Few, to whom the construction of 'specials' appeals, will not know or perhaps have seen John Bolster's fabulous 'Bloody Mary', and I recall once asking him his impressions of his first drive in her, round a field incidentally. Drawing himself up to his full height and with all the famous Bolster mannerisms flaring, including the moustache 'twitch', he replied 'Well, of course, I knew at once that I had entered the ranks of the great motor car designers of the World'.

With James Tilling, who probably knows more about 'Bloody' than anyone except John himself, I was once co-opted as 'second mechanic' to John and his brainchild at a race meeting at Oulton and it proved an experience too, for the driver/designer never ceased issuing shouted instructions throughout the day. 'Copper wire' he boomed as 'Bloody' required attention to some vital part, the existence of which only he knows. 'No, not that roll, that's the pre-war stuff, we haven't got much of that left'. And on starting technique 'Now you all know the form. Don't stop pushing immediately one engine fires. They've done the four minute mile now — you ought to be able to do three. No one who isn't lying face down on the road with a bloody nose when she goes is doing his job.' It's something that remains with you as not to be attempted too often. So John's book *Specials* is a 'must' in this section.

Three more good books are Cyril Posthumus' *The British Competition Car* and his *Classic Racing Cars* and Doug Nye's *The Classic Single Seater*. And, of course, Pomeroy's *Design and Behaviour of the Racing Car* and *Evolution of the Racing Car* even though the former is moving from the 'scarce' category to 'rare'.

Only two factors cause a book to move up the board like this. It must at least be a very good book of its type in the first place. From then on it's just a question of supply meeting the increasing demand. *The Golden Age of the American Racing Car* (Borgson) has always been popular and so has Lord Montagu's *The Gordon Bennett Races*, particularly the 1st Edition. Ludvigsen's *Mercedes Benz Racing Cars*, an American title, is a big and beautifully illustrated book if you can find it, but I wouldn't think there can be many copies floating around in UK, nice though it is. Jenkinson's *The Maserati 250 F* is another to put alongside his *Grand Prix Mercedes W 125* and, in a sense might be happier in Section D 1, but Mathieson's *Pictorial Survey of Racing Cars 1919-1939* is, in its class, surely the best. How nice to be like 'Taso' and write only two books, both of them so good.

The Racing Car — Development and Design by Clutton, Posthumus and Jenkinson, is a sister book to *The British Competition Car,* both published by Batsford and part of an excellent series they put out in the 1950s and '60s. Although I am not sure, they may have been put out later as small softbacks. Quite a number of good titles were reprinted in this form and when customers of my business used to ask me what was the minimum sum necessary on which to start a library of motoring books, I used to answer 'around £5', for these little pocket editions were always available in the markets for around 50 pence. While Batsford did *The Racing Car* (Clutton, Posthumus and Jenkinson), *The Sports Car* (Stanford), *The Racing Driver* (Jenkinson) *Starting Grid to Chequered Flag* (Paul Frere), *Veteran and Edwardian Motor Cars* (Scott Moncrieff) and *The Vintage Motor Car* (Clutton and Stanford), Pan Books rallied round with *BRM* (Raymond Mays), *Life at the Limit* (Graham Hill) and *Jim Clark at the Wheel* (Clark), to which Trust Books added *Fangio* (Fangio) with a foreword by Stirling Moss. There may well be others but what a galaxy of titles to gather together at 50 pence per time — all by well known authors.

Despite its rather grand title, *The Racing Car Explained* by Pomeroy is a small and rather insignificant looking little book, but Pomeroy knew his subject and knew how to put his knowledge into writing. Jenkinson's *Racing Car Pocketbook,* one of a series, and pocketbook size, contains a lot of his vast store of knowledge on racing. The others, by different authors, are the *Sports Car Pocketbook, Veteran Motor Car* and *Vintage Motor Car* — in other words a four volume set, all good reference and nice to have.

One that emerged almost too late for inclusion, yet must be added, is David Weguelin's *The History of English Racing Automobiles,* to assess which one must read Bill Boddy's review in the Februry 1981 issue of *Motor Sport.* The review is lengthy and comprehensive but to quote Bill's

words the book 'must rank as the best of all one make racing-car productions'. I have been loaned the book and have only had time to browse through it but have no doubt at all that what he says is right.

Some others in this section are largely pictorial and in colour, nice to scan and not too technical.

Section D 7

Racing drivers and personnel. Driving — art and technique (for autobiographies and biographies see Section G)

If one listens to a group of motor racing enthusiasts chatting over a recent Grand Prix, usually in the bar, it isn't hard to see that is usually the driver, rather than the car itself, that forms the main topic of conversation. Today, the names of Grand Prix drivers are known worldwide, even among those who follow sport in a general way.

A slight problem arises in this section in that some of the books concerning racing drivers are biographies and autobiographies and, to ensure that the reader can find the title or titles he seeks, there is probably more cross referencing here than anywhere else.

Atalanta, the late 'Sammy' Davis book on lady racing drivers came out in the 1950s via Foulis and has, for a long time, been the only book on this particular aspect of motor racing. This is rather a pity because there has always been a nucleus of lady drivers, the best of whom have, from time to time, been comparable in skill with their male counterparts, even though not in the 'top flight'. Today there are several ladies in the sport and, since they certainly add interest to the scene, it would seem that, after so long a time lag, another book on the subject could be overdue. *Atalanta* covered mainly the ladies who took part in pre-war racing.

Competition Driving by Paul Frere, a well-known driver and journalist, could be useful to those contemplating taking the plunge, particularly because the author took part in his day in so many and

The Constant Search

varied aspects of competition. Daley's *The Cruel Sport* is a large and beautifully produced book crammed with good illustrations and, though the exact opposite in size, *Drivers in Action* by Klemantaski and Frostick is also one of the best.

German Racing Cars and Drivers by Molter is a favourite of mine and *Klemantaski's Photo Album* is one of Motor Racing Publication's spirobound softbacks which will appeal to all lovers of good action photographs. Another good spirobound is Sallon's *Motor Racing Drivers Past and Present,* a first class collection of caricatures which, though for long un-noticed by collectors has now, it seems, become 'collectable'.

Denis Jenkinson's *The Racing Driver* is one of fifty books that *Motor Sport* Editor, Bill Boddy, would like to take with him were he ever marooned on a desert island and of it he says 'It may be rather scientific, and even depressing as making motor racing sound rather mathematical but I would require it so that, if ever I were rescued, I would know how to go round corners rather faster than I had done before'. So there is no doubt about that one. If Bill puts that rating on it, it's good.

I would put *A Racing Driver's World* by Caracciola high on the list because, Nuvolari apart, he was such a great pre-war driver, not only for his Grand Prix performances but also for those great drives in the huge SSK Mercedes, one lone entry pitted against massive Bentley opposition — and, with it, such a modest and unassuming man.

In another way, I have always liked Piero Taruffi's *Works Driver.* I only once saw him drive, when he took over the entry of Earl Howe's Bugatti at Brooklands but, like Caracciola, he is such a quiet and modest man that one found it hard to believe that, once in the car, he could become transformed in the way he was.

Not a very large section, but something there for everyone.

Section D 8

Motor Racing (General), Races, Record breaking and Hill climbing

In its day, I liked Rodney Walkerley's *Automobile Racing* because Rodney was not only the 'Denis Jenkinson' of his era but wrote with all his accuracy since, as *Grand Vitesse* of the *Motor,* he was always on the Grand Prix scene, meeting and living at the same hotels as the drivers. Rain or sunshine, there would be the tall willowy figure, the notebook, the drooping cigarette and the quizzical smile, always friendly, always with the latest snippets of gossip to impart and, later in the evening, always hunched over his pink gin in one corner of the bar — a 'built in' part of the motor racing scene. What Rodney didn't know about Grand Prix racing wasn't worth bothering about.

The Book of Speed put out by Batsford in 1934 may not be everyone's cup of tea, even though it is mine. Not everyone will go for it because, though its contributors include Capt.G.E.T.Eyston, Sir Malcolm Campbell and racing motorcyclist Jimmy Guthrie, the greater part of it is given up to speed in the air, by rail and on water. I like everything about this one: its sepia illustrations, text by no less than twelve different authors but most of all its 1930s look, both textwise and externally. A museum piece if you like.

Although I have Eyston's *Fastest on Earth* and *Flat Out* among my books, I have always thought of both as better reference than reading. For all his tremendous achievements both on the track and in record breaking, Eyston was the most unassuming and modest of men and one who recoiled at the thought of 'blowing his own trumpet'. This, I think, comes out in some of his books. Although I saw a lot of him at Brooklands, and he was always friendly, I have learned more about him through my friend, Bert Denly, who not only prepared and maintained his racing fleet and even led the team in building 'Thunderbolt', the giant Land Speed Record car but also was co-driver with the 'Captain' on many long distance runs. In all the time I knew and saw Eyston at the track, I never once heard him say an unkind word. The nearest he ever came to it was when, in course of one of the BRDC 500 mile races, Walter Handley was sharing the driving of the well known 1100cc MG Magnette single-seater with him. At a stage of the race when Walter was driving, the car went out of control towards the end of the Railway Straight and crashed through the fence on the offside of the track at around 130mph. It was an unusual place for such a thing to happen and remote from all help, so that I was the first to get there. Wal was shaken but unhurt and wanted the 'Captain' to be told as quickly as possible. On the way back to the pits, I met him and gave him Wal's message. Looking crosser than I'd ever seen him, Eyston replied with one word 'Idiot'! Not knowing the circumstances and feeling only relieved about Walter, there was no reply I could make!

The Land Speed Record by Posthumus is one of the scarcer books besides being well up to Cyril's usual high standard. *Magic MPH* by Goldie Gardner tells the story of his successful record runs with MG. All MG books are popular not only with MG enthusiasts but with collectors generally and this is no exception. It is a small book but, of course, the size of a book has no bearing whatever on its popularity — it's what is inside it that counts.

Mini Racing by Christabel Carlisle is a useful little book, even though softback, and it does seem surprising that, when one looks back on all the racing there has been with Minis, it should fall to a lady to write a book about it. *Motoring Sport,* with joint authors Stuck and Burgaller, is now more than just scarce and forms one of the cornerstones of many collections. But I confess that it is one with which I have never been in love and I still fail to see its appeal.

One that I did enjoy was May's *Shelsley Walsh,* out from Foulis in 1945 at the time when, since no circuits were in use, hill climbing and sprinting was all the rage. This was one that Foulis did put a date on but there were many other good ones that went out 'Not Dated' and, as time goes on, this seems rather a pity.

Speed — The Book of Racing and Records, apart from the fact that it came out in 1950, is in many respects similar to *The Book of Speed* mentioned earlier in this Chapter and for that reason, I like it as well. It does have one or two nice colour plates and contributors include, on the car side, John Cobb, Goldie Gardner, Raymond Mays, Rodney Walkerley and D.B. (Bunny) Tubbs and, on bikes, Graham Walker, Freddie Frith and (pedal powered) Reg Harris.

Speed Hill Climb was another of Austin May's nice small books and *Speed on Salt* was a larger format book describing Eyston's record runs on the salt flats in which he was aided by co-author W.F.Bradley. *Sprint* by Nicholson, focussing on sprints and hill climbs, is in many collections, and so is Bill Boddy's *World Land Speed Record* which

came out in three forms, hardback and 'spiro-bound' via M.R.P and also in near-pocketbook form.

Section D 9

Motor Racing. Results, statistics and management

What can one say concerning a section that consists largely of statistics, and who would want to read through it? Well, though it is admittedly a reference area, it is one that may be of use to authors but besides writers there are countless thousands of collectors all over the world whose libraries on motor racing would just not be complete without such books.

First, look at *Autocourse.* There are, in fact, two Autocourse productions, one which is an Annual while the second is a magazine, of which more anon. The Annual first came out in 1959 and, together with the 1960 Annual, which was in two parts, appeared in softback form, after which it came out regularly year by year. Always well produced and well illustrated with a high proportion of colour, *Autocourse* took on a new lease of life when, in 1975, Richard Poulter's company, Hazleton Securities, took over production. Since then it has gone from strength to strength, widening to a second and new production, *Motocourse,* covering the principal motorcycle races.

There is no one better to be in charge of a production like this than a really enthusiastic and knowledgeable follower of racing and since this tag fits Richard perfectly, it isn't at all surprising that since the take-over *Autocourse* has gone ahead so well in the last five years. In its present form there is certainly no better 'year by year' record of Grand Prix racing.

Next, *Behind the Scenes of Motor Racing,* which is literally a 'behind the scenes' since its author, Ken Gregory, was for years manager to Stirling Moss. *Controlling a Racing Car Team* comes from the pen of Sammy Davis who not only drove in many racing teams but also ran some. Sammy's idea of how a team should be run and controlled were definite as I once heard from the

The Constant Search

late Charles Brackenbury, a contemporary of Sammy's, for though both were close friends, Charles was a bit of a practical joker at times, with ideas that, on occasions, clashed with Sammy's, even though both had great respect for the other.

The incident that brought matters to a head was, I think, in 1935 when Sammy was manager of the team of four Aston Martins to run at Le Mans and Charles was one of the drivers. The plan was to drive all four cars from Feltham to Dover, cross on the boat and then run from Calais to Le Mans and Sammy's instructions to the drivers were to keep all four cars running at a steady seventy miles an hour from Calais to Le Mans. Charles was a very good and reliable team driver who could always be relied on to obey orders in a race, but he didn't think much of this particular plan. He was a great Francophile and loved the French way of life, so the idea of the seventy mile an hour schedule with no stops at the attractive looking bars and bistros was just 'not on'. As a result, only three cars travelled at a steady seventy non-stop and the fourth at between eighty five and a hundred, with frequent stops to catch up. Though nothing was said on the way, the three cars constantly passing and being passed by the fourth, quite a lot was said on arrival. It was rare for Sammy to be out of control and it never lasted for long.

Again, on team management, David Murray's book *Ecurie Ecosse* and John Wyer's *Motor Racing Management* are written by authors with vast first-hand knowledge, the former with his Scottish team of 'C' and 'D' Type Jaguars and the latter with the works teams of Aston Martins, among others.

Where statistics are concerned, Rodney Walkerley's *Motor Racing Facts and Figures* will provide good reference up to the 1960s and, from then on, the task was inherited by Blunsden and Brinton's *Motor Racing Year,* Anthony Pritchard then continuing with the same title in 1970.

Where the cars themselves were concerned, the demand for every volume of Denis Jenkinson's *Motor Sport Racing Car Review* speaks for itself. Only small volumes but all filled with information and good photographs. And to cover every aspect of statistics, Robin Richards' *Speed and a Microphone* covers the views and problems of the broadcaster.

Section D 10

Tracks and circuits

Since, without tracks, there can obviously be no racing, this section, though small, is quite important.

Initially, Great Britain lagged behind the rest of the world in the provision of tracks till it fell to a private landowner, Mr Locke King, to provide the country with its first and, for years, its only track, Brooklands. It has always seemed to me that this was one of the greatest acts of philanthropy ever handed to the country and its motor industry. Obviously he looked for a return on his huge outlay of capital and must have had a good idea of the sort of opposition he would meet. The following reference to the track, from Eric Parker's *Highways and Byways in Surrey* of 1908, gives a good indication of what this was likely to be :-

'By Brooklands hill but since a year,
        untrod the meadows lay.
Unspanned through musk and meadows
        sweet ran olive bright the Wey.
Blackbirds about that wind and wild,
        carolled a roguish choir
From willow green to willow grey,
        kingfishers shot sapphire.

There gay and far the Surrey sun
        spread cowslips far and gay,
Lit wide the orchid's purple flames
        the white fire of the May
And thither stole a happy boat
        to hear the ringdoves coo,
To mark again the drumming snipe
        zigzag the April blue;
To watch the darting dragon flies,
        live pine needles awing
O Brooklands meadow, there we knew
        you first knew all the spring.

And then — the change! Spade, engine, pick,
        the gangers' myriad Hun,
A thousand branches banished shade,
        flat glare of sand and sun.

From pine and stream to steam and stone,
from peace to din and pain,
From old unused to new unuse,
but never Wey again!

To his credit, if in fact he ever saw it, Mr Locke King wasn't deterred by that, or by the tremendous opposition he met, and Brooklands opened in 1907. From the start, it had an aura of mystery about it that even today still lingers on. Many books have been written about Brooklands and all that went on there but, where car racing is concerned, none has surpassed W. Boddy's *History of Brooklands Motor Course* which came out first in three separate volumes between 1948 and 1950 and then, in 1957, as 'three volumes in one'. If one has this on the shelf, nothing else is needed, for Bill is certainly the most knowledgeable of all where car racing at Brooklands is concerned and also knows a great deal about other aspects. Charles Gardner's book *Fifty Years of Brooklands* is another nice one and takes in a lot of the flying that went on there and *Wheels Take Wings* by Burn and Bradley gives good coverage of much of the early 'hassle' that took place between the local residents who hoped to prevent its birth, and the owners, the Locke Kings.

Throughout the time that the track operated, the *Brooklands Automobile Racing Club,* who organised and administered the car racing side, issued various publications including Year Books which were well illustrated and interesting. Their *Rule Books* and *Speed and Distance Tables,* though not easy to find, form part of the collections of many Brooklands devotees. Other tracks, including Indianapolis and Monza, have done the same but, in the case of Montlhéry in France, Boddy's well put together *Montlhéry* seems to have been the only real reference work.

In the case of road circuits I have always thought of Klemantaski's and Frostick's *Motor Racing Circuits of Europe* as being way ahead of the rest, although Dunlop's little softback *Famous Motor Racing Circuits* contains a lot of interest in its twenty five pages.

Airfield circuits? There were many after the war but, now, only Silverstone has survived as an entity and still goes from strength to strength, thanks to the hard work and effort put in by the British Racing Drivers' Club. In this context Carrick's book *Silverstone* is the one to include.

Section D 11

Motor Racing. Other than sections 1 to 10

There has to be a section into which to slot titles that seemed unhappy elsewhere and, though I confess that I have none of these in my own library, a number are by quite well known authors and will be well worth having. There was a time when several of these were among my own but, over the years, with space always being the problem, they have been 'culled' in order to make room for others.

Quite a number are photograph books, largely in colour, some very nice productions, but they are not books for which I have fallen. Others are on aspects of motor racing such as photography itself, which is something about which I know almost nothing.

So, even though they don't figure where I am concerned, that doesn't mean that they may not fit well into other collections. The answer here is to look for yourself.

Chapter 8   Section E

Books on cars for use on the road

Section E 1

Touring Cars

Whereas in the years after the turn of the century, this could well have been one of the largest sections of any, the position has changed. Today, motorists who tour need very little information on the subject as far as the car is concerned so, again, this becomes an area of history and reference.

While the Mini and other cars of its class and size are widely used for touring, many owners, faced with the possibility of something larger or faster, would be able to say at once what makes and horsepower they would choose without reference to a book. But even so there are one or two that are of interest and I would recommend to history lovers C.F.Caunter's *Motor Cars* Parts 1 and 2, put out by the Science Museum in conjunction with HM Stationery Office for, even though softback, they are authoritatively written, well illustrated and interesting.

A nice book to have in any general collection is the complete run of *The Observer's Book of Automobiles,* all pocket size which, while taking up minimum shelf space, give a continuous pictorial history of the development of motor cars from the mid 1950s onwards together with short but informative text. The earlier editions are becoming harder to find and autojumbles are the places to find them.

The Post War Touring Car by Graham Robson, from Haynes, is one on its own, so must merit consideration by all keen motoring tourists. Titles relating to early touring are, of course, to be found in their own particular section.

Section E 2

Sports Cars

Gregor Grant's *British Sports Cars* was for long a leader in the field, running to several editions. For me, the foreign sports car has always had a special appeal and, for this reason alone, I wouldn't be without Boddy's *Continental Sports Cars* which I have browsed through over and over again.

I don't know what it is about continental sports cars — I think that continental styling has a lot to do with it but, in this context, I have always regarded the Italians as second to none. Over the years they have produced some superbly engineered sports machines as well.

Germany has too, and I like *German High Performance Cars* by Sloniger and von Fersen and it has always seemed strange that, while this came out via Batsford, the other good one, *Italian High Performance Cars* by Pritchard and Davey was by courtesy of Allen and Unwin. The latter is becoming less easy to find and I suppose that will soon apply to both.

Haynes *Guide to Used Sports Cars* was, at the time, a must to many aspirants and is still good and useful reference fifteen years later.

I love Nick Georgano's *History of Sports Cars* and also Hough's *History of the World's Sports Cars* and the *History of the World's High Performance Cars* that he did together with Michael Frostick.

The softbacks published by Brooklands Books, which are really reprinted articles and road tests, cover many makes and give good coverage to Jaguar. Since all the information contained in them is authentic, they make both good reference and good reading. Some have pages numbered and others don't, which is a pity.

Three more good titles are Colin Campbell's *The Sports Car* and *The Sports Car — Its Design and Performance* and Stanford's *The Sports Car — Its Development and Design,* the first two possibly better as reference and the other more readable. Titles on Bodywork and Coachbuilding have always been in short supply, which will account for the demand for *Sports Car Bodywork* by Locke. *The Sports Car Pocketbook* by Bill Boddy is as good and informative as the rest of the series and a 'non space taker' as well. Even if *Sports and Classic Cars* by Borgeson and Jaderquist does take space, it is worth it for the volume of information it contains, and the same applies to Markmann and Sherwin's *The Book of Sports Cars* — but one really does need space for these big ones.

Section E 3

Veteran, Edwardian and vintage cars

Since this is really a three in one section, let's first 'recap' on the periods. 'Veteran' is pre-1905, Edwardian 1905 to 1918 and 'Vintage' 1919 to 1930, and there is plenty to choose from in each category.

Pemberton's *Amateur Motorist* is in many good collections but, though well illustrated, is rare, and not very light reading. St John Nixon's *The Antique Automobile,* though written much later, is the product of one of the best known authors, himself an early motorist and one who knew his subject as well as anyone. *Autocars* by Farman, 1896, is as heavy as almost all the books of its period but is the one I like best and *The Automobile* by Hasluck, in three volumes, is almost certainly the most comprehensive.

All the Batsford series are mainly picture, colour illustrated, not expensive and easily found. Brown's *Book of the Light Car* is delightful and, in view of its period, rare now. *The Book of the Motor Car* by Sloss is an American title and, apart from my own copy, I don't recall seeing another. The other *Book of the Motor Car* by Rankin Kennedy runs to four volumes, although the fourth is later and sometimes absent. It is quite hard to sell and easily found. The circulation must have been enormous because it is in almost every auction.

Cars and Motor Cycles, a three volume set by Lord Montagu and M.W.Bourdon, is the only one of its kind. It came out originally as a magazine in 26 parts, over a period between 1928 and 1929, in which form it may not have sold out because one almost always finds it bound in three separate volumes. It is profusely illustrated with some colour plates and covers a wide spectrum: cars, motorcycles, commercials and even steam. The text is light and readable, it is very good for reference and I love it. Filson Young's *The Complete Motorist* is acknowledged as a classic and ran to numerous editions, so that most good collections include it. *Edwardian Cars* by Carter is good, and, though it is only a small book, so is *The First Hundred Road Motors* by Kidner.

Facts Concerning Elementary Locomotion 1833 is a title that I must admit to never having seen and I am still trying to have a sight of it, first hearing of it from an old customer and friend, Mr D.M.King in USA. John Bolster's *French Vintage Cars* and Karslake's *From Veteran to Vintage* should be in any good library and so should Filson Young's *The Happy Motorist* though it isn't a great favourite of

The Constant Search

mine. I like Rolt's *The Horseless Carriage, Horseless Carriage Days* by Maxim, *Horseless Vehicles, Automobiles and Motor Cycles* by Hiscox and also St John Nixon's *Invention of the Automobile.*

My great favourite in this section is *The Modest Man's Motor* by Maj. C.G. Matson, an author no more or less pompous than others of the 1903 period who set out to write a book advising would be automobilists on how to motor at modest cost. Not long ago, I reviewed it at some length in *Collector's Review* and here are one or two short extracts:

On cost: For over a year I drove this little car daily in all weathers, mostly taking my wife for afternoon excursions but also making a few trips of thirty or forty miles to the seaside and my total expenses for that period for petrol and lubricating oil were under £10. Accumulators were charged about every two months at a cost of one shilling and sixpence and that was all.

On the engine: Have a single cylinder motor of about six and a half to eight horse power of the simplest type. i.e. with the inlet valve opening by ordinary atmospheric pressure and not by any mechanical means.

On tyres: Have solid, thick rubber tyres. Pneumatic tyres cost three times as much as all the other motor expenses combined. They are quite unnecessary for speeds up to twenty miles an hour.

On the chassis: The frame should be of wood, reinforced by steel plates. This is both light and strong and easily repaired in the case of an accident and the same cannot be said of either the stamped steel or the tubular frame (How would he have felt about monocoques?).

On transmission: In all machinery except a motor car, from a sewing machine to the enormous lathes in Woolwich Arsenal, power is transmitted from where it is generated to where it is wanted, by a belt and pulleys, and so it is on my ideal car. A flat belt about 2½ inches wide.

On repairs: There were no repairs.

On horses: One soon gets to know by a horse's eye if he is going to shy or not. If ladies, driving or riding, are met, the counsel of perfection is to shoot up a side road, or even turn round and retire a mile or two by the way which you came.

On intoxicated persons and imbeciles of both sexes: They can be negotiated.

On the Police: A friendly nod and, perhaps, a friendly lift to a stout and perspiring constable making his way to a distant village on a hot and dusty summer day is appreciated, and possibly, when you are swinging along home at a little above the legal limit you will suddenly come on him again, and he will find something of interest to observe, on the other side of the hedge, as you go by.

On noise and smell: The driver does not worry about noise — he leaves it behind him with the smell. What to do with the exhaust gas is a large question. The great thing is to get rid of it at once. If it passes out unchecked, it makes a horrible bang so it is passed through a 'silencer' full of holes which lets it trickle out. But if it doesn't get out fast enough, the piston has to push it out, which puts back pressure on the piston and slows the car.

Yes, the Major certainly knew something.

The Montagu Motor Book, and *The Motor* by Armstrong, both published in the 1910s, are good to have and so are *Motor Cars* by Wallis Tayler, 1897, and *Motor Cars and Other Motor Driven Vehicles* by Walker, 1920. *Motor Cars and the Application of Mechanical Power to Road Vehicles* by Rhys Jenkins (1902) and *Motor Cars and Their Story* by Talbot (1912), are both large and desirable books but, despite its rather grandiose title *The Motor Car — Its Nature, Use and Management* by Sir Henry Thompson, published in 1902, is a small and rather uninspiring little book. *Motoring* by Berriman is nice and the Badminton Library Series *Motors and Motor Driving,* the 1st Edition of which is 1902, is an absolute 'must' although I really don't think it matters which edition one has. Many collectors of Rolls-Royce material prefer the editions in which Chapter 9, The Caprices of the Petrol Motor, is by the Hon. C.S. Rolls (1904).

New Method of Propelling Locomotive Machines (Compressed Air), 1830, *New System of Inland Conveyance for Goods and Passengers* (Compressed Air), 1827 and *Notes on Motor Carriages,* 1896, are all titles, the details of which have been researched for me by my friend, Mr King, in the States. Their existence he has established, but none of them I have ever seen, which applies also to *Power Locomotion on the Highway. A guide to* (1896) and *Propulsion of Carriages on Common Roads other than by Animal Power* (1893).

Self Propelled Vehicles (1902) is one old title I

54

have and like and Minchin's *Silver Lady* is the story of a particular Rolls-Royce as told by herself. It has always been with my other Rolls-Royce books and is one which one can read again. I have liked all 'Bunty' Scott Moncrieff's books and his *Veteran and Edwardian Motor Cars* is almost the best in its sphere. *The Veteran Car Owner's Manual* and *The Veteran Motor Car Pocketbook* are popular but I confess that in saying this I am speaking as a dealer (retired!) and not as a Veteran enthusiast, which I am not, much as I enjoy seeing the cars in action.

Vintage? I go for *The Vintage Car 1919-1930* by Nicholson, not so often seen nowadays, *The Vintage Car Pocketbook* by Clutton, Bird and Harding but most of all, *The Vintage Motor Car* by Clutton and Stanford, which I think is a lovely book and, strangely, because it is so good, it can still be found without too much difficulty. And though they will not, perhaps, be everybody's choice, I have and like both *Woman and Her Car* (1918) and *Woman and the Motor Car* (1906). Women were so feminine and helpless then, but not so pretty as they are today.

Section E 4

Cars 1931-1939

Take heart if this Section looks lean because the reason is that these are the only titles setting out specifically to cover solely the cars of this period.

In fact there are countless books which give good coverage of, at least, the glamour cars of the 1930s and many of the 'bread and butter' models as well. If space were available to do so, one could pinpoint many of these here but, with so many titles to cover, it is only possible to give brief details of some.

Fifteen or twenty years ago there was comparatively little interest in any but the most prestigious cars of the 1930s but, with inflation at its present rate, many car collectors seek run of the mill makes of the 1930s rather than be out of the picture altogether. One has only to attend a few of the rallies held, to see how much time and effort has gone in to beautifully restoring comparatively mundane

models of Austin, Morris, Wolseley and other 1930s cars. It would be surprising, therefore, if in the next year or two, many more books of cars of the 1930s were not to appear on dealers' shelves. Though not so exciting as some of the more expensive cars, all these smaller models form links in the chain of history of the automobile.

Almost all the titles listed give good coverage of the period and particularly Camm's *Book of Motors,* which I wouldn't be without.

Section E 5

Cars — 1940 onwards

Some eighteen months ago, when talking with a fellow collector who specialises on books relating to cars of specific periods, I asked him why he thought it was that there should be more titles covering cars of the 1940s and 1950s than of the 1930s. His answer was immediate 'Well you see, it's the youngsters. They've not seen many cars of the 'thirties. To them, an old car is a car of the 'forties or 'fifties, like their dad's which they rode in as kids, and what could be nicer to own than that'.

Although that may be part of the answer I doubt whether it goes all the way. One certainly does see many young enthusiasts displaying well restored models of the 1950s at rallies, but it seems to me that interest in this era may be partly because spares are easier to find but also because the cars themselves were so very much better than those of the 'thirties.

Whatever the reason, the selection of books covering this period is certainly better and almost every book in this Section is worth having if this is the period that appeals.

Section E 6

Cars — Thoroughbred and Classic

Though many cars, both thoroughbred and classic such as Bugatti, Bentley and Rolls-Royce will not be found here, all can be found in section G 2 (Marque). The books listed in this section (E 6), will probably include examples among other makes and types.

The Automobile Book and *The Great Cars,* both by Ralph Stein, are large and are neither exorbitant in price nor too hard to find and would, I think, form a good base on which to build. Both give wide coverage and are profusely illustrated with both black and white and colour photographs.

Automobile Treasures is nice and, if you like colour illustrations, the Batsford series provides it. In a different class because, for one thing, it is in a higher price bracket, Ulyett's *The Beauty of Cars* really does live up to its title and is superbly produced. *Bodies Beautiful* by McLellan is good and, rather surprisingly, was remaindered not long ago at a price well below its new cost.

Cars of the Connoisseur by Buckley must now be rated as, at least, a mini classic and my own feeling about this one is that the author picked all the right cars to include. But that's just an opinion, of course, and may mean nothing more than that my conception of a 'connoisseur's car' is identical to his.

Again, I wouldn't be without Hough and Frostick's *History of the World's Classic Cars* and, though I'm not and never could be a 'restorer', there must be a good case for Hudson's *Post War British Thoroughbreds — Their Purchase and Restoration* because so many people have told me, over the years, that the first step in restoring is to sit down and read a good book on the subject and that to do so will save you pounds.

We dealt with *Sports and Classic Cars* in Section E 2 and it's due to its title that it is here also. *The Thoroughbred Motor Car* is the sister to *Cars of the Connoisseur* from the same publishers, Batsfords, but with Scott Moncrieff as author. I would make the same comments on it because what 'Bunty' doesn't know about such cars isn't worth knowing. He ought to — he dealt in them long enough.

Somehow, I haven't got down to reading John Bolster's *The Upper Crust* — a shocking admission which I must rectify. But everyone I know who has read it has enthused about it.

Section E 7

Cars — Design, Manufacture, Development, Tuning, Maintenance and restoration, including coachbuilding

With so many headings, I hope that there will be something here for everyone. Both of Rae's books on the American aspect are good and, even though there are books on body building, Beattie's *Complete Book of Automobile Body Design* from Haynes must meet a need, whilst Setright's *Automobile Tyres* must be almost the only one on the subject.

Automobile Design; Great Designers and their Work by Ronald Barker and Anthony Harding is excellent, with many good plates and covering no less than eleven different designers from the Bolles, Pere et Fils, right up to modern times with Alec Issigonis and Colin Chapman.

An extremely rare one is Stanley Sears' *A Collection of Interesting Cars,* a small spirobound published by himself and, one assumes, for private circulation only, evolving round his own collection of cars. Another almost in the same class is Priest's *From Chariot to Car* which, published by Barker & Co, is on the subject of body building carried out by the Company, mainly on Rolls-Royce and similar chassis. *History of the Art of Coachbuilding* by Thrupp is another which is similar but very much rarer because, for one thing, it dates back earlier and even Oliver's *History of Coachbuilding,* which came out in 1962, is extremely scarce now.

Wheatley and Morgan's *Maintenance and Driving of Vintage Cars* together with the same team's *Restoration and Preservation of Vintage and Classic Cars* are a good pair to have, for the vintage minded. Where body building and coach painting of early vehicles are concerned, *Motor Body Building* (Terry & Hall), the same title by Shepherd, nine years later, *Motor Bodywork* and *Motor Bodies and Chassis* both by Butler and *Motor Car and Coach Painting* by Oliver are virtually all that one could need in this era. *The Practical House, Wagon and Automobile Painter* by White is a delightful little book which really tries to cover everything from testing the purity of white lead to rust spots on marble — lovely.

Steering Problems and *Subtleties of Steering* put out by Automotive Products in the 'fifties are both small softbacks but, even so, have a lot of information to impart and the same applies to *Suspension Efficiencies* by Woodhead.

Technical Facts of the Vintage Bentley by courtesy of the Bentley Driver's Club, is extracted information from their Club Journal and must be tremendously useful to all owners and *W.O Bentley: Engineer* is enjoyable and interesting reading.

Section E 8

Steam Cars, Diesel and Electric

It is food for thought that one day we may be back to the steam car and comforting to reflect that, in UK at least, we shall never be short of water! Though about as 'untechnical' as anyone could be, I have to admit that on the few occasions I have seen steam powered cars in action, I've marvelled not only at their silence but also at the torque and acceleration, which still seem to be lacking in the best of diesels.

Everything was done so thoroughly and so nicely way back in the days of steam. Looking now at one of my oldest books, titled on the spine as *Steam on Common Roads* by C.F.Young, one sees the full title on the title page as *The Economy of Steam Power on Common Roads — in Relation to Agriculturalists, Railway Companies, Mine and Coal Owners, Quarry Proprietors etc — With its History and Practice in Great Britain —* By Charles Fredrick. T. Young (Mem.Soc.Engineers) and on the next page 'To an Enlightened Public in the hope of meeting with their approval and support, this work is respectfully inscribed by their obedient servant, the author'. How different it all is today!

It is a book which, till now, I have never looked at carefully, fondly imagining that way back in 1860 there wasn't much on the roads. How wrong! There seem to have been gargantuan steam contrivances hauling miniature trainloads from place to place so it's no wonder, really, that the early motorists found surfaces 'rutted and almost impas-

sable' as some of the early road guides forecast.

Although only a small section, this classification is, in its way, quite important, and I wish it had been possible to fill in more details of some of the very early titles. Maybe more will be filled by the time the book goes to print but, in the absence of all the information, it seemed right to include these early books together with what information was known about them at the time.

Section E 9

Marque Histories

For various reasons, as this manuscript took shape, it was thought better to include marque histories in section G 'Histories of All Descriptions', however titled.

Section E 10

Driving — Including annuals, yearbooks, dictionaries, glossaries and encyclopaedias. Books other than under sections E 1 to E 9

In other words, something for everyone. In 1924 there were still many people who knew very little about motoring, people who had just bought their first car or were about to do so and books like Twelvetrees' *All About Motoring* met a demand and were often interesting reading for others who had been motoring for some time. Nick Georgano, formerly Librarian at the National Motor Museum at Beaulieu, is a master when it comes to encyclopaedias and histories and his *Encyclopaedia of American Automobiles* must be of great value now that in the UK as well as in the States interest in collecting and restoring American cars is increasing apace.

The Constant Search

Left Eoin Young — author, motor racing journalist and now motoring book dealer, whose stock of literature and motoring ephemera has to be seen to be believed.

Below Richard Hunt, whose Yorkshire *Vintage Motorshop* holds, perhaps, the largest stock of motor literature in the North.

I forget exactly when it was that I started to build a run of *Automobile Year*. I think it must have been in the mid 'sixties, and from then on I added each volume year by year. Every year, when the new volume arrived, I would browse through it before putting it up on the shelf with all the others, revelling in its uniformity and thinking how nice it looked and how lucky I was to have started collecting it before some of the early volumes became hard to find. Friends of mine, most of them collectors, used to look at the run and say how splendid it was and how much they wished that they had started to collect it earlier in its life. At times, I felt almost superior till one day it suddenly dawned on me that, not only did I never read any of it but that, almost certainly, I never would!

Make no mistake, a good run of *Automobile Year* is a lovely thing to have and valuable as well, for it forms a cornerstone in any large and good collection. Though I sold my run to make room for things that I liked better I wouldn't expect nine out of ten collectors to agree and, who knows, one day I may regret it.

Eoin Young, well known as a writer and journalist for many years, and now a leading dealer, says of *Automobile Year* in his Motor Book Catalogue No.80/3 'At the German Grand Prix this summer I had the opportunity to ask *Automobile Year* founder and publisher, Aime Guichard, just why the early volumes are so difficult to find now.' The answer was simple. 'For the first Edition we published a total of 15,000 copies in French, German and English but we sold only 8,000 copies that first year, which meant that I lost a lot of money. So, for the second year — Volume 2 — we printed only 9,000 in three languages.' 'Guichard found that his second volume of *Automobile Year* sold out quickly so for the third volume he increased production to 15,000 copies and, since then, publication has risen to a steady 35,000 copies annually. It remains the most collectable run of motoring books to put together — even though some particular volumes are most elusive when you need to fill in the vital holes'. Interesting, and it explains the tremendous difference between the value of the first two volumes and particularly of the second — when compared with all the rest of the run.

Were I collecting *Automobile Year* now, I would grit my teeth and somehow buy the complete run, or at least the first half, because otherwise I could envisage a lovely run on my shelf — lacking only numbers One and Two. Speaking both as a collector and as a past dealer, I cannot emphasise too strongly that the value of a run of *Automobile Year* or, for that matter, a run of anything else lies in its completeness. No matter how much a vendor may convince himself that a couple of issues missing is of no great consequence, the view won't be shared by prospective buyers — and they will be right. I would qualify that by saying that it does depend where the shortage lies. If, for instance, in the case of *Automobile Year,* a particular run lacked say, Volume 8, the easiest of all, the problem could probably be solved at a cost of under £10. If it were Volumes 1 and 2, it would be not less than £300, so it does pay to know as much as possible about the run you intend to collect.

So many enthusiasts harbour the illusion that they know all that needs to be known regarding the use of tools that Humphries *Car Tools — How to Choose and Use,* the only book of its kind, must be good for the amateur restorer. *Cars, Cars, Cars* by Davis is one that I have enjoyed and so is *The Complete Book of Motor Cars, Railways, Ships and Aeroplanes* which Odhams put out in the 1930s.

Georgano's *Complete Encyclopaedia of Motor Cars 1885-1968* and *Encyclopaedia of American Automobiles* are two that I would include and, for some, *The Guinness Book of Car Facts and Feats.* For the legally minded, there are three in the area between 1910 and 1936, even though laws may have changed a bit since then. Cade's *Modern World Book of Motors* is easy to find and is good history and, in the same context, so is *The Motor Guide to Makes and Models 1946-1956* and, if you need to know the cars of the famous, try Garratt's *Motoring and the Mighty.*

Three very popular titles, none of them expensive, are *The Motorist's Miscellany* (Harding), *The Motorist's Week End Book* (Frostick & Harding) and *The Motorist's Bedside Book,* also by Harding, mostly short stories by well-known contributors and all good value for your money. The run of *Motor Yearbook*s put out by Temple Press between 1949 and 1957, and compiled by Laurence Pomeroy and Rodney Walkerley, is very nice and all are fairly easily found, except the first, published during 1949, which is a brute. Even so, if you can pick up all the rest, you do have a continuous, even

The Constant Search

though not complete, run and the first volume is not nearly as expensive or hard to find as in the case of *Automobile Year.*

Picnics for Motorists is a rare and a nice little book even if the picnics of 1936 were not too inspired by the standards of today, and Wake's *Successful Car Dealing* will delight many. All the World Car Catalogues make fine reference but some are harder to find than others.

Chapter 9   Section F

Autobiographies, biographies and personalities

When, some time ago, we did an analysis in *Collector's Review* of readers' interests, it was found that two types of book, motor racing and autobiographies and biographies were the most popular. In my own collection I now have more in this particular section than any other.

Alf Francis — Racing Mechanic is one of the best, not only because Alf was for years mechanic to Stirling Moss, but also because the style of writing and thinking is so obviously Alf. I like *The Amateur Racing Driver* for I not only met and knew the author at Brooklands but also admired his courageous handling of the big three litre single seater Maserati he drove. I like Bira's *Blue Wings to Bangkok* slightly more than his *Bits and Pieces* but, even better, is Lord Brabazon's *The Brabazon Story* for, among all his good qualities, I loved the noble Lord's sense of humour.

No designer of his era can have done more for motor racing than Ettore Bugatti or produced finer cars for that, and other, purposes. All I would say here is that, having owned and raced one of his products, used others on the road and having collected and read every book that I could find concerning him, Bugatti is alone among manufacturers as far as I am concerned. W.O.Bentley's *The Cars in My Life* is now a bit scarcer than his other books and, for that reason, may perhaps be considered the best among Bentley lovers . . .

Mike Hawthorn's *Champion Year* and *Challenge me the Race* are both titles to include and so, I think, is Wal Hassan's *Climax in Coventry* and Setright's *The Designers*. I loved Ferrari's *Enzo Ferrari Memoirs* and also both Jenkinson's and Merlin's books on Fangio. And, even though I now lean more towards Bugatti than Bentley, I think that both of Hillstead's books *Fifty Years with Motor Cars* and *Those Bentley Days* were superb, for both gave such a wonderful insight of the appalling worry and problems evolving round manufacturing and selling motor cars in the late 1920s. Dunlop 'Mac's *Fifty Years with Speed Kings* is another, I think, in the *Alf Francis* mould.

Fifty Years of Travel on Land, Sea, Water and Air by Frank Hedges Butler is a favourite with me. Henry Ford has always fascinated me and, though I have most of the books written about him, I like *Forty Years with Ford* by Sorensen the best, because there's no doubt that when one man has worked with, and for, another for forty years, he must not only know him well but respect him. For different and varying reasons I liked Bruce McLaren's *From the Cockpit*, Wilbur Shaw's *Gentlemen Start Your Engines*, Lord Montagu's *The Gilt and the Gingerbread*, Schildberger's *Gottlieb Daimler, Wilhelm Maybach and Karl Benz*, and Jackson's *The Great Barnato*. Wish I could give each reason, but if that was done in every case there would be a 'wordage' problem in the end. Herman Lang's *The Grand Prix Driver*, now included in this section, we assessed under D 1 and I think of both Fraser's *Harry Ferguson —*

The Constant Search

Inventor and Pioneer and *He Lit the Lamp* concerning Professor A.M.Low as highly collectable. Professor Low was not only an inventor but an extremely nice man and a brilliantly capable and tactful Chairman of Committees which I attended as a Member in the 1950s. I still recall serving on the Council of the British Automobile Racing Club, of which he was Chairman, way back in the 1950s, when one of the problems was to get motor racing restarted at the Crystal Palace. Though the LCC were in favour, there was much opposition from local residents concerning noise but, undaunted, the Chairman countered with a proposal to erect acoustic screens. The result? The residents came back with the complaint that these would prevent them seeing the racing. 'They can't have it both ways' said the Chairman, and nor did they!

Oldham's *The Hyphen in Rolls-Royce* is, I think, one of the best on Rolls and, though not all motoring, band leader Billy Cotton's autobiography does contain a lot of his motor racing and is superb. And another good thing about it is that, not realising its motor racing content, many general booksellers put it, not in the motoring section but under autobiographies — so keep a sharp look out for *I Did it My Way,* the story of an extremely nice, humorous and remarkable man.

Where racing drivers are concerned, I would rather not express an opinion because there are really no bad books and it is very much a question of personal preferences — in the Grand Prix field, at any rate. I like and still have all the 'lives' — that is to say, *The Life of: Harry Ferguson, Lord Nuffield, Sir Henry Royce* and *Sir Henry Segrave.* I haven't read, and don't have, *The Life of Ted Horn,* though, and the reverse applies to *John, Lord Montagu of Beaulieu,* that is to say I have it and I have read it. All the books concerning the Montagu family interest me for both generations have done so much for motoring. I don't know what one would do, sometimes, were it not for the National Motor Museum at Beaulieu.

Kaye Don — The Man and *Lionel Martin — a Biography,* though both written at different times, concern two famous Brooklands personalities and are both enjoyable, so are *Lord Austin — the Man* and *Louis Renault* by Rhodes, even though Lionel Martin's and Renault's biographies have a strong streak of sadness running through them, but life is sad sometimes. Segrave's *Lure of Speed* is a good

book and Ricardo's *Memories and Machines* is a lovely story. Of all books concerning Sir Malcolm Campbell, I think that Lady Campbell's *Malcolm Campbell* gives the best picture of him but, here again, sadness does creep in towards the end.

Charnock's *Mind over Motor* is widely sought as are most of his books, so I must be alone in not being an addict, even though I have tried hard to read and enjoy this one. I liked *More Equal than Others* and, though I rate John Bolster highly as an author, have never enjoyed any book of his more than *Motoring is My Business* which I still regard as absolutely great. What is so good about it? Everything, but particularly John's burning passion, not only for motoring, but to enjoy every aspect of motoring: cars, racing, touring and, above all, people. No more gregarious man ever lived. I regard him as indestructible.

Although I never used to think of Dudley Noble's *Milestones in a Motoring Life* as a 'great' book, and though there never seemed to be much demand for it, Bill Boddy rates it as such, which means that, having parted with my copy, I must now find another. I like *Motoring Memories in Peace and War* by Harris, Lord Montagu's *The Motoring Montagus* and Stanley Sedgwick's *Motoring My Way* which is a very nice way indeed.

For me, 'Sammy' Davis' *Motor Racing* is a must. In W.O's note which precedes the text of *My Life and My cars* the author, W.O.Bentley, says in speaking of his autobiography *W.O.* 'What I have done now is to revise and bring up to date the first book (*W.O.*), add some new material and include quite a lot of the material about the cars and my own life from the second book (*The Cars in My Life*) which is now out of print. This, then, if you will excuse the pretentious description, is really a sort of definitive *W.O.*' *W.O.* first came out in February 1958, with second, third and fourth impressions in March, April and May of the same year, all from Hutchinson. *The Cars in My Life* also Hutchinson in 1961, and *My Life and My Cars* (1967) came from the same source. All the additional material added sixteen pages to *My Life and My Cars.* But, in addition, Chapter headings have been changed, so that Chapter 1 of *W.O.,* which was titled 'The Charm of Steam' is, in *My Life and My Cars,* titled 'A Love of Locomotives, Chapter 2 becomes 'Realities are Faced' instead of 'On the Footplate', Chapter 3 changes from 'The Lure of

Speed' to 'From Two Wheels' and so on. But, as one looks at both books side by side, each chapter opens and continues with the same text as the other so that, in the end, one tends to conclude that a better choice of title for *My Life and My Cars* would have been *A Definitive W.O.* since the differences between the two are, in fact, pretty small.

My Life on Wheels by Maurice Wiggin is a small book, modestly priced and a 'must' for, in it, the author describes all the awful things that have happened to him from the start of his motoring and motorcycling life right to the end, and the great enjoyment is that every one of these has happened to all of us who have loved and enjoyed the motor car, and the motorcycle.

I would also recommend *My Motoring Reminiscences* (Edge), *My Motoring Milestones* (Baroness von Laurentz) both of which are rare, *My Philosophy in Industry* (Ford), *My Twenty Years of Racing* (Fangio) and *My Years with General Motors* by Sloan.

Nuvolari by Lurani is now an acknowledged classic and is scarce, *Out on a Wing* by Sir Miles Thomas is not too hard to get and well worth adding, particularly if you would like to read his descriptions of working closely with his chief, Lord Nuffield, and *Parry Thomas* by Hugh Tours is also good and quite hard to find now. Others that I would not like to be without are *Pursuit of Victory* by Mercedes driver Karl Kling, *A Racing Motorist* (Davis), *Racing Round the World* (Lurani) and *Renault* (St Loup).

Where the Rolls autobiographies and biographies are concerned, I can be of little help, for I am biased and, given the opportunity, would include them all, even though I don't have all. This applies to the story of Rolls and Royce — and Claude Johnson never ceases to fascinate me, or the story of the firm itself, without which this country would be so much poorer. Another good Rolls book was Rowbotham's *Silver Ghosts and Silver Dawn* which is one of those that I could read again and again.

Neubauer's *Speed was My Life* was, I thought, one of the very greatest, and my copy, given to me

by my friend Frank Stroud of Chater and Scott, is signed by the author and something I shall always keep. Raymond Mays' *Split Seconds* is also one that finds a place in most collections.

Charles Jarrott's *Ten Years of Motors and Motor Racing* is always a bit of a problem if you are going to include motor racing in your collection. Without it, your collection has a big gap but, in any form, it is expensive. The 1st Edition, 1906, is a collectors' piece and, as such, is out of reach of many. The later ones in 1912 and 1928 aren't cheap either but, through being slightly smaller format than the first, are, I think, nicer. But there's a ray of hope, for Foulis did a fourth in 1956 and, if ever you see this, buy it before someone else does, because the price will be much less and it is well produced and excellent. Throughout Jarrott's description of every race one feels that one is sitting in that uncomfortable little seat beside him, where sat his devoted mechanic, Bianchi, worrying about the tyres, the drive chains, the oil and water leaks and, above all, the dust. A fabulous book by any standards and a great part of motor racing history. I know I'm not alone in thinking that. Look at the date of the reprint — 1956. Exactly fifty years after the 1st Edition. My old friend, Harold Marshall of Foulis, knew all he needed to know about printing rights. Copyright expires after fifty years. I'll bet he'd had his eyes on *Ten Years of Motors and Motor Racing* for several years before that.

Although I still haven't read it, I know that Duncan Hamilton's *Touch Wood* is one to have and so is Morris's *Two Brave Brothers*, another Rolls book avidly sought by many. *Wheel Patter* by Dudley Colley is amusing and gives one a good idea of Irish motor racing, and Leasor's *Wheels to Fortune* I found enjoyable and interesting.

To wind up, H.O.Duncan's *World of Wheels*, which is really a series of short stories of every aspect of motoring and the motor and allied trades, is eminently collectable, extremely large and, usually, very expensive. One needs a lectern or, at least, a small table on which to rest it, but if you have that and a deep purse as well, you won't be short of reading matter for a long time to come.

Chapter 10   Section G

Histories (however titled)

Section G 1

Motoring

Though, in a sense, every book contained in *The Constant Search* is history, the obvious and accepted ones are here and this section is divided into three: Motoring, Marque and club, Industrial, Associations and others.

Under this first heading, Claude Johnson's *Early History of Motoring* must certainly go in and others, rather less grand but still good, are Snellgrove's *From Steamcars to Mini Cars,* Caunter's *History and Development of Light Cars,* Pratt's *History of Inland Transport and Communication in England,* Georgano's *History of the London Taxicab* and *History of Transport* and Lurani's *History of the Racing Car — Man and Machine* and, though it would be nice to have the first Lord Montagu's *History of Ten Years of Automobilism 1896-1906,* one may have to exclude it on grounds of rareness and price.

I wouldn't want to be without all three volumes of Lord Montagu's *Lost Causes of Motoring,* S.C.H.Davis' *Memories of Men and Motor Cars* or MacManus' and Beasley's *Men, Money and Motors,* an American published book describing the intricacies of their early motor industry or, for that matter, Eden Hooper's *The Motor Car — A History and Souvenir* which is another 'giant' but readable and beautifully illustrated.

At the other end of the scale, Bentley's *Motoring Cavalcade,* Henslowe's *Motoring for the Million,* Rolt's *Motoring History* and Lord Cottenham's *Motoring Today and Tomorrow* and *Motoring Without Fears* though all of different periods, are amusing and light reading and not too expensive anyway.

Private Motor Car Collections of Great Britain by Hugo, is well illustrated and produced to Dalton Watsons' usual high standard and Rose's *A Record of Motor Racing,* now seldom seen in 1st Edition form, is a foundation stone for any motor racing collection even in the form of the later edition. *The Story of the Wheel* by Boumphrey, though small, is good history and is inexpensive, and Simmons' *Transport Museums* and Stein's *Treasury of the Automobile* are both worth consideration.

Doyle and Georgano's *World's Automobiles* series are excellent reference but, as such, not light reading, and Nicholson's *World's Motor Museums* is well laid out and interesting if, like me, you find motor museums fascinating.

Marque

Before starting to review and ruminate over this section, one must think about who will be reading it, and from what angle. One would imagine that readers will come in three categories: the owner of a particular make, wanting to know what literature there is concerning it; owners of particular types such as sports or luxury cars; and lovers of histories generally, and marque in particular, hoping to find titles to add to their collections. So it would seem that in the cases of books naming makes, there can be no need to enlarge further.

Of the titles not specifying the marque, *Best Wheel Forward* centres round the French built Tracta, so called because of its front wheel drive, and Hopfinger's *Beyond Expectations* relates to Volkswagen. *Maintaining the Breed,* John Thornley's book on pre-war MG racing and competition, came out as a 1st Edition in large format, a thin book with attractively illustrated dust wrapper. Although in subsequent editions the format became smaller and fatter, it is the 1st that many collectors look for, preferably with the dust wrapper, a great part of its attraction.

Motoring Entente by Nickols and Karslake, published by Cassell in 1956, set out to unravel and explain the French alliance of Sunbeam, Talbot and Darracq and, achieving it, increased in price gradually on the secondhand market initially, before taking off on a price increase escalation that seems never likely to end. *Small Wonder* by Nelson is another Volkswagen book and Scott Moncrieff's *Three Pointed Star* is Mercedes history and among the best. *The Three Wheeler* is, of course, Morgan, *Where Have all the Blowers Gone?,* Bentley and *The Wild Wheel,* by Garrett, is Ford.

The section would not be complete without a note on the titles published by Brooklands Books for these are all of one type, made up of original material such as road tests, specifications and feature articles on the individual makes drawn from motoring periodicals of the day. All are softback and, since each contains material drawn from a number of different sources, the authors are

shown as 'various'. Though none are dated, this is really immaterial because, in many cases, the subject matter itself is dated. The principal, Mr Clarke, has had a good idea in producing the series and fresh titles on other makes are regularly being brought out.

Rolls-Royce is so fully documented that there is almost enough material for a book concerning its literature alone. There are, in fact, two titles in this section dealing solely with the literature of the make: *An Index to Rolls Royce and Bentley Periodicals* written by Tom.C.Clarke and produced by Transport Bookman Publications in the early 1970s, and *Notes for a Bibliography of the Rolls Royce Motor Car* compiled and privately published by John Schroder, historian of the Rolls-Royce Enthusiast's Club. On the title page of his book, Mr Clarke says 'I am particularly indebted to John Schroder Esq., Historian of the RREC for his hospitality and access to his superb library', which is a sentiment that I can echo, having seen John's library and enjoyed both his and Mrs Schroder's hospitality. For anyone wishing to learn not only about the history of Rolls-Royce but also about its literature these are the points at which to start. Mr Clarke's book is excellent and, I would say, slanted slightly more towards the technical side than John's but, as a book lover, *Notes for a Bibliography of the Rolls-Royce Motor Car* has rather more appeal for me. Published in 1971, its headings include: Books about Rolls-Royce, Periodicals about Rolls-Royce, Handbooks (English), Handbooks (Foreign), Spare Parts Catalogues, Sales Brochures and Catalogues, Publicity Material, Books with references to Rolls-Royce, ending with the note 'There are many other books and periodicals with minor references to Rolls-Royce. Only the more significant of those which have come to light have been included but all are of interest to the collector'. On the last of its nineteen pages there is 'To be continued, when a sufficient number of items have been added to the collection and when sufficient important fresh information has come to light'. Ten years later, I wonder whether the author feels that the time has come. I hope so.

Before leaving the subject, this must be the point at which to draw attention to titles which, though not including the name, do relate to Rolls-Royce. They include *The Early History of Motor-*

ing, Grand Tour, The Silver Lady, Two Brave Brothers, The Magic of a Name, Silver Ghosts and Silver Dawn, A Collection of Interesting Cars, The Book of the Silver Ghost, and The Book of the Phantoms.

Others containing references to the make include The Romance of Motoring, The Motor Car Lover's Companion, A History of the World's Classic Cars, The Vintage Car 1919-1930, Veteran and Edwardian Cars, Cars of the 1930s and the Montagu Motor Book. Would that some other marques, among them Bugatti, were documented so fully.

A last minute arrival, The History of English Racing Automobiles is, despite its fairly high cost, one for serious consideration by ERA enthusiasts and has already been referred to in the text accompanying Section D 6.

Section G 3

Club, Industrial, Associations and others

From the start it became obvious that a separate section would be needed for histories other than general motoring or marque. From its very early days, the motor and allied industries seem always to have been conscious of the value of this type of publicity and many and varied are the titles that have come out over the years commemorating not only anniversaries and jubilees but also recording contribution to the national effort in two World Wars. Although many of these are hardly more than brochures, most are, in fact, extremely nice and interesting books.

Bouverie Street to Bowling Green Lane, the history of Temple Press which, among its many other activities, published both The Motor and Motor Cycling, is one of the nicest and most interesting. Where Clubs are concerned, the four books put out by the British Racing Driver's Club are all interesting, particularly the Silver and Golden Jubilee Books, both of which are produced to a high standard.

Britain's Motor Industry by Castle is large format and is filled with interesting information. Rodney Walkerley's Brooklands to Goodwood traces the history of the BARC from its first base at Brooklands before World War Two, to Goodwood afterwards. It also explains how, at the time of the change, the name of the Club also changed from being the Brooklands Automobile Racing Club to the 'British', for obvious reasons, even though most of the officials remained.

Calling All Arms by Fairfax describes the contribution made by the Ford Motor Co to the National effort in World War Two, and David Brown's The Story of a Family Business, besides being a rare book, will have appeal to Aston Martin lovers. The Motor Car Industry in Germany, 1939-1945 is softback published by the Stationery Office after the War and contains a number of good photographic illustrations, mainly of the pre-war German Grand Prix cars, and The RAC Jubilee Book 1897-1947, by Dudley Noble and published by the Club, is to a typically high standard and well worth having. Its counterpart, This Motoring from the Automobile Association, is less exciting and for a long time met almost no demand on the used book market although its sister, This Pilgrimage, by the same author, is scarcer and therefore a bit more in demand. Vital to the Life of the Nation, sub-titled A Historical Survey of the Progress of Britain's Motor Industry from 1896 to 1946 and by Noble and Junner is, unlike some historical surveys, great reading and filled with good photographs. Finally in this section, Wheels of Fortune by Du Cros, which is the history of Dunlop from the very early days, a large and expensively produced book and, for history lovers, extremely collectable.

Chapter 11   Section H

Rallies, Rallying, Autocross, trials, Go-Karts and Karting

Although no expert on rallying, I am a tremendous admirer of those who take part and of those who prepare and maintain the cars. Much as one admires the skill of today's rally drivers, one can't help admiring even more the 'sang froid' of navigators and crews. As far as this branch of the sport is concerned, I confess that it holds no appeal for me whatever, for if in racing one makes a mistake, the error and its consequences are at least one's own, and so much easier to live with afterwards.

Throughout the whole of this section the titles themselves indicate clearly to which branch of the scene they apply so that there is virtually no need to devote text to it.

There is, perhaps, one title to which attention should be drawn, *Rallying to Monte Carlo* by Mike Couper. Since Mike so often used Bentley and Rolls-Royce for his affrays south, it will hold interest for specialists in those marques. This apart, the author was such a good raconteur and possessed of a sense of dry humour, even in the worst of situations, that even to non-rally types the book is enjoyable.

Chapter 12   Section I

Books other than technical

Section I 1

Children's Books

In the same way that early toys act as a magnet to many collectors, so do early books for children, on almost any subject. Although many of the later titles here will, perhaps, become collectors' items in the years to come, it is the pre-war books that merit comment.

Two with similar titles, *The Big Book of Motors* by Strang and *The Great Book of Motors* by Jackson, are from the same publisher but different in format and both are well illustrated and amusing. Aston's *Boy's Book of Motors* also put out as *The Book of Motors* is, I think, the loveliest of all. In the same way, *The Boy's Life of Sir Henry Segrave* also appeared titled *The Life of Sir Henry Segrave,* so only one or the other is needed.

Though all editions of *The Wonder Book of Motors* are equally well produced and illustrated, it is the first four or five that are collectors' pieces

and which command prices. In retrospect, it seems rather a pity that even though the number of each edition is shown, none were actually dated.

Section I 2

Novels and fiction

Almost to a man, book lovers will agree one thing — they either love fiction or they don't and though I personally fall into category two, I do have some fiction in my collection even though I seem never to read it. Where motoring is concerned, fiction does seem to have gone out of fashion today, but that wasn't so at all in the early days.

In order to know who the leading fiction writers were, read down the author column where, again and again, you come across Williamson. Of all authors of motoring fiction, the husband and wife team of Williamson were by far the most prolific and, of their books, *The Car of Destiny* and *The*

Lightning Conductor are the best known and were probably the best sellers.

I confess to not really knowing whether Marie Corelli's *The Devil's Motor* should be classified as true fiction for, in verse and with lurid and almost frightening illustration, it seems to amount more to a dramatic diatribe against motoring in all its forms. Although I don't fully understand it, I have always loved it, and it is the only book in this section that I would want to have.

The writing of fiction seems always to have attracted well known racing motorists and *All Out* by the Earl of Cottenham, *Carlotti Takes the Wheel* (Mike Hawthorn), *The Racer* (Hans Reusch), *Salute to the Gods* and *Thunder Ahead* (Sir Malcolm Campbell) and *Sicilian Circuit* (Cottenham) are some.

There are two extremely rare ones here. *Speed Fever* by Barrie Lyndon is often sought by lovers of his better known books and, even rarer, *Sing Holiday* by Peter Chamberlain. Soon after *Sing Holiday* came out in 1937, there was quite a flutter in the paddock at Brooklands where I worked, some readers of the book seeming to be convinced that, in it, they recognised not only themselves but also friends. There were certainly no recriminations so it may not have been true. Today, perhaps, few people will recall the incident.

Section I 3

Cartoons, verse and humour

As a topic, motoring has always attracted poets, prose writers and cartoonists like flies to a honey-pot. And why not because, when one thinks about it, there are probably as many, if not more, humorous aspects, not only to motoring but also to motor racing, rallying and even to touring, than most other scenes.

Most titles here are good in their particular spheres, but literature in this particular section is so much a question of personal choice that to make recommendations would be pointless. Brockbank and Fougasse are my own favourites and I never recall browsing through a book by either without enjoying it. And I loved Sammy Davis' *Casque's Sketch Book* and *More Sketches by Casque* both centring mainly on racing and rallies.

If, for instance, you have a book by Brockbank in your collection and like it, then look down the author column with a view to building up a set. I really think you could do much worse.

Chapter 13   Section J

Taxis, Buses, Trams, Commercial, Military and advertising vehicles

Although a 'vehicle' only in the sense that it conveys to its readers all that has happened in the advertising of motor cars, Michael Frostick's *Advertising and the Motor Car* is not altogether in place here. But it is such a good book that it seemed a pity to put it in, say, Category M as a title which, though good, didn't fit just because of its unusual name.

Two 'oldies', both nice, are *Decorated and Advertising Vehicles* by Harman and, for tractor fiends, The Farm Tractor Handbook. For me, Georgano's *History of the London Taxicab* is pure nostalgia, for my grandmother lived in London and the memory of hoping against hope that the first taxi on the rank would be a Napier, rather than a 'growling' Renault, an uninteresting Beardmore or one of seemingly thousands of rather uninspiring

Unics, still remains. At the time, S.F.Edge's name was on everyone's lips and maybe the wish being father to the thought I pictured a Napier taxi as being faster and probably more exciting than the others. But when, one day, it did come along, I was disappointed to find it not only slower but also a lot quieter.

Bearing in mind how few early books were written on the subject of commercial vehicles as compared with cars, there is, I think, quite a fair proportion here. But even though they are detailed here, I would expect almost all to prove hard to find because interest has increased in commercial vehicles so much recently. For years, the supply of early material went no way to meeting demand and, in this respect, the position is now much worse.

Chapter 14 Section K

Models, Model building, Model car collecting and racing

Builder, collector or racer, I would hope that there is something here for you. There is for me because I do collect models, even though in only a small way. The small diecast area is one of complete mystery to me and I marvel at the prices that some of these seem to command. I do have a few, though, because my plan has always been to have in my collection a model of every car I have owned and liked. When one has been motoring for more than fifty years, that means that 1/43rd scale is a 'must'. Space and circumstances permitting, I would love a collection of larger models, but always metal, never plastic.

Of the books here, I wouldn't be without *The Catalogue of Model Cars of the World* by Greilsamer and Azema which, for me, has long been 'the one'. And, recently, I added *The Model Cars of Gerald Wingrove* which I think is a great book written by an equally great model builder.

I like books on the subject and wish I had the temperament, the patience, and the skill to be a builder. But I never have and feel sure I never will.

Chapter 15   Section L

Mascots, Badges, Registration plates, Emblems and Insignia

For me, mascots and badges, yes. The rest, no, but it all goes back to collecting what you like. There is art in both mascots and badges and no doubt there is to the other things — it's personal choice again.

Although its coverage is described in its title, and its coverage is wide, I think Worthington Williams' book *Automobilia* is one that should be in every collection. Although I have an interest in both, I prefer mascots to badges and my second choice here would be Sirignano's and Sulzberger's

Car Mascots — An Enthusiast's Guide.

But, like diecast models, the world of mascots is a bit of a jungle. I was once told by an expert that mascots of birds with folded wings were as unpopular with collectors as birds with upstretched wings were popular. Within a year I had one of the finest collections of birds with upstretched wings ever seen, only to find that they were just as unloved as the rest, so since then I have admired the collections of others.

Chapter 16 Section M

Book Titles other than under headings A to L, Pictures, Prints and photographs

Best, perhaps, to divide the subjects here into two parts and deal with pictures and prints first and then photographs.

First, *The Art of Gordon Crosby* by Garnier. A beautifully laid out book which does great credit to a superb artist. Maybe one has to be getting on in years to recall the art of Gordon Crosby and that is why, after so long a lapse, it is so nice to see the book on his work so well and tastefully done.

Endless Quest for Speed. In the years before the second world war, Iliffe produced, in two series, a set of 24 colour prints of racing scenes as supplements to *The Autocar* and the complete series were, at one time, available in two folios in which were included descriptive texts by S.C.H.Davis. The full set of 24 consists of:

First Series
1. Jenatzy beating world's speed record 1899
2. Charron's first success with wheel steered Panhard 1898
3. Fournier with Mors No.4 in Paris-Berlin Race 1901
4. Charles Jarrott with the famous 70 Panhard 1902
5. Thery winning the Gordon Bennett Race 1905
6. Szisz's Renault in the first Grand Prix 1906
7. Felice Nazarro winning the Targa Florio 1906
8. S.F.Edge driving the Napier for 24 hours 1907
9. Sir Algernon Guinness's famous 200 Darracq 1908
10. Lautenschlager's Mercedes in the 1908 Grand Prix
11. Bablot's 3 litre Delage and Boillot's Peugeot 1911
12. Boillot's 7½ litre Peugeot and Bruce Brown's Fiat 1912

Second Series
13. Percy Lambert covers 100 miles in one hour in 1913
14. K.Lee Guinness in the 600 mile Isle of Man Race 1914
15. Lautenschlager and Boillot during the 1914 Grand Prix
16. Jimmy Murphy's Duesenberg at Le Mans in 1921
17. K.Lee Guinness' famous 12 cylinder Sunbeam
18. Felice Nazarro in the 1922 Grand Prix
19. Sir Henry Segrave winning the 1923 Tours Grand Prix
20. Ascari's Alfa Romeo in the 1924 Grand Prix
21. Parry Thomas and Eldridge at Brooklands 1925
22. A Lorraine Dietrich refilling at night at Le Mans
23. Historic crash in the Le Mans 24 Hour Race 1927
24. Materassi in the 1927 Targa Florio

All twenty-four of these were reprinted from paintings by F.Gordon Crosby and *The Autocar* folios containing them were approximately 12 inches by 10 inches.

Chapter 17   Section N

Magazines

The saying that 'old soldiers never die' doesn't always apply to magazines, for not only do they quite often die but they sometimes have the surprising habit of coming to life again.

Although almost as much research has gone into this section as to any other, and though a great deal has been learned, it must be admitted that a lot is still unexplained, even by those most knowledgeable. Magazines have the habit of starting off strongly, faltering and missing the odd issue, gaining strength and then forging on, only to suddenly disappear without trace.

The strong ones go on and on and no problems arise in tracing their runs. It is the weaker ones that provide the headaches and, for the time being, what follows here is all that is known. In the early days of motoring many, and possibly more, magazines saw the light of day than see it today, so the problem is not so much to know of their birth as to find out when and why they deceased.

At least we can be thankful for the strong ones and, of all these, *The Autocar* is probably the oldest and strongest.

Autocar (The). Always a weekly, *The Autocar* came out, first, in November 1895, the first volume running to December 1896. Even though the format was, at that time, smaller, the fact that it was a weekly meant a large Volume 1. Volume 2 ran from January to June 1897 and Volume 3 from July to December of the same year. It is current and has run in that way throughout — the longest and most consistent run of any periodical. From time to time, usually due to industrial problems, there have been very short breaks but, besides being short,

they have been extremely few and far between. Naturally, from the point of view of the collector, a complete run takes space, but what a wonderful reference to have in one's collection and what a service it has provided for the motorist over all those years.

Autosport. Another weekly, *Autosport* first appeared in August 1950. The first volume ran to December, after which Volume 2 covered January to June 1951 and Volume 3 July to December, to the end of Volume 41 in December 1970. By this time, the magazine had increased in size so that it had to be split to four volumes each year. It is current and, over the years, provides a first class record of motor sport and competition. Again, a desirable run, not so space consuming as *The Autocar* and much more specialised. It started with Gregor Grant as Editor to whom, together with John Bolster, much of its success is due.

Autocar (The) Road Test Books. Inspired, perhaps, by its rival, *The Motor*, *The Autocar* brought out its first *Road Test Book* in 1951. The books, which were softback, came out year by year and each contained some two dozen tests of current cars considered to be of most interest. Initially, the run consisted of one book a year but, in 1958, and thence onwards, two were produced and labelled Spring and Autumn.

Autocourse (magazine) and Sporting Motor. Not to be confused with the hardback Autocourse annuals, the magazine came out first in 1951. Volume 1, 1951, and Volume 2, 1952 were issued quarterly, and Volumes 3, 4 and 5 bi-monthly, after which this magazine came out monthly, initially

74

changing its title to *Autocourse and Sporting Motorist* and changing again to *Sporting Motorist* in 1959. To some extent the content changed as well, for although motor racing was still its subject, the style of reporting became rather less analytical and more chatty. The format also became smaller and more handleable but I confess that I rather preferred the style of the earlier volumes. Certainly a 'collectable' item and a nice set to have complete.

Autosport High Performance Cars Road Tests. Covering principally the sporting aspects of motoring, it was logical that *Autosport* would follow in the footsteps of *The Autocar* and *The Motor* in producing a series of Road Test Books covering high performance cars. First published in October 1955 and edited by Gregor Grant and John Bolster, with technical drawings by Theo Page, the initial volume spanned the years 1954-1955. Each subsequent volume spanned two years until 1965-1966 at least. I never recall seeing a volume later than this and enquiries have failed to reveal whether any were published. The publication differed in some respects from those of *The Autocar* and *The Motor* in that the *Autosport* series contained some brief feature articles in addition to the tests themselves. Up to twenty tests were included in each volume and the series covered some extremely interesting and fast cars.

Brooklands Track and Air. Of all periodicals, *Brooklands Track and Air* was the one most closely allied to the track and all that went on there. Though the circulation is not known, it must have been relatively small because copies have always been scarce and the full run even scarcer.

Somehow, *Brooklands Track and Air* seems to capture the atmosphere of Brooklands itself in a way that no other magazine does, to the extent that one almost feels that its editorial office must have been based at the track. The magazine, which had a very strong coverage of the aircraft side, began its life in October 1932, came out monthly and continued until, together with its Editor, Oliver Holmes, it was absorbed into the MG orientated *The Sports Car,* together with the *MG Magazine,* in April 1935.

Collector's Car. Starting where *Veteran and Vintage Magazine* ended and, as it stated on its front cover, incorporating the latter, *Collector's Car* came out with its first issue in September 1979 in format approximately the same size. From September '79 to April 1980, no mention was made concerning Volumes or issue numbers but 'Number Nine' was added to the May 1980 issue and this continued until the September 1980 issue, which was shown as Number 13. Since the October 1980 issue was labelled 'Volume 2, Number 3', it seems logical to assume that it was the publishers' intention that, despite their printed numbering, the August and September 1980 copies constituted the first two issues of Volume 2.

In the past, this has happened with other publications and it almost as though, at some point, it suddenly dawns that it would be a good idea to have volume runs instead of consecutive issues. So, in this case, the effect is that the first eleven copies, September 1979 to July 1980, made up the first volume, with the second volume starting at August 1980 despite its Number 12 designation.

The magazine was well produced and illustrated and appeared to take in a proportion of later cars of the 1950s and 1960s while still giving good coverage to pre-war and 'earlies'. In setting out to do that it did, in some respects, differ from the well established *Thoroughbred and Classic Car* and, with its previous background, it was sad that it should have ceased publication in September 1981, being absorbed by *Thoroughbred and Classic Car* from them on.

Collector's Review. A small item but with a devoted following both in the UK and Overseas, *Collector's Review* has for most of its run been the only publication to cover solely the literature of motoring. Started in February 1975, it comes out three times yearly, in February, July and October, and covers the current motor literature scene with emphasis on secondhand and early books, magazines and ephemera. Each issue, consisting of a minimum of five thousand words, covers and reports lot by lot the prices obtained at all the London motor literature auctions and a number of provincials as well. Feature articles are, from time to time, contributed by leading motoring authors and collectors and the clientele includes leading motor museums and auction houses as well as authors and private collectors all over the world. It has good support from the motor book trade, a number of whom advertise in it, and also includes in each issue a 'Forthcoming Dates' section, listing ahead the dates of motor literature Sales and Auctions, Autojumbles, Swapmeets and Book

The Constant Search

Fairs for the following four months from date of issue. Details of *Collector's Review* are regularly advertised in the Classified Section of *Motor Sport, Thoroughbred and Classic Car, Collector's Car* and other publications.

Commercial Motor (The). With *The Motor* established, having started its run three years previously, Temple Press looked further afield and, in 1909, brought out *The Commercial Motor* and it is interesting to note how the two large publishers, Iliffe and Temple Press, were catching on to the fact that interest in motoring of every sort was already not only considerable, but growing almost month by month.

A weekly, *The Commercial Motor* was, to some extent, the logical consequence of the almost instant success of *The Motor* and, following it, went on to become completely established, with two volumes a year, continuing its weekly run unbroken and becoming virtually unopposed in its field. Its appeal to all operators of commercial vehicles, whether of vans or lorries, was instant and one can hazard a guess that, for some time after it started, it will have had many subscribers who, though they may not have been transport operators themselves, will have been interested in every aspect of the design and use of motor vehicles whatever their size and type.

For years, collectors of motoring literature had very little interest in the commercial aspect, but in the 1960s interest began to grow. By the mid-1970s, perhaps spurred on by the formation of the Historic Commercial Vehicle Club, interest became almost as great as in any other area and *The Commercial Motor* of almost any period was being sought keenly. Now, in the 1980s, it is keener than ever, and both buses and trams are in vogue as well as lorries, trucks and vans.

Light Car and Cyclecar (The). Widening their motoring interest still further, Temple Press scored again, bringing out *The Light Car and Cyclecar* in November 1912. Another weekly, the magazine was instantly popular and, even though not helped by the outbreak of World War One two years later, really got into its stride after the war at a time when more and more manufacturers of light and ultra-light cars were bringing their products onto the market. The boom in light car production continued right through the early post-war years and on through the 1920s and 1930s, thanks partly to both

Austin and Morris, with *The Light Car and Cyclecar* on the crest of the wave. In the early post war-years, no sooner did one small light car manufacturer go to the wall than another sprang up, although it must be admitted that most of those who failed were in the cyclecar rather than the light car field. Sadly, the Second World War brought about changes for the magazine, which ended in 1953 after first becoming a monthly in much smaller format.

Light Car (The) Thinking, perhaps, that since interest in *The Autocar* and *The Motor* had been sufficiently large to sustain both, a second weekly focussed on smaller cars would go as well, Iliffe brought out *The Light Car* at the end of 1913. But, since it ran for less than five years, one imagines that either the success of *The Light Car and Cyclecar,* the start of the first World War, or both, encouraged them to discontinue, and production ceased.

Motor (The) Slightly junior to *The Autocar* in that it first came out some seven years later, in February 1902, *The Motor* is otherwise comparable. Published for many years by Temple Press, rivals to Iliffe who produced *The Autocar* and *The Motor Cycle, The Motor* was also a weekly with an equally fine run and is current today.

Since its coverage has always been virtually the same as that of *The Autocar* it always amounted to deciding which it was that one wanted to receive regularly, even though many enthusiasts subscribed to both. The rivalry was even extended to the motor cycle field because Temple Press countered Iliffe's *The Motor Cycle* with their own *Motor Cycling.* Yet the strange fact is that, two wheels or four, each of these great publications retained an individuality of its own throughout their long runs.

Motor Sport Although younger than either *The Autocar* or *The Motor* and, of course, a monthly throughout its run, *Motor Sport* is certainly most beloved by the sporting and early car fraternity. Even now, veteran enthusiasts like myself look forward eagerly to the first day of each month.

Throughout its run, which started in July 1924, probably no publication has enjoyed the affection of readers in the way that *Motor Sport* has through the years. The publication has run with its volumes matching years, January to December, since 1938, but before that there were changes. Volumes 1, 2 and 3 ran from July of each year to June of the

Right Ray Roberts who, though comparatively recently, joined the motor bookselling community, holds a fine stock of rare and early books.

Below Peter Richley, veteran and most knowledgeable collector of all, with just part of his library.

next. Volume 4 started in July 1927 and ended with a composite number covering August and September 1928. Volume 5 began with another covering October and November 1928. December 1928 to April 1929 were not published even though, today, there are collectors who seek them. May and June 1929 were published but it seems likely that the circulation of both was small, since either are as hard to find as almost any other item of motoring literature.

July, August, September and October 1929 were not published and the magazine began publication again in November 1929, the first issue of Volume 6. This volume ended in October 1930. Volumes 7, 8, 9, 10 and 11 ran from November each year to October of the next, and Volume 12 ran from November 1935 to end with a composite number covering October and November of 1936. Volume 13 started with the December 1936 issue and ended with the issue dated December 1937, after which volumes ran January to June each year. To its great credit, *Motor Sport* somehow managed to run right through World War Two without a break, largely thanks to the dedication of its editorial staff which, in those days, probably consisted of the Editor, Bill Boddy, and his friend and right hand man Denis Jenkinson. The thanks of a multitude of literature-starved enthusiasts are due not only to the publishers but possibly even more to these two. Fortunately, one hopes and thinks that they must have reaped their reward for, since the war, the magazine has gone from strength to strength. In addition to their association with *Motor Sport* both are now leading authors and critics and, through it all, *Motor Sport* continues to forge ahead.

It has for long been the most sought publication of its kind among collectors, understandable because within the 60 volumes covering its run it has contained virtually everything that the sporting enthusiast could need. Pre-1930 copies are hard to find and therefore astronomically costly, 1931 to 1935 extremely hard, 1936 to 1946 are all very difficult, particularly January in the case of some of the wartime issues, 1947 to 1949 are scarce but after that *Motor Sport* can be found fairly easily. Up to approximately 1978, the run from 1950 had very little value but after that time it began to appreciate in price. Since time has a habit of passing and since prices rise with the passage of time, now is a good time to buy unless, of course, you can afford the cost of going back earlier — and have the patience to find older issues.

Motor Racing Although younger still, *Motor Racing* has built up a strong following over the years and has increased in interest steadily since it first came out in January 1954, edited by Douglas Armstrong and published by Pearl Cooper, at which time it was the accredited organ of the half litre club. Like all publications of its kind, it took time to become collectable but I saw at a recent London auction a bound run of the first eleven volumes, from 1954 to 1964, sell for £190, which I would take to mean that the full run would be now worth between £250 and £300. Over the years there have been changes in both publisher and editorial staff but though in later years the layout and printing style has changed slightly, the format has remained the same. Volumes run January to December each year.

Motor (The) Road Test Books Leaders in the field, *The Motor* came out with their first *Road Test Book* in 1949 and, unlike *The Autocar*, continued to do so annually, at least until 1975, with a single book each year. It can be taken that, together with *The Autocar* and *Autocourse*, almost all models of any interest will be covered in one or the other. The run started earlier than either of the other two and, if I were collecting this sort of publication, I think that I would choose *The Motor* run for that reason. Probably only the road testing journalist or specialist would feel that he needed all three.

Old Motor Much loved as it is by collectors, *Old Motor* is a bit of a researcher's headache when it comes to unravelling its past habits.

Its start links with *Vintage Commercial* of which there was only one volume in small format size of approximately 6 x 8 inches. *Vintage Commercial* ran from September 1962 to May 1963 — 9 issues.

Volume 1 of *Old Motor* ran with the same style and format from January 1963 to June 1963, making 6 issues. Volume 2 onwards to the end of Volume 5 then came out in a format approximately 8 x 12 inches, and Volume 2 from July 1963 to June 1964. Volume 3 ran from July 1964 to June 1965 and Volume 4 from July 1965 to September 1966. But, in Volume 4 there were, in fact, only 12 issues since January and February 1966 were combined in one issue, as were March and April and also August and September. Volume 5 began healthily with all copies from October 1966 to June 1967 being published, then there was nothing more until January 1968 and again nothing until September 1968, so that Volume 5 had only 11 issues.

For a time *Old Motor* then came to a halt, restarting with even larger format to continue with Volumes 6 to 11, which took it to 1979, though not all issues were dated, some having only the volume and issue numbers. Up to that point the publishers had been Prince Marshall. In May 1979, it started again, with the first copy dated June, under the banner of Model and Allied Publications. Now a monthly, it is again going from strength to strength, but with a further change of publisher.

Profile Publications

Profile Publications

70   The Wolseley Hornet and Hornet
     Specials
71   The Healey Silverstone
72   The Porsche Type 356
73   The Racing Peugeots, 1912-1919
74   The Isotta Fraschini Tipo 8 Series
75   'Bloody Mary'
76   The touring Riley Nines
77   The V8 and Straight 8 Jensens
     1935-1949
78   The Maserati 250F Grand Prix Car
79   The 1906-1908 Grand Prix Renaults

Profile Publications

Vol.No. Subject
80   The Trojan Utility Car
81   The Miller Straight Eight
82   The Meadows-engined Lea-Francis
83   The Tourist Trophy Replica Frazer
     Nash
84   The Ferrari Tipo 340 & 375 Sports Cars
85   The Alfonso Hispano-Suiza
86   The 18/80 MG
87   The P2 Grand Prix Alfa Romeo
88   The Lincoln Continental 1940-1948
89   The BMW Type 328
90   The Ford GT
91   The Rolls-Royce Silver Ghost
92   The 2 litre AC Six
93   The 2 litre & 8 cylinder Ballots
94   The 8 & 12 cylinder Packards,
     1923-1942
95   The Traction Avant Citroens, 1934-1955
96   The V16 BRM

Profile Publications (First Series) The first series
of *Profiles* focussed on 96 different cars, each of
which was assessed as classic or historic type.
Each profile consisted of eleven pages of informative text, together with many good photographs,
including one or two pages in colour, illustrating
plan, nearside and offside profile together with
front and rear views. They are sought by collectors
seeking to build complete sets and, though all
were originally priced at 2/-, the passage of time
has again shown that, for some reason, certain
numbers are now harder to find than others. Least
difficult to find are those in the first half of the

series, with the first twenty five being easiest of all.
Most difficult are those from number 80 onwards
and the hardest of all to find, number 95. The
following list shows the numbers alongside the
cars represented. Produced by Profile Publications
Ltd., none are dated.

Profile Publications (Second Series) Slightly
larger in format but no less interesting than the first
series, the second, which is thought to be current,
at present runs to twelve.

Rapiditas Although included here in the Magazine
Section, *Rapiditas* is, in a sense, an Annual. The
run consisted of No.1 (1906), No.2 (1907), No.3
(1908-1913), No.4 (1914-1921), No.5 (1922-1923),
No.6 (1923-1924), No.7 (1925-1926), No.8
(1927-1928) and No.9 (1929-1930).

To describe it as rare and desirable would be the
understatement of the year. In the whole span of
my years spent in dealing, I was only once offered
Rapiditas and, even then, was outbid! In the field
of collecting, nothing must be rated as impossible
to find but, with hindsight, I would think that experienced collectors would probably agree that,
where *Rapiditas* is concerned, the chances of
acquiring the full run could only arise now every
twenty five years or more. Hardback and with
lovely illustrations.

Road and Track Though, generally, coverage has
been confined to items published in the UK, the
American magazine *Road and Track* has become
so popular in Europe and is so informative and
interesting that it would be wrong to omit it.

A monthly magazine which first came out in
1949, and which is still current, *Road and Track*
has strong appeal for the sports car enthusiast and
follower of racing and competition generally.

Among its best features are the excellent Road
Tests of sporting type cars and these are supple-
mented, year by year, by the issue of *Road and
Track Road Test Annuals.*

Copies of *Road and Track* of the 1960s and onwards are still not too hard to find, but all prior to
1960 are difficult and so are the Road Test books.
Although little hope can be held out of building up
the complete run, a full run from 1960 onwards is
well worth trying for.

Speed The inspiration of Alan Hess, *Speed* first
came out in June 1935. The production was to a
high standard and the subject matter evolved
round racing of every sort with, perhaps, some

emphasis on Brooklands. Well illustrated and interesting, it met a keen demand and, as a collector's item, still does today although it is now hard to find. The first volume ran from June 1935 to May 1936, with one composite copy covering November and December 1935. Volume 2 ran from June 1936 to May 1937 and Volume 3 June 1937 to May 1938. Volume 4 ran from June 1938 to April 1939, after which publication ceased although it was announced that the magazine was to be combined with *Motor Sport.* At the time, with World War Two looming on the horizon, there must have been problems for this type of magazine but *Speed* was greatly missed.

Some issues are easier to find than others and, of them all, the last four are certainly the hardest. For some reason, maybe softer paper, the covers of the 1939 issues seem to have stood the test of time less well and, even when one does find them, they are often coverless or, at least, with covers badly torn. To some extent the Brooklands flavour was accounted for by the fact that, on its front cover, *Speed* was described as 'The Official Organ of the British Racing Driver's Club' and, in addition, carried the Club's attractive badge on some issues. Later covers carried the words 'Land, Sea and Air' which was correct, for *Speed* did have a leaning towards both ships and aircraft, particularly the latter. Very desirable now, if one can find copies.

MG Magazine (The) Under the auspices of the MG Car Company, the MG Magazine first came out, bi-monthly, in May 1933, conducted by Alan Hess. Although the interest was there, even in those early days, the run was short, for publication, as an entity, ended in March 1935, being absorbed into the much better known *The Sports Car.*

Sports Car (The) Best known and rarest of all MG items, *The Sports Car* began in April 1935, absorbing not only *The MG Magazine* but also incorporating *Brooklands Track and Air* and, incidentally, its Editor, Oliver Holmes, as well. With the arrival of World War Two, *The Sports Car* came to an end in October 1939, yet it has remained, ever since, the most desirable of all MG literature to collect. Virtually impossible now to collect piece by piece, the run does come for sale very occasionally as a whole — but is extremely expensive.

Safety Fast The third and, perhaps, the most easily found of MG periodicals, *Safety Fast* first came out under the editorship of Wilson McComb in February 1959, continuing until November 1968. Nice to have, not too difficult to build up complete, but not easy either.

Thoroughbred and Classic Car One of the best and also the best established of recent productions, *Thoroughbred and Classic Car* first came out in October 1973.

If it was not immediately acclaimed, that could be because, in the past, so many new periodicals had appeared with a 'bang', only to fizzle out and disappear. The fact that this happened on more than one occasion was bad from the point of view of readers who had paid subscriptions in advance and one would think that any new production could, today, well meet with some degree of sales resistance.

From the outset, *Thoroughbred and Classic Car* was a 'monthly' the volumes running from October of one year to September of the next. By March of 1974 it was appreciated by countles collectors for what it was — an exceptionally good production — and then the scramble began among collectors to find the first six copies with which to build the complete run. Classified advertisements ran in the magazine from numerous seekers of the early copies and this had the effect of producing 'profit takers', who advertised them at prices that were simply absurd, so absurd in fact that, at one time, some dealers, including myself, ceased to trade in secondhand copies, since it was quite impossible to establish a secondhand price.

Gradually, however, the furore subsided but I think that no greater compliment has ever been paid to the excellence of a new product than this. That was eight years ago and, today, *Thoroughbred and Classic Car* must be considered the most popular of any comparatively new productions, not only for its text and good illustrations but also for its modern style and approach.

Although its title is *Thoroughbred and Classic Car* one often hears it misdescribed in conversation. Sometimes it is referred to as Classic and Thoroughbred Car, sometimes just Classic Car. The reason, of course, is that though it does carry its full title on the front cover, the word Thoroughbred is printed less prominently and is smaller than the word Classic. So make sure that in conversation you know the one that you have in mind.

The Constant Search

Torque Edited at first by P.J.Stephens and later by John Lello, *Torque,* the house magazine of booksellers F. & E.Stoneham, is a great addition to any motoring library, its subject being purely the motoring books and magazines of the period. What period? I am not sure of the start but my own run begins with Issue No.10 for October-December 1952 and ends with Issue 26, dated Christmas 1956. *Torque* was a quarterly and, in retrospect, makes fascinating reading. Format size is 8 x 5 inches and, from time to time, one can find it in the markets and autojumbles, where it is still not fully appreciated for what it is. I know that, having built up my own run in this manner, and I am still searching.

Vintage and Thoroughbred Car Motorsport apart, *Vintage and Thoroughbred Car,* the brain child of Bill Boddy, must rate as the first of its kind to cater for readers interested in that particular type of car and, without any doubt at all, it was first of its type to emerge after the war. Though not a fat product and with a smaller than usual format, it was just what enthusiasts wanted at the time and quickly became desirable and collectable.

There were four volumes from beginning to end, the first running from February in 1953 to December of the same year. Volumes 2 and 3 ran from January of each year, 1954 and 1955, to December, and the fourth and last volume, in 1956, consisted of only four copies: that is to say, January, February, March and April.

I confess I don't know, even now, why it stopped but, soon afterwards, its place was taken by *Veteran and Vintage Magazine* from the same source, headed by Lord Montagu.

Vintage and Thoroughbred was always a nice magazine to have. Now seldom seen, the first copy is the hardest of all to find, and then the last four. It is compact, binds well into two volumes — that is to say, Volumes 1 and 2 together, and Volumes 3 and 4. It is better to acquire this title complete rather than bit by bit.

Veteran and Vintage Magazine Somehow one always thinks of *Veteran and Vintage* as a consistent performer which, though it may not have set the world on fire, was nice to have and would always keep coming. In consequence it was a great shock to its many subscribers when, even though it gave everyone good notice, the day came when it ceased publication. No one had a right to think

that it would automatically always continue — it was just that since it came from Beaulieu it had always been thought of as the mouthpiece of the Museum. In a way it was rather like Brooklands: never praised when it was there but sadly lamented once it had gone.

That's the way of the world — we should think a bit more carefully about these things when we have them. *Veteran and Vintage* was a nice magazine and a good performer in that it had a good long run, never missed an issue and was enjoyable and informative in its subject coverage. Volume No.1 Issue 1 came out in August 1956 and ran till August 1957, after which all volumes ran from September of each year to August of the next. Throughout virtually all of its run, which ended in August 1979, *Veteran and Vintage* ran its own binding service. Since each volume tended to be thin, many collectors preferred to make their own arrangements for binding and, to save expense, had volumes bound in pairs. Since the run ended with Volume 23, this meant that the last volume had to be bound on its own.

The format of the magazine was uniform over its run, even though the print style was changed slightly in the 1970s, by which time the magazine had been fairly easy to acquire on the secondhand market. Then it started to become fairly valuable, and a complete bound run was sold by Christies in October 1980 for £220. It is still not too difficult to acquire and is well worth collecting but, now that it has ended, it will almost certainly continue to increase in value. Since it is the early volumes, say the first four, that are less easily found, I would suggest, initially seeking these and, once found, then continue to add and bind up with the later ones. It makes a nice run and, since in its early days Graham Walker was curator of the motorcycle section at Beaulieu, there are some extremely good and interesting motorcycle racing articles by him included in the text.

At this point perhaps we could stop for a moment to ponder on one or two aspects related to this particular section. Bearing in mind that the sub-title of this book is 'An Introduction to Motor Literature Collectors', even though I would hope that many established collectors will find it useful, I am thinking a lot of the time about collectors who are either about to start or who have started fairly recently.

Throughout the text I have used the word 'collectable' fairly freely and there are, I think, two meanings that the word can have. Till now, I have used it to convey that something is worthy of being collected but, at this point, it is still, I think, the best word to use although in a different sense. I thought long and hard before deciding what to include in the magazine section and what to leave out, and I make no bones about the fact that a great deal more could have been included. What has not been included is partly very early and partly extremely late material and this has been deliberate for two reasons.

We get back, here, to the word 'collectable'. Where the very early magazine material is concerned, it falls into two categories. Some of it is not, I think, collectable, even if it could be found, because it is to a great extent extremely heavy and dull and of no interest to all but a very few who may well not be collectors anyway. The rest, while it may have some interest, is almost never seen today and can almost be labelled 'not collectable' in the sense that it is no longer obtainable. Numerous early magazines are known to exist, and here are just a few names with their starting dates: *Automotor Journal*, 1896, *Automobile Owner*, 1907, *Automobile Engineer*, 1907, *Car Illustrated*, 1902, *Automobile Club Journal*, 1901, *Car Magazine*, 1903, and *Incorporated Institution of Automobile Engineers*, 1906. But, as a lover of completeness, I know that even though odd copies, or perhaps even odd volumes, of these may show up from time to time, one stands almost no chance of building a good run, let alone a complete one. In the rare event of a whole run coming up, one would need a very deep pocket indeed.

Not only that, but for years now, the most intense interest has lain not so much on the Veteran and Edwardian era as on Vintage, that is to say pre-1930 and, to some extent, later. And when one ponders on the fact that copies of *Motor Sport* in the 1920s have sold fairly regularly quite recently for £25 or more per copy, that is to say £300 per volume, it makes one think.

So that is why it has seemed right to confine this section to items of magazine literature that, one way or another, can still be found and sometimes acquired.

Without even making an apology, I think I will repeat here what I have said several times in my *Collector's Review*. As a group, I think that collectors sometimes tend to look back too often, rather than looking at where they are standing now. By that I mean that today's books and periodicals are buyable at today's prices — with no premium in respect of age. By all means stretch the purse strings now and again to acquire something badly wanted, at a high price in view of age but, at the same time, buy as much as possible of the best of today's to put away and mature. Magazines like *Thoroughbred and Classic Car,* for instance, which can still be collected piece by piece. At the moment, *Thoroughbred and Classic Car* is in its eighth volume and, at the start of 1981 a bound set of seven volumes covering 1973 to 1979 was sold at Christies for no less than £180. So what will that be worth when, in ten years time, it runs to 17 volumes? The same could apply to others: *Old Motor,* for instance. Yes, there are still treasures to be bought if one can pinpoint them before everyone else does the same.

So much for the 'left outs' in the early section. As regards the contemporaries, one has only to scan the shelves of any large newsagents to see how many there are. Look down the motoring section — one, two, three, four, five, six? When did each one start and how many will be running in five years' time? They may not necessarily depart but more likely will be taken over or incorporated with newer productions, maybe with a different format. Some will go from strength to strength and those will be worth keeping an eye on.

So I feel that what has been included in this section is right as things stand at the moment, but would agree that one should keep the position under review. Even with shelf space at a premium, long runs of well established periodicals that one likes are, I think, the best to have as part of one's collection as far as magazines are concerned.

Chapter 18   Section O

Club and marque bulletins, gazettes and journals

Although over the years tastes and interests change so that what in one era may be desirable to have may be less so in the next, the same general rules apply in this section as with books and magazines.

Some bulletins, gazettes and journals are produced to a higher standard than others, some have been running for a longer time, and the subjects of some have a greater appeal than in the cases of others. Enthusiasts love to start clubs and, now and then, what began life as a single sided Roneo'd broadsheet may, with the passage of time, blossom out into something artistic and nice to have in one's collection as a run.

What still applies is that in the cases of the long runs, and particularly where the subject matter has strong appeal, the early copies are difficult to find and expensive when at last tracked down. The List of Clubs following this section of the text gives some idea of the problem, but not more than that, because the records of some clubs, even post-war, are not only incomplete but, in some cases, don't exist. Fortunately, and perhaps strangely, this applies less to clubs which were founded before the War but more to those that entered the fray soon afterwards.

BARC From the year that the Brooklands Track opened in 1907 to the year when it closed in 1939, the letters BARC stood for Brooklands Automobile Racing Club and, although the BARC didn't own Brooklands, it was responsible for running the car racing. With the demise of Brooklands, the Club re-formed with many of the same officials to become the British Automobile Racing Club, performing the same functions at Goodwood and elsewhere. Throughout its life, except for the war years, the Club has issued what it termed Yearbooks (Section E 10) and, since these really amounted to journals, it seems right to include them here. The pre-war series were extensive in their coverage, taking in not only the racing and records aspect but also everything connected with the track, right down to the club house and tennis courts. They were artistically produced and illustrated and, in the 1930s at least, ran to between 60 and 80 pages, continuing in a slightly different style after World War Two.

Bentley Drivers' Club Slightly younger than the BARC but still one of the 'Senior' clubs, the Bentley Drivers' Club Review first came out in 1938 and, after a break through the war years, continued and is 'current'. Although the early copies are no less hard to find than any others of the period, the Club did thoughtfully reprint a few of the early issues together in one binding, although such is the demand that this too is hard to find now. No emphasis is needed to underline the desirability of the BDC Review, for the race history of the marque has probably been better chronicled than almost any other.

The Bugatti Owners' Club Interest in Bugatti is not only enormous but constantly increasing, which is not surprising since so many who worship at the shrine maintain that, of all designers, Ettore

Bugatti was the supreme artist.

The Bugatti Owners' Club, founded by a group of enthusiastic and knowledgeable owners headed by Colonel and Eric Giles, not only saw the light of day as far back as 1929 but issued Volume 1, Number 1 of its now celebrated magazine *Bugantics* in July 1931. Barring only the war years *Bugantics,* of all club journals, has been circulated to members with wonderful consistency, year by year. Currently it runs with four issues per year: spring, summer, autumn and winter, each year forming a volume and each copy numbered. In the early years it ran bi-monthly and there have been a few occasions when two issues came out combined as one, as for instance autumn/winter 1963 and 1964. A beautifully produced and illustrated periodical relating to a marque just as beautiful and, as a result, in strong demand always. Copies of the 1960s and 1970s can be found, those of the 1950s with difficulty, the 1940s with great difficulty, and the pre-war copies once in a blue moon. A few pre-war copies of Bugantics did come up for sale in one of the big London auctions last year, the following prices being realised:

Bugantics	1936 May, June and	
	September (3 copies)	£45.00
	1937 January to November	
	Volume 6. Complete 6 copies	£70.00
	1938 January to November	
	Volume 7 complete	£85.00
	1939 January to November	
	Volume 8 complete	£85.00

Bear in mind that *Bugantics* had been running five years previously and one gets some idea of the attraction and the value of the full run.

Christophorous A 'must' for Porsche owners and enthusiasts, *Christophorous* is one of the best produced and elaborate of all one make journals.

For a post-war make, it has one of the longest runs of all, for the first issue with English text came out in January 1956, following seventeen in German text.

It is still current but, with Porsche interest increasing, nearly all copies, and particularly the early ones, are scarce and not easy to track down. Publication occurs bi-monthly.

Early and Late From time to time, leading clubs have subdivided into Sections, marque or regional, and in the case of the Vintage Sports Car Club the proportion of Rolls-Royce owners became so great

that, in 1956, a separate journal was started for the Rolls-Royce Section.

Pre-War Rolls-Royce cars manufactured with manual rather than automatic ignition control had the control lever mounted on the steering column, marked 'Early' for advance and 'Late' for retard, and the name *Early and Late* derives from this. This journal, which is a rare item now, first came out in March 1956 and was still running at least until the late 1960s. Though nice to have in any collection it would be difficult, if not impossible, to acquire the full run.

Ferrari Although *Ferrari,* the journal of the Ferrari Owner's Club, is extremely collectable, in the sense that it is a nice item to have in any collection, it isn't in the sense that it is easily available. It is issued only to Members of the Club and, in order to become a Member, one has to be a Ferrari owner. Eight volumes, totalling 21 issues, make up the run to the beginning of 1980.

Iota Quoted here in view of its unique interest, both as the Official Organ of the 'Half Litre' Club and as a desirable item, *Iota* spanned the 500cc Formula, coming out first in April 1947 and continuing its run unbroken until April 1953. With the decline of 500cc racing, it merged with the first issue of *Motor Racing* in January 1954.

With so little of the 500cc Formula chronicled, and with interest in it not only still great but increasing, *Iota* is now more keenly sought than ever. Though very scarce now, it can still be found, but it would be hard to build up the complete run.

Mercedes Benz Gazette Though the start of the run of *Mercedes Benz Gazette* is unfortunately not known, my own run dates from January 1957 to January 1970 and this title is understood to be current. In the period that I have, the format is 5 x 8 inches. It is well produced and illustrated and has a descriptive and interesting text.

100mph As unlike the Bugatti as it could possibly be, the Invicta and particularly the low chassis 100mph model had a certain aesthetic appeal discernible to only a few, among whom were the Council Members of the Bugatti Owners Club. After the war they took the marque under their wing, embodying an Invicta section within the Club.

As an owner, at the time, of two 100mph Invictas, this recognition of the marque gave great pleasure and I still recall the first meeting of the

The Constant Search

Invicta 'clan' at a dimly lit pub in Basingstoke, under the leadership of the late Lord Ebury.

Subsequently, the Vintage Sports Car Club also smiled on the Invicta and, from all this, *100mph,* the Magazine of the Invicta Section emerged, edited by J.E.Jenkins and T.E.Laurie. It appeared in typescript but was adorned by a superbly colour illustrated cover.

Although the first issue carried no date, there is in it a report of a race meeting at Silverstone on April 23rd 1966, in which Invictas took part, and the next issue, Volume 1 No.2, is dated October 1966. Volume 1 consisted of four issues, the last of which was dated January 1968 and, thereafter, *100mph* seems to have appeared fairly regularly up to 1969, and may have continued later. A rare publication now.

On the Road In a sense the 'sister' to the Rolls-Royce Bulletin, in that it related to the Bentley car, *On the Road* is one of the rarest of all one-make journals. Since not all issues were dated, its starting date is not known but thanks to my friend Peter Richley I have been able to establish that the run, which consisted of 13 issues only, ended with the last issue in August/September 1939.

Pur Sang The journal of the United States Bugatti Owner's Club, *Pur Sang* is in style and format identical to *Bugantics,* equally well illustrated and to the same high standard. The run began in 1960, and has been continuous, with four issues per year, and is now in its twenty first year of publication. An extremely nice run to have in any collection, though rare in UK, it may be possible that copies can still be obtained on application to the Club.

Rolls-Royce Bulletin Under this heading, John Schroder said in his *Notes for a Bibliography of the Rolls-Royce Motor Car* — '' 'Rolls Royce 1928'. Published four times a year.''

Bearing in mind not only that this was written more than ten years ago and that, at the time he wrote it, John emphasised the fact that what he was setting out was, in fact, a start to his researches, one can perhaps assume that, at the time, the author himself had copies of the *Rolls-Royce Bulletin* going back to 1928 and felt pretty sure that they started earlier still. How right he was for, since then, I have seen copies of the Bulletin dated as far back as 1914.

Of all marque bulletins, this must rank as the best where quality is concerned, the most artistic and, as regards the early copies, the rarest. In a nutshell, it is in every respect like the product itself — superb.

Rolls-Royce Enthusiasts' Club Bulletin Under the Secretaryship of Lt.Col.E.Barrass, for whose help in compiling these notes I am extremely grateful, the Rolls-Royce Enthusiasts' Club continues to thrive and to issue its attractive and interesting Bulletin, the latest of which, as I write, is No.124, for February 1981.

Short runs of the *Rolls-Royce Enthusiasts' Club Bulletin* have, from time to time, come up for auction and have always met keen bidding. But, with the passage of time, they are becoming scarcer and, like many other similar items, are increasing steadily in value.

The Veteran Car Club The Veteran Car Club Gazette, titled pre-war *The Veteran Car Club (of Great Britain) Gazette,* ran to seven issues prior to World War Two, its last pre-war issue being July 1939. It continued after the war in the same 8½ x 5½ inch format and even in 1951 ran to seventy or more pages per issue, before expanding to full magazine size and becoming the *Veteran Car.* It is not so hard to find as some others, perhaps because, in view of their cost, there does seem to be rather less interest generally in very early cars and motoring than in the 'golden years' of Vintage.

Where veterans are concerned, the spectator interest is just as much there as with vehicles of other eras. But, in his heart, every spectator would really like to own a period car and, at one time at least, many 'would be' enthusiasts were so staggered at veteran car prices that they abandoned all hopes and turned their thoughts to cars of later periods. To some extent this attitude has had an effect on literature relating to the Veteran period.

The Vintage Sports Car Club Junior in years to *Bugantics* but slightly senior to the *Bentley Drivers' Club Review,* the *Vintage Sports Car Club Bulletin* first appeared as three 'Roneo'd' sheets in August 1935, blossomed out in magazine form in March 1937, with twelve pages, and continued in the same form, bi-monthly but with pages increased, until the start of the war.

One of the first clubs of its kind to re-start after the war, the VSCC has continued to go from strength to strength and with it the Bulletin, which now runs to seventy or more pages per issue and comes out quarterly. Although pre-war copies are no easier to find than *Bugantics,* post-war are not as difficult, at least in the 1950s onwards, and, if I were starting now to build up a collection of club bulletins and wondering which to choose, this is the one I would go for because the VSCC Bulletin is well produced, full of interesting material and well illustrated. The Club is large and active, runs race meetings at Silverstone and Oulton Park, among other places and, taking everything into consideration, is the one to join if early and interesting post-war cars appeal.

Here again, throughout this section, the same thoughts apply as with magazines. Ten or fifteen years ago, many of the things that are now thought of as rare were easy rather than hard to find. At that time items such as Ferrari Yearbooks and copies of *Hearsay,* the journal of the ERA Club, which are virtually unobtainable now, were already rare and in today's condition there is really no point in discussing such.

Nothing is literally unobtainable but, to acquire things that are extremely difficult, one needs more than average knowledge of where to look, patience in handling the owner once one has found it and, above all, a very deep purse in order to persuade him to sell.

It is certainly a good thing to join the club issuing the journal or bulletin in which one is interested for, no matter how rare it may be, the membership will almost certainly know who has the thing or things that one seeks and, from time to time, items may be advertised in the current issue of the journal itself.

But if one is only starting to collect, it is probably better to acquire later issues to begin with and to build the run backwards rather than wait to find early copies.

The Specialist Car Clubs

A30-A35 OWNERS CLUB
Bill Cochran, 25 Fiveheads Road,
Horndean, Portsmouth.

A40 CLUB
Miss Cynthia Hiller, Flat 12
Jasmin Court, 115 Sydney Road,
Sutton, Surrey.

A.B.C. OWNERS CLUB (section of the
Bean Car Club)
David Hales, 20 Langbourne Way,
Claygate, Esher, Surrey.
Tel. No. Esher (78) 62046

AC OWNERS CLUB
Membership Secretary
4 Portsmouth Road,
Camberley, Surrey.

A-C-D CLUB (Auburn-Cord-Duesenberg)
Gene Clark, P.O.Box 1614,
Chico, Calif. 95926, USA.

ALFA ROMEO OWNERS CLUB
Alan Taylor, 37 Amerland Road,
London SW18

ALFA ROMEO SECTION OF THE VSCC
(pre 1941 only)
Mr. & Mrs.A.Cherrett,
The Old Forge, Quarr,
Nr.Gillingham, Dorset.
Tel. No. 07476 2756

ALL-WHEEL DRIVE CLUB
J.Gearing, 220 Park Lane,
Frampton Cotterell, Bristol.
Tel. No. Winterbourne (0454) 772945

ALLARD OWNERS CLUB
Miss P.Hulse, 1 Dalmeny Avenue,
Tufnell Park, London N7 0LD
Tel. No. 01-607 3589

ALTA REGISTER
Grahame Fleming,
16 Queen Elizabeth's Walk,
Wallington, Surrey

ALVIS OWNERS CLUB
M.Cummins, The Hill House,
Rushock, Nr.Droitwich, Worcs.
Tel. No. Chaddesley Corbett (056 283) 309

(ALVIS) 12/50 REGISTER
(1920-32 models only)
A.Salt, 23 Eversley Crescent,
London N21. Tel. No. 01-360 3630

The Constant Search

CLASSIC AMERICAN AUTO CLUB OF
GT. BRITAIN
H.Shell, Old Laundry Cottage,
Eastwick Road, Hunsdon, Herts.
Tel. No. 0920 870353

PRE '50 AMERICAN AUTO CLUB
(incorporates the V8 Register)
L.Arnott, Pubs End,
Drayton Parslow, Milton Keynes, Bucks.
Tel. No. 029 672 377

AMILCAR REGISTER
Mrs.E.Drake, Inwardleigh,
Rockbourne, Nr.Fordingbridge,
Hants. Tel. No. Rockbourne (072 53) 227

AMPHICAR REGISTER
Keith H.Gould, "Park Land",
Ladburn Lane, Shilton, Oxford.
Tel. No. 0993 841999

ARMSTRONG SIDDELEY OWNERS CLUB
M.Hubbuck, 90 Alumhurst Road,
Westbourne, Bournemouth, Dorset.
Tel. No. Bournemouth (0202) 763413

ASTON MARTIN OWNERS CLUB
G.Hopkins, 293 Osbourne Road,
Hornchurch, Essex.
Tel. No. Hornchurch (49) 46841

ASTRA MOTOR CLUB
Miss B.Harris, 71 West Street,
Sittingbourne, Kent.

AUSTIN COUNTIES CAR CLUB
Ian Wheater, 82 Northfield Lane,
Wickersley, Rotherham, Yorkshire.

VINTAGE AUSTIN REGISTER
J.Stringer, 17 Grove Park Ave.,
Borden, Sittingbourne, Kent.
Tel. No. 0795 70797

AUSTIN-HEALEY CLUB
Eastern Centre: N.Stagg,
5A Westwood Road, Canvey Island, Essex.
Midland Centre & Overseas:
Mrs.Carolyn Walters, 27 Three Oaks Rd,
Wythall, West Midlands.
New Forest Centre:
Pat Martin, 104 Winchester Rd.,
Shirley, Southampton.
Tel. No. Southampton (0703) 783680
Northern Centre:
Sheila Reich, 61 Winstanley Rd.,
Sale, Cheshire. Tel. No. 061 973 9995
South Western Centre:
Carol Marks, 171 Coldharbour Road, Bristol.
Thames Valley Centre:
Tom Oakman, 14 Burnt Oak,
Wokingham, Berkshire.
Southern Centre:
Robina Matthews, 8 Cleveland,
Tunbridge Wells, Kent.
Tel. No. Tunbridge Wells 26080

(AUSTIN-HEALEY) SPRITE REGISTER
Pete Dicks, 38 Howdles Lane,
Brownhills, Walsall, Staffs.

AUSTIN SEVEN CLUBS ASSOCIATION
Ian Dunford, 280 Church Road,
Frampton Cotterell, Bristol.
Tel. No. 0454 778021

AUSTIN TEN DRIVERS CLUB
Mrs.Kate Carthew, Colwyn Cottage,
Parsonage Rd., Rickmansworth, Herts.

AUTOVIA CAR CLUB
Nigel Plant, 18 York Road, Birkdale,
Southport, Merseyside.

BEAN CAR CLUB
Mrs.Wendy Cooksey,
32 Wellington Road, Wokingham, Berks.

BENTLEY DRIVERS CLUB
Mrs.B.Fell, W.O.Bentley Memorial Building,
15 Chearsley Road, Long Crendon,
Aylesbury, Bucks.
Tel. No. Long Crendon (0844) 208233

BERKELEY ENTHUSIASTS CLUB
D.Price, 17 Cherry Tree Avenue,
London Colney, St.Albans, Herts.

B.M.W. CAR CLUB
Peter Samuelson, The Old Cottage,
Upper Green, St.Helens, Isle of Wight.
Tel. No. Bembridge (098 387) 3966

BOND OWNERS REGISTER
10 Baber Drive, Feltham, Middlesex.

BORDERS VINTAGE AUTOMOBILE CLUB
Michael Bruce, "Meadowfield",
Ormiston Farm, Hawick.

BORGWARD DRIVERS CLUB
R.R.D. Richmond-Jones, 22 Warburton Rd.,
Canford Heath, Poole, Dorset.

BRISTOL OWNERS CLUB
Bernard Lee, 2 Middle Green Road,
Langley, Slough.

BRITISH SALMSON OWNERS CLUB
Tim Grisdale, 36 Station Road,
Ridgmont, Beds.
Tel. No. Ridgmont (052 528) 548

BROOKLANDS SOCIETY
Mrs.Mirian Peddle, Yarnhams,
Rectory Close, Stanton St.Quintin,
Nr.Chippenham, Wilts.
Tel. No. Hullavington (066 63) 666

BROUGH SUPERIOR CLUB
J.Wallis, 11 Meadow View,
Potterspury, Towcester, Northants.

BSA FRONT WHEEL DRIVE CLUB
Peter King, 81 Beverley Drive,
Edgware, Middlesex.

BUCKLER REGISTER
Malcolm Buckler, Fairy Oak,
Regaby, Isle of Man.

BUGATTI OWNERS CLUB
Geoffrey Ward, Prescott Hill,
Gotherington, Cheltenham, Glos.
Tel. No. Bishops Cleeve (024 267) 3136

BUICK CLUB OF AMERICA (UK CHAPTER)
Dave Norton, 8 Clarence Rd., London E17

LONDON BUS PRESERVATION GROUP
Cobham Bus Museum, Redhill Rd.,
Cobham, Surrey. Tel. No. Cobham 4078

CALTHORPE REGISTER
D.Bristow, 11 Rock Lane,
Warminster, Wilts. Tel. No. 098 52 3525

CITROEN CAR CLUB
A.Bowden, "Pilgrims", Pilgrims Way,
Kemsing, Sevenoaks, Kent.

(CITROEN) TRACTION OWNERS CLUB
Mrs.Maria Hogehiss, 94 Oving Road,
Chichester, W.Sussex.

CLAN OWNERS CLUB
Robert Russell, 77 Ashby Road,
Woodville, Burton-on-Trent,
Staffs. Tel. No. 0283 217361

CLASSIC AND HISTORIC MOTOR CLUB
Mrs.Tricia Burridge, "Ashford",
Ham Lane, Paulton, Bristol.

CLYNO REGISTER
J.Salt, New Farm, Startley,
Chippenham, Wilts.
Tel. No. Seagry (0249) 271

HISTORIC COMMERCIAL VEHICLE CLUB
M.Banfield, Iden Grange,
Cranbrook Road, Staplehurst, Kent.
Tel. No. Staplehurst (0580) 892369

CONSUL CAPRI OWNERS CLUB
Peter Owens, 15 Gyllyndune Gdns.,
Seven Kings, Ilford, Essex.

CORNWALL VINTAGE VEHICLE SOCIETY
B.Murrish, The Bron, North Hill,
Chacewater, Truro, Cornwall.

CROSSLEY REGISTER
G.Lee, Arlyn, 4 Brickwall Lane,
Ruislip, Middlesex.
Tel. No. Ruislip (71) 36757

The Constant Search

DAIMLER AND LANCHESTER OWNERS CLUB
Barry Thorne, 57 Northcote Road,
London SW11. Tel. No. 01-228 6835

DAVRIAN REGISTER
Alan Rodwell, 47a Ross Road,
Wallington, Surrey.

DE TOMASO CLUB
Marianne Anderson, Drottninggatan 11,
244 02 Furulund, Sweden.

DELAGE SECTION OF THE VSCC
C.Hamilton Gould, The Grange,
Great Horwood, Milton Keynes.
Tel. No. Winslow (029 671) 2354

DELLOW REGISTER
John Temple, c/o Douglas Temple Studios Ltd.,
104b Old Christchurch Road,
Bournemouth, Dorset.

DIVA REGISTER
Steve Pethybridge, 8 Wait End Road,
Waterlooville, Hants.

DKW OWNERS CLUB
Kurt Sozen, 18 Rutland Court,
Denmark Hill, London SE5

DUTTON OWNERS CLUB
P.Briee, 58 Hollingdean Terrace,
Brighton.

ELVA OWNERS CLUB
Roger Dunbar, 124 Marine Crescent,
Goring-by-Sea, Worthing,
West Sussex.

ENFIELD & DISTRICT VETERAN
VEHICLE TRUST
C.Glazebrook, 76 Baker Street,
Enfield, Middlesex.
Tel. No. 686 333 X2776

ERA CLUB
Guy Spollon, Arden Grange,
Tamworth-in-Arden, Warks.
Tel. No. Tamworth-in-Arden (056 44) 2271

FACEL VEGA OWNERS CLUB
Mrs.P.Witkowska, 17 Crossways,
Sutton, Surrey.

FAIRTHORPE SPORTS CAR CLUB
Barry Gibbs, Rose Cottage,
The Hollington, Long Crendon, Bucks.

FERRARI OWNERS CLUB
Godfrey Eaton, 10 Whittox Lane, Frome,
Somerset. Tel. No. Frome (0373) 2987

FIAT REGISTER (pre-1950 only)
Alan Cameron, 7 Tudor Gardens,
West Wickham, Kent. Tel. No. 01-777 4729

500 OWNERS ASSOCIATION
B.Brant, 38 Bushmore Road,
Hall Green, Birmingham.
Tel. No. 021 778 3435

(FORD) CORTINA OWNERS CLUB
Roger Tyrell, Pantiles, 30 Perth Rd.,
Bridgemarg, Gosport, Hants.

FORD CLASSIC OWNERS CLUB
John Cantwell, 48 Church Road,
Manor Park, London E12

FORD 1600E CLUB
Bert Mainey, 17 Bowland Ave.,
Ashton-in-Makerfield, Wigan.
Tel. No. 0942 74046

(FORD) GT40 OWNERS CLUB
Bryan Wingfield, South Gibcracks Farm,
East Hanningfield, Chelmsford, Essex.
Tel. No. Danbury (024 541) 5369

(FORD) Mk I CONSUL, ZEPHYR, ZODIAC
OWNERS CLUB
Dave Barry, 25a Junction Rd.,
Burgess Hill, Sussex.
Tel. No. Burgess Hill (044 46) 44521

(FORD) Mk II CONSUL, ZEPHYR, ZODIAC
OWNERS CLUB
Dave Debenham, 26 Burwash Road,
Plumstead, London SE18

(FORD) MODEL T REGISTER
Alan Meakin, 14 Brickfarm Lane,
Taverham, Norwich.

FORD POPULAR REGISTER
B.Palmer, 13 St.Bernards,
Chichester Rd., Croydon, Surrey.
Tel. No. 01-686 3179

FORD SIDEVALVE OWNERS CLUB
(incorporates 100E Owners Club)
John Norris, 6 Thakeham Close,
Bexhill-on-Sea, Sussex.
Tel. No. 0424 220183

(FORD) V8 PILOT OWNERS CLUB
Howard Stenning, 65 Butler House,
Burdett Road, London E14

FRAZER NASH SECTION OF THE VSCC
C.R.Newton, 8 Edgehill Road,
Four Oaks, Sutton Coldfield,
W.Midlands. Tel. No. 021-353 0534

GENTRY REGISTER
Vincent French, 9 Emerald Gardens,
Beacontree Heath, Essex.
Tel. No. 01-595 6945

GILBERN OWNERS CLUB
Richard Bonnie, Bucklers Hard,
55 Hempstead Road, King's Langley,
Herts. Tel. No. King's Langley (40) 62731

GINETTA OWNERS CLUB
Stephen Greenwood, 10 Crossways,
Colne Engaine, Colchester, Essex.

GORDON-KEEBLE OWNERS CLUB
Mrs.A.Lakas, Gordon-Keeble Car Centre,
Westminster Rd., Brackley, Northants.
Tel. No. Brackley (0280) 702311

GT40 OWNERS CLUB
Bryan Wingfield, South Gibcracks Farm,
East Hanningfield, Chelmsford, Essex.
Tel. No. Danbury (024 541) 5369

ASSOCIATION OF HEALEY OWNERS
Neil Mackay, 26 Main Street,
Burton Joyce, Nottingham.

HEINKEL/TROJAN CLUB
29 Hurst Road, Earl Shilton, Leics.

HILLMAN AERO-MINX REGISTER
(pre-war only)
A.Demaus, Cadmore Close, St.Michael's,
Tenbury, Worcs.

HILLMAN REGISTER
Clive Baker, 16 Parklands,
Wootton-under-Edge, Glos.
Tel. No. Wootton-under-Edge (045 385) 3438

HISPANO-SUIZA CLUB
D.Brookbank, Twitten House,
Furners Green, Uckfield, Sussex.

HISTORIC SPORTS CAR CLUB
David Wormak, 3 Laurel Close, Hutton,
Nr.Brentwood, Essex.

HONDA S800 REGISTER
Rosalind Rackham, 9 Hetley Gardens,
Fox Hill, Upper Norwood, London SE19

HONDA S800 SPORTS CAR CLUB
Chris Martyn-Wilson, 64 Gatley Road,
Gatley, Cheshire.

THE (HONDA) Z CLUB
Eddie Miller, 3 Ashview Close,
Ashford, Middlesex.

HORSHAM LIONS
Nick Symes, Greenfields, Lyons Road,
Slinfold, Nr.Horsham, Sussex.

HRG ASSOCIATION
Ian Dussek, Wellhampton House,
Upper Green Road, Shipbourne,
Tonbridge, Kent.
Tel. No. Plaxtol (073 276) 359

HUMBER REGISTER (pre-1931)
P.Diffey, The White House,
Chalk Hill, Dunstable, Beds.
Tel. No. Dunstable (0582) 68355

91

The Constant Search

POST VINTAGE HUMBER CAR CLUB
David Edgar, The Warehouse,
Serpentine Road, Southsea, Hampshire.

ISETTA OWNERS CLUB
Mike Kensdale, Lukifynd,
29 Vine Road, Tiptree, Essex.

JAGUAR DRIVERS CLUB
Norfolk Hotel, Harrington Road,
London SW7. Tel. No. 01-584 9494/5

JENSEN OWNERS CLUB
Roy Tomlin, 29 Little Norsey Road,
Billericay, Essex.

JOWETT CAR CLUB
Dr.Harry Brierley, 5 Farne Avenue,
Gosforth, Newcastle-upon-Tyne.

JUPITER OWNERS AUTO CLUB
Steve Keil, 16 Empress Avenue,
Woodford Green, Essex.
Tel. No. 01-505 2215

LAGONDA CLUB
Mrs.V.May, 68 Savill Road, Lindfield,
Haywards Heath, Sussex.
Tel. No. Haywards Heath (0444) 72274

INTERNATIONAL LAMBORGHINI CLUB
Armin Johl, Karl Seeger, GMbH,
P.O. Box 592, 6050 Offenbach, W.Germany.

LANCIA MOTOR CLUB
Mrs.B.Rees, New Grass, Down Ampney,
Cirencester, Glos.

THE LAND-ROVER REGISTER (1947-51)
T.Hutchings, Bridge Cottage,
11 Tilmore Road, Petersfield,
Hants. Tel. No. Petersfield (0730) 4977

LEA-FRANCIS OWNERS CLUB
W.Adams, Amberway, Oxhill, Warwick.

LINCOLN ZEPHYR OWNERS CLUB
Colin Spong, 22 New North Road,
Hainault, Ilford, Essex.

CLUB LOTUS
Margaret Richards, 22A High Street,
Watton, Thetford, Norfolk.
Tel. No. 0953 883314

HISTORIC LOTUS REGISTER
Victor Thomas, Badgerswood,
School Road, Drayton, Norwich.
Tel. No. 0603 867464

CLUB ELITE
D.Jinks, Chestnut Cottage,
Water Lane, Storrington, Sussex.

LOTUS SEVEN CLUB
Seven House, Town End,
Caterham-on-the-Hill, Surrey.

MAGENTA REGISTER
Steve Johnson, The Station,
Lealholm, Whitby, N.Yorks.

MARCOS CLUB
Colin Feyerabend, 61 Middle Road,
Higher Denham, Uxbridge, Middlesex.

MARENDAZ SPECIAL CAR REGISTER
John Shaw, 23 Vineries Close,
Leckhampton, Cheltenham, Glos.
Tel. No. Cheltenham (0242) 26310

THE MASERATI CLUB
M.Miles, The Paddock, Salisbury Road,
Abbotts Ann, Andover, Hants.
Tel. No. Abbotts Ann (026 471) 312

MERCEDES-BENZ CLUB
Mrs.J.Gupwell, The Firs, Biscombe,
Churchstanton, Taunton, Somerset.
Tel. No. Churchstanton (082 360) 385

INTERNATIONAL FEDERATION OF
MESSERSCHMITT CLUBS
Ian Andrews, 43 St. Nicholas Road,
Witham, Essex.

METROPOLITAN OWNERS CLUB
W.Dowsing, 4 Burham Road, Knaphill,
Surrey. Tel. No. Brookwood (048 67) 4841

MG CAR CLUB
The Secretary, 67 Wide Bargate,
Boston, Lincs.

MG OWNERS CLUB
Roche Bentley, 13 Church End, Over,
Cambs. Tel. No. Swavesey (0954) 31125

(MG) OCTAGON CAR CLUB
Harry Crutchley, 36 Queensville Avenue,
Stafford, Staffs.
Tel. No. Stafford (0785) 51014

REGISTER OF UNUSUAL MICRO-CARS
FOR G.B.
Mrs.Jean Hammond, 28 Durham Road,
Sidcup, Kent.

MILITARY VEHICLES CONSERVATION GROUP
P.Gray, 15 Tarring Road,
Worthing, Sussex.

MINI COOPER OWNERS CLUB
Ray Holman, 9 Walesbeach,
Furnace Green, Crawley, W.Sussex.

MINI-MARCOS OWNERS CLUB
Bob Manifold, 33 Stoneleigh Drive,
Hoddesdon, Herts. Tel. No. 09924 61375

MONOPOSTO RACING CLUB
Julian Pratt, The Lodge, Thornden,
Cowfold, W.Sussex.

MORGAN SPORTS CAR CLUB
Charles Smith, 23 Seymouth Avenue,
Worcester, Worcs. Tel. No. 0905 52995

MORGAN THREE WHEELER CLUB
D.Ellis, 105 Mays Lane, Earley,
Reading, Berks.

MORRIS REGISTER (pre 1940)
Bob Beaumont, 20 Chestnut Avenue,
Gosfield, Halstead, Essex.

BULLNOSE MORRIS CLUB
David Williams, 123 Lakeside Close,
Hough Green, Widnes, Cheshire.

MORRIS MINOR OWNERS CLUB
Paul Davis, 10 Beech Avenue,
East Leake, Loughborough, Leics.
Tel. No. East Leake (050 982) 3226

MINI SEVEN RACING CLUB
H.Hartley, c/o Axleline Eastern Ltd.,
Phoenix Mill, Fydell Crescent,
Boston, Lincs.
Tel. No. Boston (0205) 67005

OCTAGON CAR CLUB
Harry Crutchley, 36 Queensville Avenue,
Stafford, Staffs.
Tel. No. Stafford (0785) 51014

PACKARD CLUB
C.Juneau, Box 2808, Oakland,
California 94618, USA.

THE ASSOCIATION OF PANHARD OWNERS
P.Watkins, 10 New Upperton Road,
Eastbourne, Sussex.

PEERLESS/WARWICK OWNERS REGISTER
Dudley Thompson, Redbeech Cottage,
Church Lane, Friesthorpe, Lincoln.

PIPER CLUB
Clive Davis, 9 Myrtle Close,
East Barnet, Herts.
Tel. No. 01-368 6460

PORSCHE CLUB OF GREAT BRITAIN
Roy Gillham, 64 Raisins Hill,
Pinner, Middlesex. Tel. No. 01-866 7110

PULSAR OWNERS CLUB
John Smith, 47 Melody Road,
Biggin Hill, Kent. Tel. No. 095 94 75505

RAILTON OWNERS CLUB
B.McKenzie, Fairmiles,
Barns Hall Road, Burncross, Sheffield.

RALEIGH SAFETY SEVEN AND
EARLY RELIANT OWNERS CLUB
Nicholas Symes, Greenfields, Lyons Road,
Slinfold, Horsham, W.Sussex.
Tel. No. Slinfold (0403) 790262

The Constant Search

RAPIER REGISTER
John Batt, 48 Ampthill Road,
Maulden, Beds.
Tel. No. Ampthill (0525) 402935

RELIANT SABRE AND SCIMITAR
OWNERS CLUB
Roger Tipler, The Old Bakery,
1 Silver Street, Brixworth, Northants.
Tel. No. Northampton (0604) 881173

RENAULT OWNERS CLUB
E.Smith, 15 Lowshoe Lane,
Romford, Essex.

RILEY MOTOR CLUB LTD.
A.Farrar, The Gables,
Hinksey Hill, Oxford.

RILEY REGISTER
I.Thorpe, 26 Hillcrest Close,
Tamworth, Staffs.

RILEY RM CLUB
John Horn, 20 Greenwood Meadows,
Chinnor, Oxfordshire.
Tel. No. Kingston Blount (0844) 52983

ROCHDALE REGISTER
Derek Bentley, 259 Junction Road,
Burgess Hill, Sussex.
Tel. No. 04446 41125

ROLLS-ROYCE ENTHUSIASTS CLUB
Lt.Col.E.Barrass, Lincroft,
Montacute Road, Tunbridge Wells, Kent.
Tel. No. Tunbridge Wells (0892) 26072

ROLLS-ROYCE AND BENTLEY OWNERS
DRIVERS GUILD
The Coach House, Whistlers Wood,
The Ridge, Woldingham, Surrey.
Tel. No. Woldingham (905) 3251

ROVER P4 DRIVERS GUILD
Daniel Young, 60 Woodville Road,
London NW11. Tel. No. 01-455 6992

ROVER SPORTS REGISTER
Pre 1950: Geoffrey Moore, Yew House,
Fisher Lane, Chiddingfold, Godalming,
Surrey. Tel. No. Wormley (042 879) 3250
Post 1950: Adrian Mitchell, 42 Cecil Road,
Ilford, Essex. Tel. No. 01-478 1204

SAAB OWNERS CLUB OF GB
P.Parfitt, 49 Rogers Road,
Tooting, London SW17

CLASSIC SALOON CAR CLUB
P.Deffee, 7 Dunstable Road,
Caddington, Luton, Beds.

SCOOTACAR CLUB
S.Boyd, Pamanste, 20 Jayns Close,
Aylsham, Norwich. Tel. No. 026 373 3861

750 MOTOR CLUB
Dave Bradley, 16 Woodstock Road,
Witney, Oxon. Tel. No. Witney (0993) 2282

ASSOCIATION OF SINGER CAR OWNERS
Barry Paine, 41 Folly Road,
Wymondham, Norfolk.

SINGER OWNERS CLUB
John Oliver, Dormer Cottage,
Woodham Park Way, Woodham, Weybridge,
Surrey. Tel. No. Byfleet (09323) 46359

SKODA OWNERS CLUB
Ray White, 78 Montague Road,
Leytonstone, London E11.
Tel. No. 01-539 8288

STAG OWNERS CLUB
June Armstrong, 82 Amyand Park Road,
Twickenham, Middx. Tel. No. 01-892 4323

STANDARD MOTOR CLUB
Les Fish, 1 York Gate,
Southgate, London N14

STAR, STARLING, STEWARD AND
BRITON CAR REGISTER
D.Evans, 9 Compton Drive, Dudley,
W.Midlands. Tel. No. Dudley (0384) 54768

SUNBEAM ALPINE OWNERS CLUB
Justin Harrington, 32 Kingswood Court,
West End Lane, London NW6.
Tel. No. 01-624 9412

SUNBEAM RAPIER OWNERS CLUB
David Parrott, 185 Milton Road,
Cowplain, Hampshire.

SUNBEAM TALBOT ALPINE REGISTER
John Tolhurst, 201 Havant Road,
Hayling Island, Hants.
Tel. No. 07016 2679

SUNBEAM TALBOT DARRACQ REGISTER
(pre 1937)
Jeremy Grammer, 39 Broad Walk,
Wilmslow, Cheshire. Tel. No. 0625 524589

SUNBEAM TIGER OWNERS CLUB
R.Murray, 25a The Drive, Ilford, Essex.
Tel. No. 01-518 0709

SWIFT REGISTER
John Harrison, 5 Oakfield Road,
Ashtead, Surrey.

SIMCA ARONDE OWNERS REGISTER
Robert Friendship, The Flat,
4 Queen Annes, High Street, Bideford.

THE LONDON VINTAGE TAXI ASSOCIATION
L.Percival, 7 Clifton Close,
Addlestone, Surrey.

TORNADO REGISTER
Dave Malins, 48 St.Monicas Avenue,
Luton, Beds. Tel. No. Luton (0582) 37641

TRACTION OWNERS CLUB
Mrs.Maria Hogehiss, 94 Oving Road,
Chichester, W.Sussex.

TR REGISTER
Val Simpson, "Beechcroft", Seymour Road,
Northchurch, Berkhamsted, Herts.
Tel. No. Berkhamsted (04427) 5906

PRE-1940 TRIUMPH CLUB
A.Noble, 20 Station Road,
Littlethorpe, Leicester.

TRIUMPH MAYFLOWER CLUB
Philip Hall, 75 Morley Road,
Staple Hill, Bristol.

TRIUMPH RAZOREDGE OWNERS CLUB
Stewart Langton, 25 Mawbys Lane,
Appleby Magna, Burton-on-Trent, Staffs.
Tel. No. Measham (0530) 71640

TRIUMPH ROADSTER CLUB
R.Fitsall, 11 The Park, Carshalton,
Surrey. Tel. No. 01-669 3965

TRIUMPH SPORTS SIX CLUB
Steve Jarmyne, 69 Stanley Road North,
Rainham, Essex. Tel. No. 040 27 55674

(TRIUMPH) STAG OWNERS CLUB
June Armstrong, HRS, 73/77 Britannia Road,
Fulham SW6. Tel. No. 01-731 3287

TRIUMPH 2.5 PI OWNERS CLUB
Steven Stepney, 23 Berkeley Road,
Street, Somerset.

TROJAN OWNERS CLUB
A.Hacking, Upper Woodhouse,
Billingshurst, Sussex.

TURNER REGISTER
David Scott, 21 Ellsworth Road,
High Wycombe, Bucks.
Tel. No. High Wycombe (0494) 445636

TVR CLUB
Douglas R.Manuel, 21 Fishers Road,
Staplehurst, Nr.Tonbridge, Kent.
Tel. No. Staplehurst (0580) 891838

UNIPOWER OWNERS CLUB
G.Hulford, 8 Coppice Road,
Horsham, Sussex.
Tel. No. Horsham (0403) 66432

VANDEN PLAS OWNERS CLUB
C.Dawe, 10 Playses Green,
Hambridge, Langport, Somerset.

The Constant Search

VAUXHALL OWNERS CLUB
Ron Shier, 41 Oxleys Cottages,
Haynes West End, Bedford.
Tel. No. Bedford (0234) 741215

VAUXHALL REGISTER (pre 1931 only)
M.Applebee, 83 Finborough Road,
London SW10

VETERAN CAR CLUB
Mrs.Joan Innes-Kerr, Jessamine House,
15 High Street, Ashwell, Herts.
Tel. No. Ashwell (046 274) 2818

VINTAGE SPORTS CAR CLUB
P.Hull, 121 Russell Road, Newbury,
Berkshire. Tel. No. Newbury (0635) 44411

VOLKSWAGEN OWNERS CLUB
R.Sleigh, 28 Longnor Road,
Brooklands, Telford.

HISTORIC VOLKSWAGEN CLUB
R.Shaill, 194 Old Church Road,
Hollington, St.Leonards-on-Sea, E.Sussex.

VOLKSWAGEN CABRIOLET OWNERS
CLUB OF GB
Tim Barnes, 12 Victoria Street,
Maidstone, Kent.
Tel. No. Maidstone 670714

VOLVO OWNERS CLUB
Mrs.Rosemarie Nettleton,
19 Broadhurst Gardens, Eastcote,
Ruislip, Middlesex.

WARWICK/PEERLESS OWNERS REGISTER
Dudley Thompson, Redbeech Cottage,
Church Lane, Friesthorpe, Lincoln.

WOLSELEY REGISTER
Dave Allen, Glenville, Glynde Road,
Bexleyheath, Kent.

WOLSELEY HORNET SPECIAL CLUB
R.Banks, Taliesin Heath Road,
Horsell, Woking, Surrey.

Note: These names and addresses are subject to frequent change and should always be checked before contact is made. The data published was correct at the time when the manuscript was completed by the author.

Chapter 19   Section P

Items other than under headings N and O

At the time that the Classification Index was drawn up, it was thought that there may be items of literature that would not fit happily into sections N and O.

In the event this was not the case, so there are no notes or entries to be recorded in this section.

Left W. (Bill) Boddy, Motoring Historian, Author, and Editor of *Motor Sport*.

Below Lord Montagu of Beaulieu, whose contribution to preserving not only the history of early motoring and motorcycling but also its literature, must surely rate highest of all.

Chapter 20 Section Q

Sales literature and Commemorative brochures

Sales Literature

Although not surprising, in view of its originality, interest in collecting sales literature is as enormous as the subject itself.

The principal problems of collecting in this area are the size of the subject, the eighty five year period it covers, the storage problem and the cost involved.

I must confess that, much as I love sales literature, the problems as I see them have·prevented me from starting to collect. I do have a small collection of catalogues relating to cars that over the years I have owned and liked, but that is as far as it goes. The other reason why I have never become involved is that, much as I love original publications, I enjoy reading rather than browsing. It has always seemed to me that, whereas one can read a book, one can only browse through a catalogue or brochure unless, of course, one is technically minded — and I am not.

One comes back to the question of collecting what you yourself like but, if one is going to collect sales literature, it is worth giving the matter careful thought before starting. One can collect sales literature and nothing else, which immediately makes the problem much simpler, or one can build up a section as part of a general library.

If the latter is the case, thought should be given to the proportion of sales literature in relation to the rest. In the past ten years interest in the collection of sales literature has increased enormously, with the result that even certain post-war catalogues now command high prices.

Bearing in mind that it is the sports and prestige type of car that is of the greatest interest, one can go some of the way by dividing the general picture into three categories as far as the post-war era is concerned.

1 *Makes of car where sales literature values are highest* Allard, Alvis, Armstrong Siddeley, Aston Martin, Bentley, Bristol, Cooper, Facel Vega, Ferrari, Frazer Nash, Gordano, Gordon Keeble, Iso Grifo, Iso Rivolta, Lamborghini, Maserati, MG, Pegaso, Rolls Royce.

2 *Makes where sales literature values are middle range* AC, Alfa Romeo, Audi, Austin Healey, BMW, Bond, Borgward, Buick, Chevrolet, Chrysler, Citröen, Daimler, De Soto, Dodge, Elva, Fairthorpe, Fiat, Frisky, Goggomobile, Healey, Holden, Honda, Invicta, Jaguar, Jensen, Jensen Healey, Jowett, Lagonda, Lancia, Lanchester, Lea Francis, Lincoln, Lloyd, Lotus, Mercedes, Messerschmidt, Metropolitan, Morgan, Moskvich, Nash, NSU, Ogle, Oldsmobile, Opel, Packard, Peugeot, Plymouth, Pontiac, Porsche, Reliant, Renault, Riley, Rover, Singer, Sunbeam, Tornado, Trident, Triumph, TVR, Wartburg.

3 *Makes where sales literature values are lowest*

The Constant Search

Austin, Ford, Hillman, Humber, Morris, Renault, Saab, Simca, Skoda, Standard, Vauxhall, Volkswagen, Wolseley.

This is an assessment in general terms and there are qualifications. Jaguar XK models, early E Series and early post-war Lagonda could fit better into Category 1, and Morris '1000' could equally well go from 3 up to 2. But as a yardstick, it is a fair assessment. On this basis one would envisage the least expensive catalogues in Category 3 to be priced at £1 and the dearest in Category 1 at not more than £100.

The pre-war era of sales literature is more complicated but again it is possible to give an indication.

1 *Makes of car where sales literature values are highest* Alvis, Aston Martin, Armstrong Siddeley, Alfa Romeo, Alta, Albion, Atalanta, Alldays, Bentley, Benz, Berliet, BMW, Brasier, Bugatti, Daimler, De Dietrich, De Dion, Delage, Delahaye, Dennis, Delaunay Belleville, Diatto, Duesenberg, Farman, Hispano Suiza, Invicta, Isotta Fraschini, Itala, Lagonda, Locomobile, Maserati, Maudslay, Maybach, Mercedes Benz, Metallurgique, MG, Minerva, Napier, Panhard et Levassor, Peerless, Renault, Rolls Royce, Stanley, Stutz, Voisin, Vulcan, White, Zust.

2 *Makes where sales literature values are middle range* ABC, Adler, Amilcar, Angus Sanderson, Ansaldo, Arrol Aster, Arrol Johnston, Auburn, Austin (7hp), AV, Ballot, Bantam, British Salmson, Bean, Beardmore, Belsize, Beverley Barnes, Bianchi, BNC, Bradshaw, Brocklebank, Brough Superior, BSA, Buick, Cadillac, Chenard Walcker, Chrysler, Clement, Constantinesco, Cord, Cottin Desgouttes, Crossley, Crown Magnetic, Cubitt, Darracq, DFP, D'Yrsan, Frazer Nash, GN, HE, Hotchkiss, HRG, Lammas, Lanchester, Lancia, Lea Francis, Marendaz, Moon, Morgan, Newton Ceirano, OM, Packard, Peugeot, Railton, Raymond Mays, Riley, Rover, Ruston Hornsby, Salmson, Schneider, Sizaire Berwick, Squire, Star, Straker Squire, Sunbeam, Talbot, Unic.

3 *Makes where sales literature values are lowest* AJS, Argyll, Ariel, Austin (over 7hp), Calcott, Calthorpe, Carden, Chevrolet, Citroën, Cluley, Clyno, Coventry Victor, De Soto, Derby, Dodge, Durant, Enfield Allday, Eric Campbell, Erskine, Essex, Fiat, FN, Ford, Graham Paige, Guy, GWK, Gwynne,

Hampton, Hillman, Horstman, Hudson, Humber, Hupmobile, JMB, Jowett, Lincoln, Marlborough, Marmon, Marquette, Matford, Mathis, Maxwell, Mercury, Metropolitan, Morris, Nash, New Hudson, Opel, Overland, Plymouth, Pontiac, Raleigh, Simca, Singer, Standard, Studebaker, Swift, Tamplin, Terraplane, Triumph, Trojan, Vauxhall, Wanderer, Waverley, Whitlock, Willys, Windsor, Wolseley

Just some of them. One is thinking of those in the first category as being mainly in the early years, except a few such as Rolls-Royce which has value in all periods. In this sphere one would envisage the lowest priced catalogue at, say, £5 and the most expensive, in Category 1, at £300 or thereabouts. That isn't too high by any means — it has happened more than once already.

Lastly comes the question of storage and I doubt whether one can improve on Clearview plastic wallet books, from and into which one can always slip catalogues easily.

Commemorative Brochures

Throughout the history of the British Motor Industry, the publicity and sales side has always been conscious of boosting business by the issue of commemorative booklets and brochures relating to record breaking and competitive successes. Even though the amounts of any particular issue varied, a lot have survived and are rated highly among specialists and by enthusiasts for particular marques.

There is sound reasoning behind the idea because nearly all such items were attractively designed and always well illustrated. At the same time they often had texts written by well-known motoring authors of the day, and by racing drivers and well known personalities in the world of motoring.

Sunbeam. Grand Prix de France 1923

The Sunbeam Motor Company was among the first to recognise the value of this type of publicity advertising and in 1923 produced an extremely artistic 20 page brochure which included many good photographs illustrating the company's participation in the Grand Prix de France.

203mph! The Supreme Sunbeam
Sunbeam Motor Company 1927. Few events in the world of motor racing and record breaking can have made such enormous impact on the motoring public, not only of Great Britain but also the world, as the successful World Land Speed Record attempt made by the Sunbeam company. Their gargantuan twin-engined, chain-driven car, driven by Major H.O.D. (later Sir Henry) Segrave, resulted in the record being taken at 203.7mph. Describing, in his book *The Lure of Speed,* his first sight of the monster running at the Sunbeam works in Wolverhampton, Segrave said 'From the first I had no doubt whatever that the car could attain the terrific speed it had been built for. I shall never forget my sensations when I first heard its engines running 'all out' in a 'cradle' at the works at Wolverhampton. The whole enormous body, looking like a mechanical nightmare rather than the product of human hands, was gripped in a vice-like contrivance with its wheels off the ground. The engines were started up and the whole building shook. No words can describe the unimaginable output of power which the 1000hp machinery seemed to catapult into the building. It was one continuous deafening roar. The very walls quivered while the tiles seemed to dance on the roof. The wheels were spinning round like semi-visible discs at 210mph. Even then we knew that the engines behind them were not putting forth all they were capable of. I think I stood and stared at the monster rather as a child would have done. Racing cars I had seen and driven by the dozen but this was something more gigantic than any yet dreamed of. It fascinated me. The thought that I was to drive it, control it, unleash all its potentialities was, one must admit, a little unnerving. It is the only time I can honestly say when I have stood in front of a car and doubted human ability to control it.' But control it he did and, in 1929, went on to go faster still.

Progress on Land and Water. The 'Golden Arrow' and 'Miss England'
The Sunbeam Motor Company 1929. 19 pages illustrated. The next World Land Speed Record car that Segrave was to drive, the Golden Arrow, was

as beautiful as the earlier one had been grotesque, and it was no surprise when the record fell again at 231mph. Segrave then set his sights on the World's Water Speed Record with Miss England. Sadly, it was to lead him to his end, even though the memories of his achievements still live. Both these giant cars now rest safely in the National Motor Museum at Beaulieu and the brochures describing them and their achievements form part of World Land Speed Record history.

Commemorative Brochures — MG
Of all pre-war manufacturers, the late lamented MG Car Company was probably not only one of the most active and successful in competition but also one of the most 'publicity aware' in exploiting its numerous well-deserved successes. Concurrently with its attractive sales literature, the Company regularly put out increasingly attractive publicity hand outs which increased in number, size and interest as time went on, all of which contributed to building up fervour for the marque to the point that it is today.

To See Ourselves as Others See Us 1929, a list of testimonials from owners, some well-known motoring personalities, and a comprehensive list of competition successes. 12 pages, illustrated

About George by Malcolm McIntyre, concerning the Sports M type MG Midget. With drawings by Peter Crosby

An Epic of the Double Twelve issued by the Company in December 1930 and again, revised, in February 1931. 6 sides, illustrated

At the Sign of the Octagon issued by the Company in 1932. 32 pages, illustrated

A Chequered Career by H.S.Linfield and E.C.Lester. 14 pages, illustrated. Issued 1932

The Luck of the Game by Cecil Kimber. Foreword by Capt.G.E.T.Eyston. 20 pages, illustrated. Issued 1932

Mille Miglia by H.E.Symons. 48 pages, illustrated. Issued 1933

The Luck of the Game Again by Barrie Lyndon, describing MG participation in the 1934 Tourist Trophy Race. 24 pages, illustrated. Issued 1934

Supremacy Listing and describing 1934 competition successes. 16 pages, illustrated. Issued 1934/1935

This Is Motoring by Barrie Lyndon. Relating to the new MG Magnette. 14 pages, illustrated. Issued 1935

The Constant Search

Action Race participation and results. 16 pages, illustrated. Issued 1935

What I think of the MG Car Opinions of well-known owners and racing drivers. Foreword by Earl Howe. 34 pages, illustrated. Issued 1934

The Greatest Achievement of the Year 30 pages, illustrated. Issued 1939

There were others, among them *The Fun of the Thing* and *Safety Fast in the Making,* the only hardback. All fulfilled their purpose and, not only that, they are still avidly sought by collectors of MG literature today.

Were I to expand my collection (which Heaven prevent!), I confess that I would be very tempted to include publications such as these which are, to me, attractive and interesting records of landmarks in motoring and motor racing history. I can well understand anyone being keen to build up such a collection.

Brooklands Automobile Racing Club, Souvenir of the
Published by *The Car Illustrated* dated July 6th

1907 and edited by the Club's Vice-President, Lord Montagu, this must rate as one of the rarest and most desirable of all commemorative brochures, since it sets out to describe the thoughts that led to the construction of Brooklands Track, its design, construction and inaugural meeting, as well as the personalities involved.

An excellent reprint, edited and revised, was produced for the Brooklands Society by Peter Roddis Productions Ltd in 1977, abridged in that its pages totalled 63 instead of the 83 of the original and easily identifiable by its back cover. The original has a full page advertisement by the Daimler Motor Co (1904) Ltd, whereas the reprint omits this and makes clear its origin.

With reprinting techniques to such a high standard today, it is good to see a production of this type done not only so well but also making crystal clear that it is a contemporary reprint, unlike some others which state the fact but not always so clearly.

Chapter 21 Section R

Service Literature

Though a book of this nature must obviously contain a section relating to service literature, it cannot in any sense be considered as 'collectable' in the sense that one would set out to build up a library of it.

Nevertheless there is a strong and constant demand, particularly for early handbooks and workshop manuals and a steady one for later items both from private owners of cars and from specialists in the maintenance and repair of early and classic type cars.

The demand exceeds supply to a greater extent than with sales literature because, whereas maybe a dozen or so catalogues may originally have been issued in order to sell a new car, probably only or or possibly two handbooks will have been issued in order to maintain each car.

Even so, the price of the average handbook can be taken to be some ten to fifteen per cent less than the corresponding catalogue, whatever the age or type of vehicle.

With 'run of the mill' models of the 1950s and 1960s now advertised for sale as collector's pieces, the section has been laid out to include books and literature generally for these periods. No further comment or explanation seems necessary.

Chapter 22   Section S

Motorcycling

Section S 1

Road and Touring

Once a motorcyclist, always a motorcyclist, so they say. And the opposite also applies, in that if you aren't a motorcycle enthusiast in the days of your youth, the chances are that you never will be. So, though this section will have appeal for many, there will also be a large band for whom it holds no interest.

Although I have it, I have never read *Across America by Motor Cycle*, which is a fairly large book. No reason for the omission — it's just the matter of time. I loved Sheridan's *Across Europe with Satanella* and could read it again, for Satanella was an elderly vee-twin Ariel and surprisingly well behaved, bearing in mind her years and the distance covered. Although there is not a lot of motorcycle content in *The Adventures of a Despatch Rider,* it was another that I enjoyed, purely because of the adventures which were, at times, hair raising.

Around the World with Motor Cycle and Camera, though of a much later period, was good, the machine was a Triumph, and Soboleff's marathons described in *Cossack at Large* and *Nansen Passport,* riding an Ariel single were, I think, the best of all. Although I read *From Leipzig to Cabul* a long long time ago, I can't recall much about it or even whether I enjoyed it. But I did enjoy Battson's *The Land Beyond the Ridge,* a small

book, not too well illustrated but enjoyable because it was written by an obviously 'incurable' enthusiast.

We have covered *My Life on Wheels* already in one of the car sections, for it is a record of one man's motorcycling and motoring 'loves' — and his 'hates' as well. The 'hates' only fell into that category after he had bought them. He loved them all at the time of purchase and some of them all the time. It is a lovely story, particularly for its humour and because all the awful things that happened to the author have happened to almost every motorcycling and motoring enthusiast. Particularly so is the discovery that every time you want a change of steed, everyone is seeking the one you want to buy while the one you want to trade in has suddenly, and unaccountably, become valueless!

Three Wheeling Through Africa — by courtesy of two elderly Triumph sidecar outfits — was a good account of a bleak marathon ride but, again, I have to admit that I have only scanned through the others in this section. The last title here, *With a Motor Bike in the Bush,* though shown as illustrated, does in fact have only one illustration opposite the title page, but I am told that the story is good.

Almost, but not quite, too late to be included here was Bob Currie's new book, *Motor Cycling in the 1930s.* I loved this, not so much for the comic photograph I found of myself, blissfully unaware of a nearly flat rear tyre in the 'Hutchinson 100' at Brooklands, but for the way it captures the atmosphere of the nineteen thirties as no other contemporary book seems to have done, and for the numerous fine photographs which contribute so much to a book of this kind.

Section S 2

Racing — all aspects

Of all books on motor cycle racing that should be reprinted, *The Art of Motor Cycle Racing* by Mike Hailwood and Murray Walker is the one, and I say this not only as a great admirer of Mike's but because the book is far and away the best. Even though it came out in 1963, almost everything in it still applies.

Swift's *Ride it! The Complete Book of Big Bike Racing* is another good bet and is readable and instructive as well. I enjoyed Barry Briggs' autobiography, *Briggo,* even though I know very little about speedway. In its day, Higgins' *Britain's Racing Motor Cycles* was a mini classic, but Jeff Clew's *British Racing Motor Cycles* brings the picture up to date and must therefore rate even better.

Brooklands and Beyond, my own autobiography, is partly bike racing and partly car, mainly pre-war at Brooklands, but also carrying on through the post-war period. The follower on from that, *Brooklands: Behind the Scenes* covers the long races held at Brooklands, 200 Mile Solo and Sidecar, in the 1925 to 1930 era and was the most enjoyable of any I have done because, having written up the history of the races in the first half, I then took a tape recorder to talk to some of the veterans who had taken part in them and the vivid recollections they had astonished me. While on the subject of Brooklands, I thoroughly enjoyed Bert Perryman's *A Clubman at Brooklands* even though I thought he was almost too modest because, although he certainly did start at the track as a clubman, he soon blossomed out as one of the regulars.

Continental Circus, by Ted Mellors and Geoff Davison, was an excellent account of pre-war continental bike racing and Jeff Clew's *Francis Beart: A Single Purpose* was tremendous, I thought, 'single purpose' being Francis Beart's determination to win, of course, which he usually did. Noel Pope's *Full Chat* was a surprise when it came out, not only because none of us knew that he was doing it but because, of all at the track, he was the last that one

would imagine getting sufficiently organised to get down to writing a book. But he did and *Full Chat* is amusing, original and good.

Griffith's *Historic Racing Motor Cycles* will delight enthusiasts with its good illustrations and *Hailwood,* by Macauley and Hailwood, published by Transport Bookman, is one that I could read again and again because, besides being such a very nice man, Mike is absolutely 'the greatest' I think. If you can find them, both of Basil Brindley's books on Irish motorcycle racing are first class to have in one's library — but they are hard to track down. I enjoyed Ivan Mauger's *World Speedway Book* but liked, even more, his autobiography *Triple Crown Plus* because, even with little knowledge of speedway, it was interesting to see how the speedway riders meet all the same sort of problems on the way up, among them the difficulty of finding a good and reliable chap to look after the machines.

With years of experience of motorcycling journalism behind him, Vic Willoughby's *Classic Motorcycles* and *The Racing Motorcycle,* both by courtesy of Hamlyn, are certainly two of the best in this section.

A Million Miles of Racing, by Phil Heath and McGowan, is another of those lovely little books published by TT Special, that wonderful newspaper that, thanks to Geoff Davison, has come out every year in the Isle of Man during the TT period. The book is just as good as all the others of the series and without TT Special where would we have been. While on the subject, let's pinpoint the others in the series, all of which are good to have in a collection. They are *The Racing Game, Racing Reminiscences, Racing Through the Century, The Racing Year, The Story of the TT, The Story of the Ulster, The TT Races — Behind the Scenes* and *TT Tales,* all by Davison, and *Short Circuits* by Davison and Smith — a great series and all well worth looking for.

Younger, by comparison, and different because it is the 'sister' to *Autocourse, Motocourse* is a 'must' for the follower of road racing because, coming out annually, it gives a superb account of each season's racing. There is literally nothing to compare with it in its field and, in producing it, Hazleton Securities, via their enthusiastic chief, Richard Poulter, have rendered a tremendous service to all followers of road racing.

The Constant Search

Phil Read's *Phil Read — The Real Story* is one that I enjoyed, from the pen of a great rider. Higgins' *Private Owner* is another, though cast in a different mould, since it tells of the trials and sacrifices that had to be made by anyone keen to get into racing before and immediately after the war. Sprouts Elder's *Romance of the Speedway* and Stenner's *Thrilling the Million* both tell the story of the start of speedway in this country. Both great books, and what a wonderful period it was. They had the machines, they had the tracks and they had the 'know how' from Australia, where speedway was all the rage. What they didn't have were riders, and thinking initially that TT stars would fill the bill, they tried them and found them disappointing. So, throwing it open to all comers, they started 'test days', when anyone could come along and have a go. How I wished that I'd been born just five years earlier! Surtees' book, *Speed,* is good but hard to find now and must rate a bit of a collector's piece.

Harwood's *Speed and How to Obtain It* ran to countless editions and was the bible for us all when it first came out and, for the 'tuners', Phil Irving's *Tuning for Speed* is another good one. Jim Redman's *Wheels of Fortune* was excellent and my own *We Went Racing* was good fun to write and told the story of my sponsorship of a great rider, Griff Jenkins, who rode my Manx Nortons and 7R AJSs in 1963 and 1964, winning the Senior Manx Grand Prix at the then record average of 96mph.

Section S 3

Motocross, scrambles and trials

Most of the books in this section are 'moderns' and since in the evening of life one doesn't think too much about entering for motocross or trials events, my comment must, to some extent, be limited.

On the other hand, of course, looking at the section with almost no knowledge, one starts with a clean sheet and has no bias. Looking through the books listed here, I would go for Melling's *Ride it! The Complete Book of Motocross,* Smith's *Ride it! The Complete Book of Trials* and Mick Andrews' and Beezley's *The Book of Trials,* go out and buy my machinery and 'have a go' were I faced with the situation. If not too successful, I would then turn up the section again to make a second choice!

Though never a participant in any of these activities, I did, when I was sponsoring Griff Jenkins, take him to see a scramble, with the idea of getting a bike for him to ride during the winter in order to keep him fit. At the time I thought the idea was good and that we would both enjoy it but, after watching the first scramble heat, Griff turned to me with 'You want me to do this? Sorry, I always want to please you but, no — it's too dangerous'. And that after his record Manx win in 1963.

Smith's *The Greatest of all Trials the Scott,* is one that I have, and I also enjoyed Jeff Clew's *Sammy Miller: The Will to Win,* the biography of Sammy Miller, which was lent to me at the time it came out.

If one isn't too well informed on a particular subject, it always seems best not to express strong opinions and I have Jeff Clew to thank for pointing out the excellence of *The Art of Moto Cross* by Jeff Smith and Bob Currie which, when one delves into it, is probably the best of all.

Section S 4

Marque

Again, in this section, I must acknowledge the great help I have had from Jeff Clew who not only helped me to draw the dividing line between the true marque history type of book and others that deal more with the service and maintenance aspect, but also took enormous trouble in producing many additional titles for this, and other, sections from his own personal collection, many of which would not otherwise have been included.

One would think that, having spent a great part of one's business life in the field of motoring and motorcycling literature, this would present no problem but the answer to that is that no one surveying the scene from a general angle can have the same amount of knowledge as a specialist collector. Although you may feel reasonably confident of having most of the answers, the specialist often proves you to be wrong and the answer to that is not to be cross with yourself but grateful for having specialist collectors among your friends.

Marque histories have, for years, been among the most popular of all books where motoring is concerned but, when it comes to motorcycling, among the most neglected. Jeff Clew blazed the trail with his Velocette (*Always in the Picture*), Douglas (*The Best Twin*) and Scott (*The Yowling Two-Stroke*) marque histories, picking the right makes and making the very best of the enormous research involved, and no one has done more towards contributing to the motorcycle literary scene.

Other professionals, including Bob Holliday, Bruce Main-Smith and Bill Boddy, also contributed to the marque scene, but it wasn't until the 1970s and 1980s that new authors to motorcycling, such as Leonard Setright, Michael Frostick, Ryerson, Champ and Peter Hartley, joined in, so that now we have marque histories for Brough Superior, AJS, Douglas, Norton, BSA, Scott, Sunbeam, Morgan, Matchless and Triumph — and still they come.

So the marque scene is now much brighter than it was even a few years ago, and still is improving.

Section S 5

Sales literature

Interest in collecting motorcycle sales literature is no less than in the car field, and in the post-war era is more, perhaps because the collectors are, as a rule, younger.

As with all original material, it is hard to find but the best sources are certainly the numerous autojumbles and swapmeets held up and down the country, mainly in the summer. Subdividing the scene into sections we get:

Makes of most interest
ABC, AJS, AJW, Ascot Pullin, Brough Superior, BSA, Cotton, Excelsior, McEvoy, Norton, HRD, Triumph, Grindlay Peerless, Rex Acme, Rudge, OEC, Velocette, Sunbeam, Vincent, Zenith.

Types of most interest
Sporting, large capacity vee-twins, marques listing overhead valve and overhead camshaft models, particularly TT replicas, marques having a history of racing and rare and unusual machines.

Types of least interest
Mopeds and small capacity two-strokes.

Although increasing in value, prices of motorcycle brochures and catalogues are generally lower than for cars, but the margin is closer between pre- and post-war. The standard of production of post-war catalogues is generally lower than pre-war and what is now rated a catalogue would, pre-war, be rated a brochure. At the time that I was dealing in these, our definition of a catalogue was an item of literature the pages of which were numbered and which turned, as with a book. A brochure folded, probably twice, and unfolded to show the contents, so its sides were not numbered.

Early sales catalogues and some, even, of the 1930s were collector's items in the true sense. Triumph, for instance, produced catalogues in the 1910s that almost amounted to softback books, with 50 pages or more. In these, every model in the range was illustrated, its full specification given together with price and the methods of construction shown, with illustrations of the factory. There were also lengthy pages listing racing and competition successes and more of riders' and owners' opinions. Even in the mid-1930s, Norton catalogues, usually titled *The Roadholder*, were put out in the same size and on the same lines so that, in a sense, they amounted more to commemorative brochures.

One could expect, today, to see post-war catalogues priced at between £1 and £5 according to make and type. Pre-war are usually priced between £2 and £10 but catalogues of the type just described could be priced at £20 or, in some cases, more.

Although the supply position of early and better type catalogues is generally less good even than in the car field, caches of early ones do seem to turn up more often than with car catalogues. If one is lucky enough to be around when this happens, it is better not to waste time because the word gets around quickly.

Section S 6

Service Literature

To a great extent, the same guidelines apply to motorcycle service literature as with cars in that, although not 'collectable' in the sense that one would build up a collection to read and enjoy, there is, nevertheless, a good demand for it.

Again, autojumbles and swapmeets provide the best supply and the reason is probably that, since most of the vendors are not really traders but private exhibitors who have 'turned out' the garage to provide stock, the supply source is to some extent maintained as more and more 'ex owners' jump on the band wagon and have a go.

A very large proportion of what comes to light is 'run of the mill' material and one sees piles of this on every stall. But, now and again, there are useful items buried in with it and 'digging' is the answer if one knows what one is looking for.

Again, values fit in with the car side and the price of any particular item can be taken as about ten per cent below the corresponding catalogue for the same model. Condition of motorcycle service literature tends, as a rule, to be rather worse than in the case of cars, almost certainly because, in the case of bikes, more maintenance has been done out in the open rather than in the garage and, at times, in the rain. So, before putting down money, it is as well to check that all pages are in situ.

For some reason, motor bike service literature doesn't seem to come up in caches every so often, as with sales literature — it's just always around in the markets. Where makes and types of machine are concerned, exactly the same applies as with sales material. The same makes and types are popular and unpopular.

Service data is particularly hard to find in respect of a few post-war makes and types, and International and Manx Norton and 7R AJS are two examples.

All these observations apply, of course, to pre-war and early post-war machines and models. Where more recent makes are concerned there is no problem at all, since the Haynes Publishing Group have, for years, specialised in producing superb manuals covering virtually every make and model of any consequence. Even though they are, of course, my publishers in this case, I make no apology for mentioning this because, not only are they leaders in the field but specialists in other types of motorcycle literature as well.

Where restoration, rather than maintenance, is concerned, I can strongly recommend Jeff Clew's *Restoration of Vintage and Thoroughbred Motor Cycles* because anyone who has set eyes on his own private collection can have no doubts whatever concerning his qualifications and knowledge of the subject.

Two others in this section, the three volume set of *Modern Motor Cycles* and Molley's *Motor Cycle Repair and Upkeep,* are both 'musts' in a different way. The former is great reading for the lover of pre-war motor bikes, is good reference and is illustrated with many fine photographs. During the time I traded, I sometimes parted with something of my own in order to be able to supply a good customer with something that he badly wanted and this was in that category. At the time I felt sure that I would sooner or later find it again and replace it, but now, two years later, I still haven't been able to do so, despite searching through many autojumbles, including two at Beaulieu. Sooner or later it will come up, but I am beginning to wonder what the price is likely to be when it does.

Motor Cycle Repair and Upkeep is in a different class, not something that one can pick up to read and enjoy, but by far the best of its kind for the lover and restorer of pre-war machines, many of which have individual chapters to themselves. It was published originally as a 14 issue part-work.

Section S 7

Novels, fiction and humour

A small section, since motorcyclists are probably not, as a breed, readers of fiction and derive sufficient humour from their own company to need no more.

While confessing that I share their views, I have no doubt that, if one looked hard enough and had time to give to searching, more could be found.

With the exception of Jack Gawne's *Motorcycle Moonshine* and *Gawne Crazy* which is humour, the others here are all novels and, though all repose among my own books, I know I shall never read them. I keep them because, in each case, they are exceptionally nice copies so retain their places on the basis of condition rather than content.

I can only hope not to be classed a Philistine by the purists and, if I am, hope that others who share my view will stand by and protect me.

Section S 8

Magazines

Whatever the shortage of books on the subject of motorcycling, there has never been a dearth of magazines and today there is almost a glut, even though by no means all of them can be rated 'collectable'.

In the years up to the start of the Second World War, the fact that there were only two made no difference, because both were so old-established and good, and gave such wide coverage, that between them they met the needs of every enthusiast, whether touring, racing, trials or speedway. They were, of course, *The Motor Cycle,* affectionately known to all as the 'Blue 'un', and *Motor Cycling,* the 'Green 'un', from Iliffe and Temple Press respectively. What, in retrospect, is strange is that two weekly magazines, both covering identical aspects of motorcycling, and therefore competing directly against each other, could have survived years, including the recession of the 1930s, only to depart from the scene thirty years later at a time when interest in almost every aspect of motorcycling was on the increase.

To be frank, research into the history of almost every magazine on motorcycling has proved baffling and has revealed only one thing, and that is that as fast as one traced one ex-Editor, he would pass one on to another, who had sometimes taken over the editorship of his magazine at the same time as he took over the editorship of another from someone else. At the time, all that looked quite promising, if it hadn't been for the fact that not one of them could recall the exact time at which these changes took place. To a man, they were all most anxious to help and at the start of each conversation not one of them had the slightest doubt they had the exact answers to hand. But they hadn't, because they all had the same reference in mind — the *Handbook of the Guild of Motoring Writers,* which didn't have the answers itself. No disrespect to the Guild, though, who really couldn't be expected to supply such information so far back in the dim, dark ages. But some information did eventually emerge:

Motor Cycle (The)
Published by Iliffe & Sons, Dorset House, Stamford Street, London E.C.4. Started its run as a weekly magazine in March 1903 and continued the run, unbroken, until, it is believed, the late 1960s when it ceased circulation as a magazine, continuing as a weekly newspaper.

Motor Cycling
Published by Temple Press Ltd, Bowling Green Lane, London E.C.1. Started its run as a weekly magazine in November 1909 and continued the run, unbroken, until the mid-1960s, when it ceased.

Motor Cycle Sport
Published by Teesdale Publishing Ltd, Standard House, Bonhill Street, E.C.2. Started its run as a weekly newspaper with two editions, North and South, in 1961 under the editorship of Cyril Quantrill. Changed to become a monthly magazine in 1962 and is currently running.

Classic Bike
Published by EMAP National Publications Ltd, Park House, 117 Park Road, Peterborough, PE1 2TS. Started its run as a quarterly with Issue No 1, in March 1978. Subject matter is as indicated by its title. Now monthly.

As with the car side, others are arriving on the shelves of retailers and in time may be interesting enough with runs sufficiently long to be worth collecting. There are also motorcycle newspapers but, since this section covers magazines only, these are not included.

Vintage Motor Cycle (The)
The Official Journal of the Vintage Motor Cycle Club. Commencing in 1953 and still current, *The Vintage Motor Cycle* is issued monthly. There are some illustrations.

Section S 9

Items other than under Sections 1 to 8

With less motorcycle literature than car to catalogue, rather more items have ended up under this heading than with the car section.

The Constant Search

Cars and Motor Cycles, by Lord Montagu and M.W.Bourdon, has already been mentioned under heading E 3 so all that is necessary here it to repeat that it is one to include. Jeff Clew's biography of Harry Weslake, *Lucky all My Life,* is another, for not only was Weslake an interesting and unusual man but, throughout his life, was involved in particularly interesting and unusual aspects of engine development.

If caricatures appeal, there is nothing to compare with Sallon's *Motor Cycle Personalities Past and Present,* put out by Shell Mex in 1957, and, for history, both Caunter's *History and Development of Motor Cycles* and his *Motor Cycles, A Technical History* are well worth having. *Motor Cycles, Sidecars and Cyclecars,* by Page, is another if it can be found, and so are the *Motor Cycling Yearbooks and Sports Yearbooks.*

Though they include a fairly high proportion of four wheel coverage, the *Achievement* books, put out by Castrol and Shell year by year throughout the 1950s and 1960s, do contain a good amount on motorcycle racing and competition generally and most of them are not too hard to find, even now. Brindley's *On Two Wheels and Four* and Wingrove and Wilson's *Yarns of the Speedway* are both good as well.

In this section lies what I have always thought of as the finest book on the subject of motorcycling ever produced — *The Motor Cycle Book for Boys.* Dated 1928 and brought out under the banner of that great magazine The Motor Cycle at a time when it was becoming accepted that school leavers should own and ride motor bikes, its intention and aim was to underline the fact and popularise ownership of motorcycles by youngsters. Every aspect of motorcycling is covered — touring, racing, maintenance, the beauty of the countryside that was theirs for the seeking — and all so simply set out and excitingly illustrated. One illustration consists of a full page map of Southern England, from London to Land's End, to illustrate how far a gallon of petrol would take the rider on machines of varying capacity, showing the 1000cc sidecar outfit running out of fuel at Mere (106 miles), the 500cc sidecar at Ilchester (127), 1000cc solo at Ilminster (139), 750cc solo at Honiton (157), 350cc sidecar at Exeter (172), 500cc Solo at Tedburn St Mary (179), 350cc solo, Bridstowe (201), 250cc solo, Bodmin (236) and the 150cc solo at Land's End, 292 miles. They may not have had the performance of today's machines but they hadn't the thirst either. Another lovely feature of the book is the centre spread, which features photographs of 32 fuel tanks of machines of the period, each in its correct colour. Of all motorcycle books, I love it best and my own copy, a birthday present, has never left my collection which, in itself, is unique.

Chapter 23   Section T

Cycling — all aspects

Although opinions may vary as to whether cycling really forms part of this book, it seems to me that without some mention of it the story is incomplete, because if one takes 1895 to be the start of motoring and motorcycling, one has to bear in mind that the first motorcycles were little more than pedal-powered machines with some form of engine added.

Glancing down the list of titles making up this section, one can get some idea of the progress made in cycling by noting that the earliest cycling title is dated 1870 and the next 1879. There are one each in 1884, 1885 and 1886, two in 1887, one each in 1888 and 1890 and in the period after 1895, two in 1896, four in 1897 and one in 1898 and 1899.

So, in fact, not only is cycling much better documented than motorcycling but it was more fully covered for no less than twenty five years before the arrival of powered vehicles. Although cycling is an aspect of road transport that does hold some interest for me, I am far from being an expert and the titles contained here are only those that I have seen from time to time or have in my own collection.

My favourite of them all is Stevens' *Around the World on a Bicycle,* the two volumes of which came out in 1887 and 1888. The mind boggles at the idea of anyone going round the world on a 'Penny Farthing' even today, let alone nearly a hundred years ago. Although Stevens' round the world journey was way out on its own, there were many other long trips taking place by pedal power even then.

To decide when the bicycle came into being, one first has to define a bicycle. The first two wheeled machines were termed 'Hobby Horses' and were without pedals, the rider sitting astride and pushing himself and the machine along. Although, in the strict sense, these must have been 'bicycles', the accepted form of propulsion is by pedals, which puts the date as around 1850.

Most of us started our 'wheeled' life on the road with bicycles and some may end it the same way, so I hope that this short chapter will be thought of as not altogether out of place.

Chapter 24

Summary and Assessment

Throughout the whole span of my years spent in bookdealing, the demand for books not only exceeded supply but, towards the end, began to outstrip it, so I spent more than three quarters of my time searching for the right titles on the basis that if I could find stock in good condition selling would look after itself.

Concurrently with dealing, I built up over the years a good collection of my own books, mostly in fine condition. Obviously I learned a great deal about motoring literature in all its forms but, having written and read back through this book, not quite as much as I had imagined. Since I was, to all intents and purposes, a 'one man band' my bookdealing business took up every minute of my time including weekdays, many week ends and some evenings. It meant that perhaps ninety per cent of each day was spent in business and only ten per cent as a private collector.

Although I have always enjoyed reading, I had almost no time at all to read throughout those years. In retrospect, I learned more concerning the value of books than of the books themselves. The writing of the 'Constant Search' involved my spending more time in reading than I had spent in all the years that I was dealing so, to be honest, though I now know far more than I did, my knowledge of book prices when I started to write was greater than the content of the books themselves.

I found quite quickly that I had gone completely against my first principle — collect what *you* like — imagining that I was collecting what I liked although what I was actually doing was collecting what the most knowledgeable of my customers liked. To a great extent our tastes coincided, but not always, and having now come to the end of the book I do know what I like and I am collecting it.

For various reasons, I am reasonably happy with *The Constant Search.* I know it will be subject to criticism, particularly by specialist collectors, because the whole spectrum is far too great for any one person to be able to know everything about every section. Throughout all the time that I traded, I did know when to talk to a customer about books — and when to listen — for, over the years, I met many customers who knew far more about their own particular interest than I did. When in their presence I tried always to get them to talk while I did the listening and could learn.

I doubt very much whether anyone except a dealer in motoring books could have written and classified in detail what is contained here, for it seems to me that no one, private collectors included, could have through their hands the rare, scarce, good and not so good books as a dealer would. In that context, I am glad to have completed my self-appointed task. A few details such as author or publisher are lacking, particularly in the case of some early books. In such cases it seemed better to include whatever information I had, rather than leave it out, in the hope that the gaps may eventually be filled.

As with most things, the literature of motoring has had its golden years. To me, the years between 1910 and 1920 were pure gold because, at the start of that era, the motor car had become a 'usable' vehicle with some degree of reliability which enabled it to make journeys that had never before been possible. At the end of this period, it had lost much of its spidery appearance and had, in many cases, become a thing of great beauty.

I thought that, with a few notable exceptions, the 1930s and 1940s were rather barren, and the 1950s and 60s much better. But it wasn't until the late 1970s and onwards that real gold began to re-appear and I really do think that, with the passage of time, the period we are in now will become rated a truly golden era, at least as far as books are concerned.

Maybe you will agree, maybe not, but not long ago, when lunching with Denis Jenkinson, I asked him which in his opinion were the golden years of motor racing. Without a moment's hesitation he replied 'I'm not sure which ones have been but I'm sure we're among them now' which surprised me and made me realise how out of touch with the Grand Prix Scene I must be.

I do think that the same applies concerning the literature of motoring. More lovely books on motoring, particularly marque histories and those about motor racing, are appearing now than ever before. More new and knowledgeable authors are coming forward, backed by publishers like Dalton Watson, David and Charles and, on the motorcycle front, Haynes/Foulis and others.

Having written this book and, in doing so, having looked carefully through my own collection, I feel confident enough to weed out some books that I shall never read in order to finance the purchase of at least some of the best of today, even though I confess that there are some older titles for which I shall still constantly search.

Classified alphabetical index by subject

Section A

Technical books, other than those under specialist headings

Title	Author	Publisher	1st Ed'n	Later Ed'ns	Pages	Illus	Index	Rate	Text
A.B.C. of Motoring	Brown	Drane	1901		89	•		C	•
Automobile Motors and Mechanism								B	
Carburation	Brewer	Crosby Lockwood	1913		253	•	•	C	•
Carburetters & Fuel Injection Systems	Judge		1957		496	•		D	
Carburetters, Vapourisers and Distributing Valves	Butler	Griffin	1909		176	•	•	C	
Carburetter Handbook	Knott	Pitman	1925		403	•	•	D	
Catechism of the Motor Car	Knight	Crosby Lockwood		6th 1920	109	•	•	C	
Complete Hints and Tips for Automobilists	Autocar	Iliffe		4th 1910		•	•	D	•
Electrical Equipment of British Cars	Hall	Foulis	1968		241	•	•	E	
Electricity and the Motor Car	Hutton	Iliffe	1916		144	•	•	C	•
Gas Engine Troubles and Installation	Rathburn	Stanton & Van Liet	1918		447	•		D	

Title	Author	Publisher	1st Ed'n	Later Ed'ns	Pages	Illus	Index	Rate	Text
Introduction to Internal Combustion Engineering	Sneeden	Longman	1938		267	•	•	D	
Liquid Fuels for Internal Combustion Engines	Moore	Crosby Lockwood	1918		200	•	•	C	
Manual of Petrol Motors & Motor Cars	Strickland	Griffin		2nd 1914	372	•		D	
Motor Mechanic's Handbook	Watson & Heron Rogers	Cassell	1919		267	•	•	D	
Mechanics of Road Vehicles	Steeds	Iliffe	1960		286	•	•	E	
Modern Gas and Oil Engines	Grover	Technical	1897	1909	373	•		A	•
Modern Machine Shop (The)	Rankin Kennedy		1907 4 vols					F	
Modern Motor Car Practice	Berry	Hodder & Stoughton	1921		582	•		D	
Motor Car Mechanism & Management Simplified	Shepherd	Crosby Lockwood		6th 1930	175	•	•	D	
Motor Car Red Book (The)	Bersey Adoran	Tech Pub Co.	1916		216			C	
Petroleum — Motive Power of the Future	Tower & Roberts	Hodder & Stoughton	1912		245	•		D	
Sparking Plugs	Young & Warren	Pitman	1922		106	•		D	
Triumphs of Engineering	Various	Odhams	ND		256	•	•	E	

Section B

Books on Touring and Travel

Title	Author	Publisher	1st Ed'n	Later Ed'ns	Pages	Illus	Index	Rate	Text
Across Africa on a Lorry	Redmayne	Marshall, Morgan & Scott	1937		128	•		C	
Across the Kalahari Desert	Makin	Arrowsmith	1929		288	•		D	
Across the Sahara by Motor Car	Haardt & Dubreuil	Fisher, Unwin	1924		255	•		C	•
Adventurer's Road	Nicholson	Cassell	1957		235	•	•	E	
Adventures of Imshi	Prioleau	Jarrolds	1922		358	•		E	•
Africa in a Jeep	Cuervost	Staples	1956		206	•		F	
Age of Motoring Adventure 1897-1939	Nicholson	Cassell	1972		170	•		F	
Around France in an 8hp Car	Budd	Stonevale	1950		212	•	•	E	•
Australia Through the Windscreen	Hatfield	Angus & Robertson	1939		303			E	•
Automobilist Abroad (The)	Milntoun	Brown/Langham	1907		381	•	•	C	•
Auto Nomad in Barbary	McArthur	Cassell	1950		350	•	•	F	•
Auto Nomad in Spain	McArthur	Cassell	1953		245	•	•	F	•
Auto Nomad in Sweden	McArthur	Cassell	1948		275	•	•	F	•

116

Title	Author	Publisher	1st Ed'n	Later Ed'ns	Pages	Illus	Index	Rate	Text
Auto Nomad through Africa	McArthur	Cassell	1951		330	•	•	F	•
Balkan Roads to Istanbul	Motte	Hale	1960		189	•	•	E	
Black Journey, The	Haardt & Dubreuil	Bles	1928		316	•		C	•
By Bus to the Sahara	West	Travel	ND		232	•		D	
By Camel and Car to the Peacock Throne	Powell	Appleton Century	1939		391	•	•	D	
By Car to India	Forbes Leith	Hutchinson	1925		232	•		D	•
By Car in Norway	Stren	Oppi	1950		87	•		C	
By Road to Moscow and Yalta	Bell	Redman	1959		294	•	•	D	
By Road to Tangier and Marrakesh	Bell	Redman	1960		303	•	•	D	
By Way of the Sahara	Tweedy	Duckworth	1930		247	•		C	
Cairo to Persia and Back	Tweedy	Jarrolds	1933		288	•		C	
Camping with Motor Car and Camera	Barker	Dent	1913		302	•	•	D	
Canyons, Cans and Caravans	Hassell	S.P.C.K.	1930		320	•		E	
Cape Cold to Cape Hot	Pape	Odhams	1956		256	•		F	
Caravan. How to Choose and Use a	Leonard	Haynes	1977		174	•	•	F	
Cape to Cairo	Court Treatt	Harrap	1927		247	•		D	•
Caravanning (Motor) The Complete Book of	Park	Haynes	1979		152	•	•	F	
Cape to Cowley via Cairo	Belcher	Methuen	1932		237	•		D	•
Cathedral Cities of the South — A Tour for Motorists	Bland	Burrow	ND 1930s		220	•	•	D	
Charm of the Road (The)	Hissey	Macmillan	1910		421	•	•	F	
China to Chelsea	McCallum	Benn	1930		283	•	•	D	•
Coleman's Drive	Coleman	Faber & Faber	1962		260	•	•	E	
Continental Motoring	Scott		1947		128	•		E	

Title	Author	Publisher	1st Ed'n	Later Ed'ns	Pages	Illus	Index	Rate	Text
Cornwall in a Light Car	Filson Young	Mills & Boon	1926		73	•		D	
Crazy Journey	Hess	Foulis	1953		124	•		F	
Desert Encounter	Holmboe	Harrap	1931		281	•		D	•
Desert Journey	Rodger	Cresset	1944		151	•		E	•
Desert Watches (The)	McArthur	Hart Davis	1954		272	•		E	
Diabolical (The)	McWilliams	Duckworth	1934		311	•		D	
Double Crossing America	Wild	Hale	1938		288	•		D	
Drive Round the World	Baudot & Seguela	Macdonald	1962		221	•	App	E	•
East Africa by Motor Lorry	Campbell	Murray	1928		318	•		C	
Eastern Odyssey (An)	Le Fevre	Gollancz	1934		368	•		D	
Enchanted Ways	Prioleau		1933		287	•	maps	E	
English Holiday (An)	Hissey	Macmillan	1908		419	•	•	F	
En Route	Trevor	Stanford	1908		303	•	•	C	•
Escape from Peace	Moncrieff	M.R.P	1949		120	•		D	•
Europe from a Motor Car	Richardson	Rand McNally	1914		227	•		C	
Express to Hindustan	Ellis	Bodley Head	1929		308	•	•	D	•
Family Motor Tour Through Europe (A)	Baekeland	Horseless Age	1907		366	•	•	B	
Fill 'er Up	Partridge	McGraw Hill	1952		235	•	•	D	
First Overland	Slessor	Companion	1957		271	•		E	
Five Roads to Danger	Nicholson	Cassell	1960		186	•		E	
Four on a Tour	Shackleton	Duckworth	ND 1920s		347	•	•	C	•
From Alaska to Cape Horn	Weise	Hale	1960		192	•	•	E	
From Coast to Coast by Motor	Vernon	Black	1929		115	•	•	D	
From Dolomites to Stelvio	Waters	Methuen	1926		272	•	•	D	
Grand Tour	Balfour	Long	1934		318	•		C	•

Title	Author	Publisher	1st Ed'n	Later Ed'ns	Pages	Illus	Index	Rate	Text
Hissey, J.J. (Works by)									
Coaching & Driving Titles									
Old Fashioned Journey (An)	Hissey	Bentley	1884		375	•	•	E	
Drive Through England (A)	Hissey	Bentley	1885		390	•	•	E	
On the Box Seat	Hissey	Bentley	1886		404	•	•	E	
Holiday on the Road (A)	Hissey	Bentley	1887		408	•	•	B	
Tour in a Phaeton (A)	Hissey	Bentley	1889		400	•	•	E	
Across England in a Dog Cart	Hissey	Bentley	1891		413	•	•	E	
Through Ten English Counties	Hissey	Bentley	1894		406	•	•	E	
On Southern English Roads	Hissey	Bentley	1896		423	•	•	E	
Over Fen and Wold	Hissey	Macmillan	1898		447	•	•	E	
Motoring Titles									
Untravelled England	Hissey	Macmillan	1906		459	•	•	F	
English Holiday (An)	Hissey	Macmillan	1908		419	•	•	F	•
Charm of the Road (The)	Hissey	Macmillan	1910		421	•	•	F	
Leisurely Tour in England (A)	Hissey	Macmillan	1913		400	•	•	F	
Road and the Inn (The)	Hissey	Macmillan	1917		440	•	•	F	
Imshi in New Europe	Prioleau	Bles	1924		224	•	•	D	•
Into the Blue	Ferguson	Collins	1955		254	•	App	D	
Italian Highways and Byways from a Motor Car	Miltoun	Hodder & Stoughton	1909		374	•	•	C	•
Jeopardy in a Jeep	Rogers	Hale	1959		191	•		E	
Journey to Turkistan	Teichman	Hodder & Stoughton	ND 1930s		221	•	•	D	
Libyan Sands	Bagnold	Hodder & Stoughton	1935		351	•	•	D	
Light Car Odyssey (A)	Davies	'India'	1932		175	•	•	D	•

The Constant Search

Title	Author	Publisher	1st Ed'n	Later Ed'ns	Pages	Illus	Index	Rate	Text
Lift Luck on Southern Roads	Edwardes	Methuen	1910		301	•		D	
Little Motor Tours	Prioleau	Secker	1927		181	•	maps	D	
Little Wheels	MacQuarrie	Bodley Head	1935		272	•		C	
Locust and the Ladybird (The)	Birt	Sampson Low	1911		235	•		C	
Mine Host America	Cottenham	Collins	1937		473	•	•	D	
More Motoring Abroad	Walkerley	Temple Press	1954		190	•	•	E	
Morocco From a Motor	Vernon	Black	1927		184	•		D	•
Motor Caravanning	Wilkinson	David & Charles	1968		156	•	•	F	
Motor Caravanning at Home and Abroad	Lyons	Yeoman	1973		142	•		F	
Motor Flight Through Algeria and Tunisia (A)	Ayer	McClurg	1911		445	•	•	C	
Motor Flight Through France (A)	Wharton	Macmillan	1908		201	•		C	
Motoring Abroad	Presbury	Outing	1908		294	•		C	•
Motoring Abroad	Walkerley	Temple Press	1950		223	•		E	•
Motoring Holidays in the Rhineland and Black Forest	Lascelles	Barker	1964		174	•	•	D	•
Motoring in the Balkans	Hutchinson	Hodder & Stoughton	1910		340	•	•	D	•
Motoring in East Anglia	Harper	Burrows	ND 1910s		187	•		D	•
Motoring in France	Barrett	Methuen	1925		206	•	•	C	•
Motoring in Italy	Barrett	Methuen	1928		223	•	•	D	•
Motoring in Sussex and Kent	Stawell	Hodder & Stoughton	ND 1920s		384	•	•	D	•
Motoring in the North of England	Harper	Burrows	ND 1910s		238	•		D	•
Motoring in the West Country	Stawell	Hodder & Stoughton	ND 1920s		312	•	•	D	•

Title	Author	Publisher	1st Ed'n	Later Ed'ns	Pages	Illus	Index	Rate	Text
Motoring in the West of England	Harper	Burrows	ND 1910s		164	•		D	•
Motoring in West Sussex									
Motoring on Irish Byways	Trent	Foulis	1965		182	•	•	E	•
Motoring on Scottish Byways	Trent				150	•	•	E	•
Motoring on the Continent	Freeston	Burrows	ND		132	•	•	D	•
Motorist's Companion (The)	Prioleau	Dent	1936		503	•	•	E	
Motorist's Companion on the Highways of England	Trent	Newnes	1955		174	•	•	D	
Motorist's Interpreter (The)	'Anon'	Haynes	1968		89			F	
Motor Rambles in Central Europe	Rimington	Methuen	1927		235	•	•	D	
Motor Rambles Through France	Rimington	Constable	1925		250	•		D	
Motor Routes of England 1909 (Southern Section)	Home	Black	1909		334	•	•	D	•
Motor Routes of England (Western Section)	Home	Black	1911		337	•	•	D	•
Motor Routes of France	Home	Black	1909		444	•	•	D	•
Motor Routes of Germany	Heck	Black	1914		456	•	•	D	•
Motor Tour Through Belgium & Germany (A)	Xenier	Mills & Boon	1913		310	•		C	•
Motor Tour Through Canada (A)	Wilby	Bodley Head	1914		290	•	•	C	•
Motor Tour Through France and England (A)	Yardley	Paul	1911		242	•		C	•
Motor Tour Through the Cathedral Cities of the South (A)	Bland	Burrow	1933		220	•		C	•
Motor Tours in the West Country	Stawell	Hodder & Stoughton	1910		227	•		D	•
Motor Tours in Wales and the Border Counties	Stawell	Hodder & Stoughton	1908	1909	280	•		D	•

The Constant Search

Title	Author	Publisher	1st Ed'n	Later Ed'ns	Pages	Illus	Index	Rate	Text
Motor Tours in Yorkshire	Stawell	Hodder & Stoughton	1910		228	•	•	D	•
Motor Tramp	Heygate	Cape	1935		342	•		D	•
Motor Ways at Home and Abroad	Abraham	Methuen	1928		252	•	•	D	
Motor Ways in Lakeland	Abraham	Methuen	1913		307	•	•	D	
Motor Ways in Wales & The Border Counties	Stawell	Hodder & Stoughton	ND 1910s		280	•	•	D	
Motor Ways in Yorkshire								D	
My Two African Journeys	Gray	Methuen	1928		271	•	•	C	
Nature Jottings of a Motorist	Mortimer Batten	Jenkins	1926		312	•		D	
Nine Thousand Miles in Eight Weeks	Bruce	Cranton	1927		254	•		C	•
On Wandering Wheels	Gordon		1929		336	•		D	
Pampas and the Andes (The)	Blake	Cassell	1952		190	•		C	
Paradise of Fools (The)	Mason	Hodder & Stoughton	1936		282	•	•	C	
Poor Me — Diary of a Motor Car	Friedlander	Argus	1911		132	•	•	B	
Roadside Camera	Ware	David & Charles	1974		112	•	•	F	
Round England in an £8 Car	Horsley	Nicholson & Watson	1932		223	•		D	•
Round France in a Motor	Neville	Combridge	1906		146	•		C	
Round the World in a Baby Austin	McQuarrie	Hodder & Stoughton	1933	1936	383	•		C	•
Round the World in a Motor Car	Mann	Bell	1914		238	•		C	•
Round the World in a Motor Car	Scarfoglio	Richards	1909		368	•		B	•
Rumania Through a Windscreen	Forman	Sampson Low	ND c1938		250	•	•	C	•
Sahara is Yours (The)	Stevens	Constable	1969		270	•	•	E	

Title	Author	Publisher	1st Ed'n	Later Ed'ns	Pages	Illus	Index	Rate	Text
Savage Sahara	Sleigh	Wingate	1956		134	•		E	
Seeing Britain and the Continent from an Austin	Murray	Austin	ND 1930s		213	•		D	
Seeing Britain from an Austin	Murray	Austin	ND 1930s		180	•		D	
Seven Across the Sahara	Ingrams	Travel	1950		231	•	•	E	
Seven Years with Samantha	Ball	Stevens	1974		246	•		E	
Sheep & the Chevrolet (The)	Elek	Elek	1947		176	•		E	
South Bound Car (The)	Llewellen & Raven Hill	Methuen	1907		281	•	•	C	•
Spain in a Two Seater	Ross	Faber & Gwyer	1925		260	•		C	
Sudan Sand	Court Treatt	Harrap	1930		251	•	•	C	
Three Men in a Motor Car	Maxted	Treherne	1904		126	•		B	•
Three Men in a Motor Car	Scarritt	Dutton	1906		268	•		B	•
Three Thousand Miles in a Motor Car	Maxted	Treherne	1905		144	•		B	•
Through Brazilian Jungle Lands with the Book	Glass	Pickering & Inglis	ND 1920s		200	•		C	•
Through East Anglia in a Motor Car	Vincent	Methuen	1907		406	•	•	C	•
Through Europe and the Balkans	Etherton & Dunscombe Allen	Cassell	1928		308	•	•	C	•
Through Persia in a Motor Car	Anet	Hodder & Stoughton	1907		281	•		A	
Through the Alps to the Appenines	Konody	Paul, Trench, Trubner	1911		370	•	•	C	•
Through Western Canada in a Caravan	Hassell	S.P.G	1927		254	•		D	
To Menelek in a Motor Car	Halle	Hurst & Blackett	1913		311	•		C	
Tour by Motor Car Through England, Wales and Scotland	Sisson	Bank N.S.W.	1953		377	•		D	
Touring Abroad	Wisdom	Odhams	1960		340	•		E	

1

2

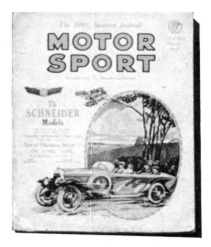

3

4

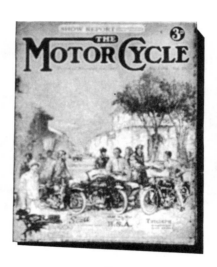

5

6

7

8

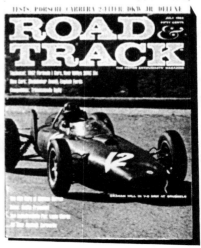

9

Title	Author	Publisher	1st Ed'n	Later Ed'ns	Pages	Illus	Index	Rate	Text
Touring England, by Road and Byway	Jones	Batsford	1927		140	•	•	C	
Touring in England								D	
Touring Through France	Shackleton	Penn	1925		407	•	•	C	
Tourist's Handbook	Shelton	Pitman	1936		101	•	App	C	
Towards the Sunshine	Owen John	Cassell	1919		182	•		C	
To Venice and Back in a Two Seater	Ross	Cassell	1924		239	•		C	
Toy for the Lion (A)	Nicholson	Kimber	1965		139	•	•	E	
Travel	Brereton	Batsford	1931		88	•	•	C	•
Travel and Invention in the Modern World	Shears		ND		388	•		C	
Travel and Transport Through the Ages	Lee	Cambridge	1951	1955	187	•	•	E	
Travel in England	Burke	Batsford	1942	1949	154	•	•	E	
Travels of a Capitalist Lackey	Basnett	Allen & Unwin	1965		223	•		E	•
Triptyque	Graves	Nicholson & Watson	1936		240	•	•	D	
Turn Left for Tangier	Smith	Temple Press	1960		58	•		E	•
27000 Miles Through Australia	Cranley	Travel	1963	1963	188			E	
Two Americans in a Motor Car	Gunnison	Brooklyn	1905		114	•		C	
Two Roads to Africa	Symons	Travel	1939		319	•		D	•
Untravelled England	Hissey	Macmillan	1906		459	•	•	F	
Under My Bonnet	Minchin	Foulis	1950		183	•		D	•
We Lived on Wheels	Duncan	Rich/Cowan	1955		184	•		D	
Wheels Round the World	Hess	Neame	1951		94	•	•	F	
When Motoring was a Sport	Lovell	Campbell	ND 1930s		96	•		D	
Wheels Round the World	Hess	Neame	1951		94	•	•	F	
With Your Car in the South of France	Noble	Muller	1959		176	•	•	E	

Section C

Books on roads, road maps and guides and road transport

Title	Author	Publisher	1st Ed'n	Later Ed'ns	Pages	Illus	Index	Rate	Text
Along the Rivieras of France and Italy	Home	Dent	1926		328	●	●	D	
Alps for the Motorist (The)	Freeston	AA & Cassell	ND 1920s		175	●	●	D	●
Ancient Roads of England (The)	Oliver				245	●	●	E	
Automobile Handbook 1904	RAC of Gt. Britain & Ireland	RAC of Gt. Britain & Ireland			288	●		C	
Automobile Handbook 1908	RAC of Gt. Britain & Ireland	RAC of Gt. Britain & Ireland	1904	1908	287	●		C	
Balkan Roads to Istanbul	Motte	Hale	1960		189	●	●	E	
Beauty of Britain			1935		248	●		E	
Best Ways out of London	Montagu	Car Illustrated	1904	maps	75	●	●	C	
Car and Country	Prioleau	Dent	1929		244	●		E	
Causes and Prevention of Road Accidents	Cohen	Preston	1968		252	●	●	E	
Contour Road Book of Great Britain	Inglis	Gall & Inglis	1926		848		●	D	

Title	Author	Publisher	1st Ed'n	Later Ed'ns	Pages	Illus	Index	Rate	Text
Cream of Europe for the Motorist (The)	Freeston	Cassell	1928		215	•		D	
Dunlop Book (The)	Dunlop	Burrow	ND 1920s		546	•		D	•
English Inns and Road Houses	Long	Werner Laurie	1937		271	•	•	D	
France for the Motorist	Freeston	Cassell	1927		207	•	•	D	•
From Track to Highway	Jackson	Nicholson & Watson	1935		260	•		E	
Great Motor Highways of the Alps	Merrick	Hale	1958	1961	272	•	•	D	
Great North Road (The)	Morley	Hutchinson	1962		324		•	E	
Great Winding Road (The)	Pike		1928		234			E	
HARPER'S ENGLISH ROADS *Charles G.Harper*		(series)							•
The Brighton Road	Harper	Chatto & Windus	1892		272	•	•	E	•
The Marches of Wales	Harper	Chapman & Hall	1894		368	•		E	
The Dover Road	Harper	Chapman & Hall	1895		363	•	•	E	
The Portsmouth Road	Harper	Chapman & Hall	1895		372	•	•	E	
The Exeter Road	Harper	Chapman & Hall	1899		318	•	•	E	
The Great North Road Vol.1 London—York	Harper	Chapman & Hall	1901		301	•		E	
Vol. 2 York—Edinburgh	Harper	Chapman & Hall	1901		310	•	•	E	
The Norwich Road	Harper	Chapman & Hall	1901		323	•	•	E	
The Cambridge, Ely & King's Lynn Road	Harper	Chapman & Hall	1902		336	•	•	E	
The Holyhead Road Vol.1 London—Birmingham	Harper	Chapman & Hall	1902		314	•		E	
Vol.2 Birmingham—Holyhead	Harper	Chapman & Hall	1902		333	•	•	E	
The Newmarket, Bury, Thetford & Cromer Road	Harper	Chapman & Hall	1904		358	•	•	E	
The Oxford, Gloucester & Milford Haven Road Vol.1 London—Gloucester	Harper	Chapman & Hall	1905		295	•		E	
Vol.2 Gloucester—Milford Haven	Harper	Chapman & Hall	1905		307	•	•	E	

The Constant Search

Title	Author	Publisher	1st Ed'n	Later Ed'ns	Pages	Illus	Index	Rate	Text
The Manchester and Glasgow Road									
Vol.1 London — Manchester	Harper	Chapman & Hall	1907		358	•		E	•
Vol.2 Manchester — Glasgow	Harper	Chapman & Hall	1907		332	•	•	E	
Highway (The)	Schieldrop	Hutchinson	1939		248	•	•	E	
Highway and Its Vehicles (The)	Belloc	Studio	1926		200	•		D	
Hills of Lakeland (The)	Cooper	Warne	1938		125	•	•	E	
In Scotland Again	Morton		1934		414	•		F	
In Search of Scotland	Morton		1935		288	•		F	
In Search of Wales	Morton		1932		269	•		F	
Newnes Motorist's Touring Guide	Newnes	Newnes	ND 1920s		376	•		D	•
Open Road (The)	Devesant & Lampitt	Oxford University	1962		43	•		E	
Open Road Abroad (The)	Prioleau		1932		206	•		E	
Passes of the Pyrenees (The)	Freeston	Kegan Paul	1912		196	•	•	D	•
Paterson's Roads	Mogg	Various		18th 1822	715		App	C	•
Regency Road (The)	Selway	Faber & Faber	1957		118	•	•	D	•
Reminiscences of a Highway Surveyor	Chapman	Chapman	1932		148	•		C	
Riviera of the Corniche Road (The)	Treeves	Cassell	1923		315	•	•	D	
Road Book and Guide (The)	Montagu	Car Illustrated	1905		346	•	•	C	
Road Goes On (The)	Scott Giles	Epworth	1946		218	•		E	
Roadmender (The)	Fairless	Duckworth	1902	20th 1921	121	•		E	
Road Transport. History & Development of	Paterson	Pitman	1927		118	•	•	D	
Road. Story of the	Gregory	Maclehose	1931		309	•	•	E	
Road Passenger Transport	Pilcher	Pitman	1937		383	•	•	D	

Title	Author	Publisher	1st Ed'n	Later Ed'ns	Pages	Illus	Index	Rate	Text
Roads and Their Traffic 1750-1850	Copeland	David & Charles	1968		205	•		D	
Roads. Story of	Hughes Hartmann	Routledge	1927		194	•		E	
Roads and Vehicles	Bird	Longmans Green	1969		250	•	•	E	
Roads of England (The)	Anderson	Benn	1932		236	•	•	D	
Roads of England and Wales (The)	Howard	Letts	1884		423	•		C	
Roads of Spain (The)	Freeston	Toulmin	1930		270	•	•	D	•
Road. Romance of the	Aldin	Eyre & Spottiswoode	1929	1933	123	•		C	•
Routes des Alpes	Waterlow	Iliffe	ND 1920s		240	•	•	D	
Scotland for the Motorist	Inglis Ker	Cassell	1930		328	•	•	D	
Scotland for the Motorist		AA	1922		260	•		D	
Wild Roads	Nicholson	Jarrolds	1969		302	•		E	

Section D

Books on motor racing

Title	Author	Publisher	1st Ed'n	Later Ed'ns	Pages	Illus	Index	Rate	Text
Flying Horse on the Ground	Fittipaldi	Kimber	1973		256	•		E	
Ford Grand Prix Engine — The Story of the	Blunsden & Phipps	Bentley	1971		224	•	App	E	
Formula One	Pritchard	Allen & Unwin	1966		336	•	•	E	
Formula One — A Story of	Jenkinson	Grenville	1960		159	•		D	•
Formula One Cars and Sports Prototypes	Gibson	Orbis	1973		96	•		E	
Formula One Record Book (The)	Thompson, Rabagliati & Sheldon	Frewin	1974		240	•	•	E	•
For Practice Only	Klemantaski & Frostick	Bodley Head	1959		54	•		D	•
French Grand Prix (The)	Hodges	Temple Press	1967		253	•	App	E	
German Grand Prix (The)	Posthumus	Temple Press	1966		143	•	•	D	•
German Grand Prix Cars 1934-1939	Earl	HMSO	1947		143	•	App	C	•
Graham Hill Grand Prix Racing Book (The)	Hill	Shell	1967		25	•		F	
Grand Prix (The)	Setright	Nelson	1973		320	•	•	E	
Grand Prix 1959	Stanley	Allen	1960		199	•		D	•
Grand Prix 1960	Stanley	Parrish	1961		192	•		D	•
Grand Prix 1961	Stanley	Barnes	1962		208	•		D	•
Grand Prix 1962	Stanley	Barnes	1963		191	•		D	•
Grand Prix 1963	Stanley	Barnes	1964		192	•		D	•
Grand Prix 1964	Stanley	Macdonald	1965		196	•		D	•
Grand Prix 1965	Stanley	Macdonald	1966		208	•		D	•
Grand Prix 1966	Stanley	Macdonald	1967		208	•		D	•
Grand Prix 1967	Stanley	Macdonald	1968		208	•		D	•
Grand Prix No.10	Stanley	Allen	1969		252	•		D	
Grand Prix No.11	Stanley	Allen	1970		200	•		D	

The Constant Search

Title	Author	Publisher	1st Ed'n	Later Ed'ns	Pages	Illus	Index	Rate	Text
Grand Prix Car (The) Vol.1 1906-1939	Pomeroy	M.R.P	1949		419	•	App	B	•
Grand Prix Car (The) Vol.2 1947-1954	Pomeroy	Temple Press	1956	1960/5	344	•	App	B	•
Grand Prix Car 1954-1966 (The)	Setright	Allen & Unwin	1968		422	•	•	D	•
Grand Prix Championship	Pritchard	Weidenfeld & Nicholson	1971		120	•		E	
Grand Prix Championship Courses and Drivers	Borgeson	Norton	1968		226	•	•	D	
Grand Prix Driver (The)	Lang	Foulis	1953		143	•	•	D	•
Grand Prix Ferrari	Pritchard	Hale	1974		381	•	•	E	
Grand Prix Gift Book	Young World	Young World	ND		141	•		F	
Grand Prix Guide 1974	Sil Sports	Sil Sports	1974		263	•		E	
Grand Prix Mercedes-Benz Type W.125	Jenkinson	Leventhal	1970		75	•		E	•
Grand Prix 1934-1939	Walkerley Fellowes	M.R.P	1948	1950	108	•	App	D	•
Grand Prix 1968-1969	BRDC	Hamlyn	1969		128	•		D	
Grand Prix Racing 1906-1914	Mathieson	Connoisseur Automobile	1965		296	•		C	•
Grand Prix Racing — Facts and Figures	Monkhouse & King Farlow	Foulis	1950	1953/9	462	•	•	C	•
Grand Prix Racing — The Story of	Fothergill	Day	1948		27	•		D	
International Grand Prix Book of Motor Racing	Frewin	Souvenir	1965		302	•		F	
John Cooper — Grand Prix Carpetbagger	Bentley & Cooper	Haynes/Foulis	1977		230	•	•	F	
Monaco Grand Prix	Hodges	Temple Press	1964		133	•		E	
Motoraces	Monkhouse	Newnes	1937		120	•		C	•
Motor Racing with Mercedes Benz	Monkhouse	Newnes	1938	& later	167	•		C	•
Power and the Glory (The)	Court	Macdonald	1966		353	•	•	C	•

Title	Author	Publisher	1st Ed'n	Later Ed'ns	Pages	Illus	Index	Rate	Text
Private Entrant	Cooper Evans	Cassell	1965		194	•		E	
Racing Coopers (The)	Owen	Cassell	1959		243	•		D	
Return to Power	Frostick	Allen & Unwin	1968		132	•		D	
Six Days in August	Cooper Evans	Pelham	1968		133	•		E	
16 on the Grid	Garnier	Cassell	1964		139	•		D	
Such Sweet Thunder	Blunsden & Phipps	M.R.P	1971		224	•		F	
Vanishing Litres (The)	Hays	Macmillan	1957		192	•	•	D	•
Vanwall	Jenkinson & Posthumus	Stephens	1975		176	•	•	E	
Vanwall Story (The)	Klemantaski & Frostick	Hamish Hamilton	1958		64	•		D	•
V-16. Story of the BRM Engine	Rivers Fletcher	M.R.P	1954		25	•		D	•
World Champions (The)	Pritchard	Frewin	1972		265	•		E	
World Championship	Grant	Autosport	1959		194	•		E	

Section D 2

Formula Racing

Title	Author	Publisher	1st Ed'n	Later Ed'ns	Pages	Illus	Index	Rate	Text
British Racing Green 1946-1956	Klemantaski & Frostick	Bodley Head	1957		60	•		D	•
500 cc Motor Racing Yearbook 1952	Pearl & Armstrong	Pearl Cooper	1954		144	•	App	D	•
500 cc Racing	Grant	Foulis	1950		178	•	•	D	•
Formula 3. A Record of 500 cc Racing	May	Foulis	1951		210	•		D	•
Formula Junior	Blunsden	M.R.P	1961		160	•	•	E	
Formula 3 Year Book 1953-1954	Pearl & Armstrong	Pearl/Cooper	1954		144	•	•	D	•

Title	Author	Publisher	1st Ed'n	Later Ed'ns	Pages	Illus	Index	Rate	Text
Formula 2	Grant	Foulis	1953		128	•	•	E	•
Go Formula Ford	Smith	Foulis	1969		134	•	•	F	
Iota. Edited Highlights of F.3 500 cc		Transport Bookman	1980		NN	•		F	•
Racing Voiturettes	Karslake	M.R.P	1950		376	•	•	C	•

Section D 3

Sports car racing and races

Title	Author	Publisher	1st Ed'n	Later Ed'ns	Pages	Illus	Index	Rate	Text
Behind the Wheel	McKay	Kaye	1961		222	•		E	
Ford — The Dust and the Glory	Levine	Macmillan	1968		630	•	•	D	•
Ford versus Ferrari	Pritchard	Pelham	1968		176	•	•	C	•
Formula One Cars and Sports Prototypes	Gibson	Orbis	1973		96	•		E	
Jaguar: Motor Racing and the Manufacturer	Berry	Aztex	1978		94	•	•	E	•
Racing a Sports Car	Mortimer	Foulis	1951	1951/7	138	•		E	•
Racing Sports Cars	Klemantaski & Frostick	Hamilton	1956		60	•		D	•
Racing Sports Car (The)	Pritchard	Pelham	1970		368	•	•	E	
Source Book of Racing and Sports Cars (A)	Georgano	Ward Lock	1973		144	•		E	
Sports Car Championship	Pritchard	Norton	1972		240	•	•	E	
Tourist Trophy	Hough	Hutchinson	1957		255	•	•	C	•
World's Sports Car Championship (The)	Posthumus	McGibbon & Kee	1961		194	•		C	•

Section D 4

Long distance road & track races. Sports and racing cars.

Title	Author	Publisher	1st Ed'n	Later Ed'ns	Pages	Illus	Index	Rate	Text
American Automobile Racing	Bochroch	Viking	1974		260	•	•	D	•

10

11

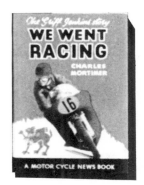

12

13

14

15

16

17

18

19

20

21

The Constant Search

Title	Author	Publisher	1st Ed'n	Later Ed'ns	Pages	Illus	Index	Rate	Text
American Road Racing	Reuter	Barnes	1964		139	•	App	D	•
Blue and Yellow	Chula	Foulis	1947		175	•		D	•
Death Race Le Mans 1955	Kahn	Barrie & Jenkins	1976		158	•		F	
Famous Motor Races	Walkerley	Barker	1963		192	•		E	
500 Miles to Go	Bloemkr	Muller	1962		278	•		D	
Grand Prix	Lyndon	Miles	1935		264	•	•	C	•
Great Auto Races	Helek	Abrams	1975		266	•	•	D	•
Great Motor Races	Carter	W & N	1960		192	•		E	
Great Road Races 1894-1915 (The)	Villard	Barker	1972		248	•	•	D	
Great Savannah Races (The)	Quattlebaum	Bryan	1957		133	•		D	
Indianapolis Race History	Clymer	Clymer	1946		318	•		D	
Indianapolis 500	Engel		1970					D	
Indy '500' (The)	Dorson	Bond Parkhouse	1974		229	•		D	
Le Mans	Klemantaski & Frostick	Hamilton	1960		60	•		D	
Le Mans '53	Scannell	M.R.P	1953		36	•		E	
Le Mans '59	Moss	Cassell	1959		115	•		C	•
Le Mans Story (The)	Fraichard	Bodley Head	1954		175	•	•	E	
Le Mans 24 Hour Race (The)	Hodges	Temple Press	1963		140	•	•	E	
Mexican Road Race. Book of the	Goodman	Clymer	1950		148	•		D	
132 of the Most Unusual Cars that Ever Ran at Indianapolis	Engel	ARCO	1970		159	•	•	D	
On the Starting Grid	Frere	Batsford	1956		224	•	•	D	
Pekin to Paris in a Motor Car	Barzini	Grant Richards	1907	1977	645	•	App	B/E	•
Porsche. Double World Champions. 1900-1977	von Frankenberg & Cotton	Haynes/Foulis	1977		280	•	•	E	

Title	Author	Publisher	1st Ed'n	Later Ed'ns	Pages	Illus	Index	Rate	Text
Road Racing 1936	Chula	Foulis	1937	1946	176	•		D	•
Road Star Hat Trick	Chula	Sun	1939		215	•		D	•
Sebring Story (The)	Ulman	Chilton	1969		203	•		E	
Shell Book of Epic Motor Races (The)	Roberts	Kaye & Vane	1964		128	•		F	
Targa Florio	Bradley	Foulis	ND		164	•	•	C	•
Targa Florio	Owen	Haynes/Foulis	1979		232	•	•	F	•
Twenty Four Hours at Le Mans	Gregoire	Cassell	1957		199			D	
200 Miles Race (The)	Boddy	Grenville	1947		155	•		C	•
Viva Alfa Romeo	Owen	Haynes/Foulis	1976		272	•	•	F	
Wheels at Speed	Chula	Foulis	1949		112	•		D	•

Section D 5

Veteran, Edwardian, Vintage and Historic car racing

Title	Author	Publisher	1st Ed'n	Later Ed'ns	Pages	Illus	Index	Rate	Text
Batsford Colour Book of Historic Racing Cars	Harding	Batsford	1975		62	•		F	•
Circuit Dust	Lyndon	Miles	1934		300	•	•	C	
Combat	Lyndon	Heinemann	1933		332	•	•	C	
Ford GT 40. (The)	Hodges	Leventhal	1970		83	•		E	
Full Throttle	Birkin	Foulis	1932	1933 & later	290	•		D/E	•
Historic Motor Racing	Pritchard	Weidenfeld & Nicholson	1969		120	•		E	
Historic Racing Cars — 1907-1960	Pomeroy & Oliver	Evelyn	1963		NN	•		D	
Mad Motorists (The)	Andrews	Harrap	1964		256	•	•	E	•
Moments That Made Racing History	Walkerley	Temple Press	1954		111	•		E	

The Constant Search

Title	Author	Publisher	1st Ed'n	Later Ed'ns	Pages	Illus	Index	Rate	Text
Motor Racing	Howe	Seeley Service	ND 1950s		256	•	•	D	•
Motor Racing	Davis	Lonsdale	ND 1950s		313	•	•	C	•
Motor Racing Memories	Bradley	M.R.P	1960		192	•	•	C	•
Other Bentley Boys (The)	Nagle	Harrap	1964		224	•	•	D	
Racing an Historic Car	Hull	Batsford	1960		160	•		D	•
Racing Cars and the History of Motor Sport	Roberts	Octopus	1973		144	•		E	
Racing Cars 1898-1921	Nicholson				169	•	•	E	
Racing History of The Bentley Car 1921-1931	Berthon	Bodley Head	1956		143	•		C	•
Record of Motor Racing 1894-1908 (A)	Rose	M.R.P		1949	325	•	App	C/D	
Romance of Motor Racing (The)	Campbell	Hutchinson	ND		299	•		D	•
Romantic Story of Motor Racing (The)	Campbell	Hutchinson	ND		300	•		D	•
Tribute By Trophy	Hays	MacGibbon & Kee	1958		165	•	•	E	•

Section D 6

Racing cars, design, construction (including Specials), development, evolution, tuning. (For Histories, see Section G)

Title	Author	Publisher	1st Ed'n	Later Ed'ns	Pages	Illus	Index	Rate	Text
Austin '7' Specials, Building, Maintenance and Tuning	Williams	Foulis	1958		160	•	•	E	•
British Competition Car (The)	Posthumus	Batsford	1959		256	•	•	D	•
Building and Racing my '750'	Stephens	Foulis	1953		111	•	•	E	•
Classic Racing Cars	Posthumus	Hamlyn	1977		160	•		E	•
Classic Single Seater (The)	Nye/Goddard	Macmillan	1975		143	•	•	E	•
Competition Cars of Europe	Pritchard	Hale	1970		208	•	•	E	
Construction of Ford Specials (The)	Mills	Batsford	1960		128	•	•	E	

Title	Author	Publisher	1st Ed'n	Later Ed'ns	Pages	Illus	Index	Rate	Text
Design and Behaviour of the Racing Car (The)	Moss & Pomeroy	Kimber	1963		285	•	•	C	•
Design and Tuning of Competition Engines	Smith	Foulis	1953		399	•		E	•
Design of Racing and Sports Cars	Campbell	Chapman & Hall	1973		257	•	•	E	
English Racing Automobiles Ltd. The History of	Weguelin	White Mouse	1981		288	•	•	F	•
Evolution of the Racing Car	Pomeroy	Kimber	1966		240	•	•	D	•
Famous Racing Cars	Hodges	Temple Press	1962		89	•		E	
Famous Racing Cars of the World	May	Muller	1957		142	•		E	
Ford Competition Cars	Frostick & Gill	Haynes/Foulis	1976		183	•	•	E	
Ford Specials	Stephens				198	•	•	E	•
Ford Ten Competition Engine (The)	Smith	Foulis	1958		136	•	•	E	•
German Racing Cars & Drivers	Molter		1950		190	•		D	
Golden Age of the American Racing Car (The)	Borgson	Sidgwick & Jackson	1966		288	•		C	•
Gordon Bennett Races (The)	Montagu	Cassell	1963		251	•	•	D	•
Grand Prix and Sports Cars	Hays	Cassell	1964		70	•	profiles	D	
High Speed Internal Combustion Engine (The)	Ricardo	Blackie	1923	1944	434	•		C	
History of the Racing Car Man and Machine	Lurani	Crowell	1972		319	•	•	D	
Maserati 250F (The)	Jenkinson	Macmillan	1975		80	•	•	E	•
Mercedes Benz Racing Cars	Ludvigsen	Bond/Parkhurst	1971		260	•	•	D	•
Mercedes & Mercedes Benz Racing Car Guide 1901-1955	Posthumus	Transport Bookman	1978		14	•		E	
Motor Racing Mavericks	Nye	Batsford	1974		198	•	•	E	
One Off	Havart	Foulis	1953		168	•		E	•

The Constant Search

Title	Author	Publisher	1st Ed'n	Later Ed'ns	Pages	Illus	Index	Rate	Text
Pictorial Survey of Racing Cars 1919-1939	Mathieson	M.R.P	1963		224	•	App	C	•
Racing and Sports Car Chassis Design	Costin/Phipps	Batsford	1961		145	•		D	
Racing Car Design	Walkerley	Weidenfeld & Nicholson	1966		128	•	•	D	
Racing Car. The Development & Design of the	Clutton, Posthumus & Jenkinson	Batsford	1956		288	•		D	•
Racing Car Explained (The)	Pomeroy	Temple Press	1963		87	•	•	D	•
Racing Car Pocket Book (The)	Jenkinson	Batsford	1962		225	•		D	
Racing Cars	Hough	Hamlyn	1966		152	•	•	E	
Racing Cars	Roberts	Octopus	1973		144	•	•	F	
Racing Cars		Orbis	1971		80	•		F	
Racing Cars of the World	Roberts	Hippo	1962		126	•		E	
Special Builder's Guide	Various	750 Motor Club	1952		73	•	•	D	
Specials	Bolster	Foulis	1949		170	•		C	•
Turbocharging and Supercharging for Maximum Power and Torque	Setright	Haynes/Foulis	1976		125	•		F	•
Supercharging Cars and Motorcycles	Brierley	Lodgemark	ND		54	•		E	
World of Racing Cars (The)	Dymock	Hamlyn	1972		128	•		F	
World's Racing Cars (The)	Armstrong	Macdonald	1958		208	•	•	E	
World's Racing Cars (The)	Twite	Macdonald	1964		196	•	•	E	
World's Racing Cars. A History of	Hough/ Frostick	Allen & Unwin	1965		190	•		D	

Section D 7

Racing drivers and personnel. Driving — art and technique.

Anatomy of a Grand Prix Driver (The)	Garrett	Barker	1970		160	•	•	E	

Title	Author	Publisher	1st Ed'n	Later Ed'ns	Pages	Illus	Index	Rate	Text
Atalanta	Davis	Foulis	ND		189	•	•	D	•
Competition Driving	Frere	Batsford	1963		144	•	•	E	•
Competitive Driving	Roberts	Paul	1964		141	•	App	E	
Cruel Sport (The)	Daley	Studio Vista	1965		224	•		D	•
Drivers in Action	Klemantaski & Frostick	Bodley Head	1955		62	•		D	•
Driving for Sport	Watkins	Autosport	1960		79	•		E	
Fastest Men on Earth (The)	Clifton	Jenkins	1964		207	•		D	
Fast Ones (The)	Miller	Paul	1962		240	•		E	
German Racing Cars and Drivers	Molter		1950		190	•		D	•
Great British Drivers	Davis	Hamilton	1957		102	•		E	
Great Racing Drivers	Hodges	Temple Press	1966		176	•		E	
Great Racing Cars and Drivers	Fox		1972		252	•		E	
High Speed Driving	Haynes	Haynes	ND		103	•		D	
High Performance Driving For You	Wisdom	Odhams	1966	1967	158	•		E	
How to Watch Motor Racing	Moss	Gentry	1975		151	•	•	E	
Jackie Stewart: World Champion	Stewart & Dymock	Pelham	1970		191	•	•	E	
Jody: An Autobiography	Scheckter	Haynes/Foulis	1976		128	•		F	
Jackie Stewart: World Driving Champion		Arco	1970		159	•		E	
Klemantaski's Photo Album	Klemantaski	M.R.P	1947		46	•		D	•
Men (The)	Gill	Frewin	1968		223	•		E	
Men at the Wheel	Miller	Batsford	1963		128	•		E	
Motor Racing Champions	Drackett	Purnell	1974		61	•		E	
Motor Racing Drivers, Past and Present	Sallon	Shell/B.P	1956		68	•		E	•

The Constant Search

Title	Author	Publisher	1st Ed'n	Later Ed'ns	Pages	Illus	Index	Rate	Text
New Matadors (The)	Baumann & Purdy	Paul	1968		152	•		E	
Race Drivers	Muller	Motor Presse Verlag	1963		89	•		D	
Racing Driver (The)	Jenkinson	Batsford	1958		207	•	•	D	•
Racing Driver's World (A)	Caracciola	Cassell	1962		232	•		C	
Sir Malcolm Campbell's Book of Famous Motorists	Campbell	Blackie	1937		177	•		D	
Speed With Style	Revson & Mandel	Kimber	1974		220	•		E	
Technique of Motor Racing (The)	Taruffi	M.R.P	1960		121	•		D	
Trio at the Top	Mahoney	Hale	1970		191	•		E	
Unbelievable Unsers (The)	Scalzo	Regnery	1971		307	•		D	
Vroom!!	Manso	Funk Wagnalls	1970		225	•		D	
Works Driver	Taruffi	Temple Press	1964		222	•	•	C	•

Section D 8

Motor racing (general). Races, record breaking and hill climbing

Title	Author	Publisher	1st Ed'n	Later Ed'ns	Pages	Illus	Index	Rate	Text
Automobile Racing	Walkerley	Temple Press	1962		230	•	•	E	•
Bluebird and the Dead Lake	Pearson	Collins	1965		188	•		E	
Book of Speed (The)	'Various'	Batsford	1934		150	•		D	•
British Racing Green	Pritchard	Allen & Unwin	1969		263	•	•	E	
Checkered Flag (The)	Helck	Scribners	1961		178	•		E	
Chequered Flag (The	Rutherford	Collins	1956		223	•		E	
Fastest on Earth	Eyston	Miles	1939		175	•		C	•
Flat Out	Eyston	Miles	1933		219	•		D	•
Graham Hill's Motor Racing Book	Hill	Stephens	1970		72	•		F	
Hill Climbing and Sprinting — The Complete Book of	Boucher	Haynes/Foulis	1977		123	•		F	

Title	Author	Publisher	1st Ed'n	Later Ed'ns	Pages	Illus	Index	Rate	Text
How to Go Saloon Car Racing	Brittan	P.S.L	1967		128	•		E	
Indianapolis Records (The)	Hess	Stuart/Richards	1949		104	•		E	
Into the Water Barrier	Campbell	Odhams	1955		239	•		E	
Jack Brabham's Motor Racing Book	Brabham	Muller	1960		123	•		F	
Land Speed Record (The)	Posthumus	Osprey	1971		256	•	•	D	•
Magic MPH	Gardner	M.R.P	1951		161	•	App	C	•
Mini Racing	Carlisle	Harrap	1963		58	•		E	•
Motoring Sport	Stuck & Burgaller	Foulis	ND		206	•		C	•
Motor Racing. A History of	Boddy	Orbis	1977	1979/80	332	•	•	E	
Motor Racing and Record Breaking	Eyston & Lyndon	Batsford	1935		116	•	•	D	
Power and Speed	Dean	Temple Press	1938		250	•		D	
Racing and Sports Cars. A Source Book of	Georgano	Ward Lock	1973		144	•		E	
Racing and Sports Cars	Georgano	Pan Books	1974		144	•		E	
Racing Cars. 70 Years of Record Breaking	Bernabo	Orbis	1971		80	•		F	
Racing Cars Today	Walkerley	Barker	1962		127	•		E	
Record Breakers (The)	Villa	Hamlyn	1969		160	•		E	
Sands of Speed	Williams	Davies	1973		80	•		D	
Record Makers (The)	Robertson & Rugg	Oxford	1936		160	•		D	
Shelsley Walsh	May	Foulis	1945		135	•		E	•
Short Circuit Racing. Drive it! The Complete Book of	Huggett	Haynes/Foulis	1980		191	•		F	
Speed	Densham							C	
Speed. The Book of	'Various'	Batsford	1934		150	•		C	•
Speed — The Book of Racing and Records	Reynolds	Temple Press	ND		136	•		D	•

The Constant Search

Title	Author	Publisher	1st Ed'n	Later Ed'ns	Pages	Illus	Index	Rate	Text
Speed Hill Climb	May	Foulis	1962		190	•		E	•
Speed — 1930s Air, Land and Water. Motor Cycle & Car					142	•		C	
Speed on Salt	Eyston & Bradley	Batsford	1936		84	•	•	D	•
Speed, Space and Time	Summerfield	Nelson	1935		299	•		D	
Sprint	Nicholson	David & Charles	1969		273	•	•	E	•
Swift Picture Book of Motor Racing	Roberts	Longacre	1961		NN	•		F	
Tackle Motor Sport This Way	Berg	Paul	1962		128	•		F	
With Campbell at Coniston	Knowles	Kimber	1967		160	•		E	
World's Land Speed Record (The)	Boddy	M.R.P	1965		99	•		D	•

Section D 9

Results, statistics and management

Title	Author	Publisher	1st Ed'n	Later Ed'ns	Pages	Illus	Index	Rate	Text
Autocourse (Annual)									•
1959		Trafalgar			168	•		C	
1960 Part 1		Trafalgar			79	•		C	
1960 Part 2		Trafalgar			164	•		C	
1961-1962		Trafalgar			216	•		C	
1962-1963		Trafalgar			200	•		C	
1963-1964		Autocourse			240	•		C	
1965		Haymarket			208	•		C	
1966		Haymarket			192	•		C	
1966-1967		Haymarket			216	•		D	
1967-1968		Haymarket			215	•		D	
1968-1969		Haymarket			215	•		D	
1969-1970		Haymarket			215	•		D	

22

23

24

25

26

27

28

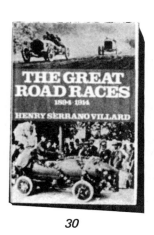

29

30

31

32

The Constant Search

Title	Author	Publisher	1st Ed'n	Later Ed'ns	Pages	Illus	Index	Rate	Text
1970-1971		Haymarket			215	•		E	
1971-1972		Haymarket			199	•		E	
1972-1973		Haymarket			200	•		E	
1973-1974		Haymarket			200	•		E	
1974-1975		Haymarket			200	•		E	
1975-1976		Hazleton			209	•		E	
1976-1977		Hazleton			256	•		E	
1977-1978		Hazleton			245	•		E	
1978-1979		Hazleton			264	•		E	
1979-1980		Hazleton			240	•		E	
1980-1981		Hazleton			240	•		F	
Autosport Directory. 1955		Autosport	1955		360	•		E	
Behind the Scenes of Motor Racing	Gregory	MacGibbon & Kee	1960		296	•		E	•
Controlling a Racing Car Team	Davis	Foulis	1951		119	•		E	•
Ecurie Ecosse	Murray	Paul	1962		179	•		C	•
Encyclopaedia of Motor Racing	Pritchard & Davey	Hale	1969		288	•		E	
International Motor Racing Book	Drackett	Souvenir	1967		143	•		E	
International Motor Racing Book No.2	Drackett	Souvenir	1968		143	•		E	
International Motor Racing Book No.3	Drackett	Souvenir	1969		143	•		E	
International Motor Racing Book No.4	Drackett	Souvenir	1970		143	•		E	
John Player Motor Sport Yearbook 1972	Gill	Queen Anne	1972		352	•	•	E	
John Player Motor Sport Yearbook 1973	Gill	Queen Anne	1973		420	•	•	E	

Title	Author	Publisher	1st Ed'n	Later Ed'ns	Pages	Illus	Index	Rate	Text
John Player Motor Sport Yearbook 1974	Gill	Queen Anne	1974		349	•	•	E	
John Player Motor Sport Yearbook 1975	Gill	Queen Anne	1975		328	•	•	E	
Motor Racing 1946	Eason Gibson	M.R.P	1948		63	•		C	
Motor Racing 1947	Eason Gibson	M.R.P	1949		94	•		D	
Motor Racing 1948-9	BRDC	M.R.P	1951		56	•		D	
Motor Racing Book of Track Tests	Blunsden	Knightsbridge	1966		47	•		E	
Motor Racing Directory 1955-56	Motor Racing	Pearl/Cooper	1956		220	•		E	
Motor Racing & Motor Rally Directory 1957	Motor Racing	Pearl/Cooper	1957		300	•	•	E	
Motor Racing Facts		Clipper	1970		120	•		E	
Motor Racing Facts and Figures	Walkerley	Batsford	1961		196		•	D	•
Motor Racing Management	Wyer	Bodley Head	1956		152	•	•	D	•
Motor Racing Register 1964	Dempsey	Foulis	1964		189	•		E	
Motor Racing Register 1965	Dempsey	Foulis	1965		204	•		E	
Motor Racing Register 1966	Dempsey	Foulis	1966		218	•		E	
Motor Racing Year 1961	Blunsden & Brinton	Knightsbridge	1961		117	•		E	•
Motor Racing Year 1962-3	Blunsden & Brinton	Knightsbridge	1963		118	•		E	•
Motor Racing Year 1963-4	Blunsden & Brinton	Knightsbridge	1964		115	•		E	•
Motor Racing Year 1964-5	Blunsden & Brinton	Knightsbridge	1965		115	•		E	•
Motor Racing Year 1965-6	Blunsden & Brinton	Knightsbridge	1966		116	•		E	•
Motor Racing Year 1966-7	Motor Racing	Knightsbridge	1967		132	•		E	•
Motor Racing Year 1967-68	Motor Racing	Knightsbridge	1968		132	•		E	•
Motor Racing Year 1970	Motor Racing	Knightsbridge	1970		120	•		F	•

Motor Racing Year

Title	Author	Publisher	1st Ed'n	Later Ed'ns	Pages	Illus	Index	Rate	Text
No.1	Pritchard	Pelham	1970		239	•		F	•

The Constant Search

Title	Author	Publisher	1st Ed'n	Later Ed'ns	Pages	Illus	Index	Rate	Text
No.2	Pritchard	Pelham	1971					F	•
No.3	Pritchard	Pelham	1972		270	•		F	•
No.4	Pritchard	Pelham	1973		318	•		F	•
Motor Sport Racing Car Review									
	Jenkinson	Grenville	1947		121	•		D	•
	Jenkinson	Grenville	1948					D	•
	Jenkinson	Grenville	1949		116	•		D	•
	Jenkinson	Grenville	1950		104	•		D	•
	Jenkinson	Grenville	1951		120	•		D	•
	Jenkinson	Grenville	1952		124	•		D	•
	Jenkinson	Grenville	1953		132	•		D	•
	Jenkinson	Grenville	1954					D	•
	Jenkinson	Grenville	1955					D	•
	Jenkinson	Grenville	1956					D	•
	Jenkinson	Grenville	1957					D	•
Race Report	Guba	Fountain	1971		160	•		E	
Speed and a Microphone	Richards	Kimber	1958		217	•		E	•

Section D 10

Tracks and circuits

Title	Author	Publisher	1st Ed'n	Later Ed'ns	Pages	Illus	Index	Rate	Text
Brooklands	Wallace	Ballantine	1971		160	•		D	
Brooklands — Fifty Years of	Gardner	Heinemann	1956		160	•	•	C	•
Brooklands. History of Vol.1	Boddy	Grenville	1948		272	•	•	C	•
Vol.2	Boddy	Grenville	1949		272	•	•	E	•
Vol.3	Boddy	Grenville	1950		256	•	•	E	•

Title	Author	Publisher	1st Ed'n	Later Ed'ns	Pages	Illus	Index	Rate	Text
Brooklands. History of 3 Vols in one	Boddy	Grenville	1957		368	•	•	E	•
Brooklands to Goodwood	Walkerley	Foulis	1961		280	•	•	E	

Brooklands Society — For the preservation of. Bulletin Issued 1970 and continuing. See Section 'O'.

Brooklands Yearbooks (Brooklands Automobile Racing Club)

Title	Author	Publisher	1st Ed'n	Later Ed'ns	Pages	Illus	Index	Rate	Text
	BARC	BARC	1930		68	•		C	
	BARC	BARC	1931		64	•		C	
	BARC	BARC	1932		68	•		C	
	BARC	BARC	1933		68	•		C	
	BARC	BARC	1934		64	•		C	
	BARC	BARC	1935		64	•		C	
	BARC	BARC	1936		64	•		C	
	BARC	BARC	1937		68	•		C	
	BARC	BARC	1938		60	•		C	
	BARC	BARC	1939		60	•		C	

And for most previous years back to 1907

Title	Author	Publisher	1st Ed'n	Later Ed'ns	Pages	Illus	Index	Rate	Text
Brooklands. A Pictorial History	Georgano	Beaulieu	1978		112	•		E	•
Brooklands Automobile Racing Club Rules. Bye Laws and Clubhouse Rules			1935		22			C	
Brooklands Automobile Racing Club. Racing Rules			1932		14			C	
Brooklands Automobile Racing Club. Speed and Distance Tables	BARC	BARC							
Brooklands Automobile Racing Club. Souvenir of	Montagu	Car Illustrated	1907		87	•		C	
Indianapolis Yearbooks			1947*					D	

Issued annually, illustrated and with between 110 pages in the earlier editions rising to 175 in later ones. Known to have run continuously to 1967

The Constant Search

Title	Author	Publisher	1st Ed'n	Later Ed'ns	Pages	Illus	Index	Rate	Text
From Brands Hatch to Indianapolis	Tommasi	Hamlyn	1974		239	•		E	
Goodwood. The Sussex Motor Racing Circuit	Garnier	Beaulieu	1980		120	•		F	
History of Monza Track 1922-1972	Autodromo di Monza		1972		180	•		C	
Montlhéry	Boddy	Cassell	1961		169	•	•	D	•
Monza Yearbooks: Autodromo Nazionale di Monza									
			1960		146	•	•	D	
			1961		148	•	•	D	
			1962		150	•	•	D	
			1963		143	•	•	D	
			1964		144	•	•	D	
			1965		146	•	•	D	
			1966		150	•	•	D	
Motor Racing Circuits of Europe	Klemantaski & Frostick	Batsford	1958		95	•		D	•
The Racing World — A Guide to Some of the Famous Motor Racing Circuits	Dunlop	Dunlop	1956		25	•		C	•
Silverstone	Carrick	Pelham	1974		174	•	•	E	•
Wheels Take Wings	Burn & Bradley	Foulis	ND 1930s		247	•	App	C	•

Section D 11

Motor racing. Other than under Sections 1 to 10

| All Colour Book of Racing Cars (The) | King | Octopus | 1973 | | 74 | • | | F | |

Title	Author	Publisher	1st Ed'n	Later Ed'ns	Pages	Illus	Index	Rate	Text
Australian Motor Racing. The Book of	Tuckey	Murray	1965		158	•	•	E	
Batsford Book of Racing Cars	Bensted Smith	Batsford	1962		70	•	•	E	
Big Race (The)	Demand & Roseman	Nest Verlag	1955		128	•		D	
B.P. Book of Motor Racing (The)	Boyd	Paul	1959	1959	100	•		F	
Cars at Speed	Daley	Foulis	1961		303	•	•	E	
Castrol Guide to Motoring Sport	Walton	Stephens	1971		128	•		E	
Come Motor Racing With Me	Nickols	Muller	1954		160	•		F	
Come Motor Racing With Me	Walkerley	Muller	1961		208	•		F	
Day I Died (The)	Kahn	Gentry	1974		91	•	•	F	
Devil Behind Them (The)	Bentley	Angus & Robertson	1959		253	•	•	E	
Dicing With Death	Lewis	Daily Mirror	1961		93	•		F	
Eagle Book of Cars and Motor Sport (The)	Roberts	Longacre	1958		191	•		E	
Everybody's Book of British Racing Cars	Posthumus		1947		18	•		D	
First and Fastest	Hough	Allen & Unwin	1963		150	•		E	
Four Wheel Drift	Carter	Bodley Head	1959		192	•		E	
Motor Racing	Boyd	Paul	1959		100	•		E	
Motor Racing in Safety	Henderson	Stephens	1968		167	•		E	
Motor Racing	Carter, Frostick & Klemantaski	Bodley Head	1955		91	•		D	
Motor Racing Camera 1894-1916	Georgano	David & Charles	1976		102	•		E	
Motor Racing Story (The)	Garrett	Paul	1969		196	•		E	
Motor Racing the International Way No.1	Brittan	Kaye & Ward	1970		120	•		E	
No.2	Brittan	Kaye & Ward	1971		88	•		E	

The Constant Search

Title	Author	Publisher	1st Ed'n	Later Ed'ns	Pages	Illus	Index	Rate	Text
No.3	Brittan	Kaye & Ward	1972		88	•		E	
No.4	Brittan	Kaye & Ward	1973		88	•		E	
Omnibus of Speed	Beaumont/Nolan	Paul	1961		223	•		D	
Speed Camera	Tompkins	Foulis	ND		100	•		E	
Sun on the Grid	Stewart & Reigh	Keartland	1967		232	•	•	E	
World of Motor Sport (The)	Tracey & Hudson Evans	Purnell	1971		93	•		E	

Section E

Books on cars for use on the road

Title	Author	Publisher	1st Ed'n	Later Ed'ns	Pages	Illus	Index	Rate	Text
Section E 1									
Touring Cars									
American Car Spotter's Guide. 1940-1965 (The)	Burness	Motorbooks International	1978		358	•		E	
Breath of Life (Air Pollution)	Carr	Norton	1965		175			E	
Modern Motor Cars	Grant	Temple Press	1949		115	•		F	
Modern Motor Cars	Hunt	Temple Press	1952		88	•		F	
Motor Car (The)	Brabazon				254	•		C	
Motor Cars Part 1	Caunter	HMSO						F	•
Motor Cars Part 2	Caunter	HMSO	1959		187	•	•	F	•
Motor Cars	Turner	Temple Press	1958		128	•	•	F	
Motor Cars	Walker	Pearson	1920		127	•	•	F	

153

The Constant Search

Title	Author	Publisher	1st Ed'n	Later Ed'ns	Pages	Illus	Index	Rate	Text
Observer's Book of Automobiles (The)	Parsons	Warne	1955		286	•	•	D	•
	Mainwaring	Warne	1956		288	•	•	D	•
	Mainwaring	Warne	1957		288	•	•	D	•
	Albert	Warne	1958		288	•	•	D	•
	Mainwaring	Warne	1959		288	•	•	D	•
	Mainwaring	Warne	1960		288	•	•	E	•
	Mainwaring	Warne	1961		288	•	•	E	•
	Mainwaring	Warne	1962		288	•	•	E	•
	Mainwaring	Warne	1963		288	•	•	E	•
	Mainwaring	Warne	1964		288	•	•	E	•
	Mainwaring	Warne	1965		288	•	•	E	•
	Mainwaring	Warne	1966		288	•	•	E	•
	Mainwaring	Warne	1967		288	•	•	E	•
	Mainwaring	Warne	1968		288	•	•	E	•
	Mainwaring	Warne	1969		288	•	•	E	•
	Olyslager	Warne	1970		288	•	•	F	•
	Olyslager	Warne	1971		288	•	•	F	•
	Olyslager	Warne	1972		239	•		F	•
Believed not published			1973						
	Olyslager	Warne	1974					F	•
	Olyslager	Warne	1975					F	•
	Olyslager	Warne	1976					F	•
	Turner	Warne	1977		177	•		F	•
	Olyslager	Warne	1978		192	•		F	•
	Olyslager	Warne	1979		182	•		F	•
Post War Touring Car (The)	Robson	Haynes/Foulis	1977		129	•		F	•

33

34

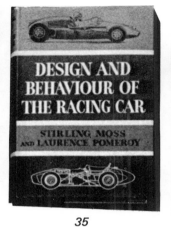

35

36

37

38

39

40

41

42

43

44

Section E 2

Sports cars

Title	Author	Publisher	1st Ed'n	Later Ed'ns	Pages	Illus	Index	Rate	Text
Batsford Book of Sports Cars	Barker	Batsford	1962		71	•		E	
British Sports Cars	Grant	Foulis	1947		186	•	•	E	•
British Sports Cars since the War	Watkins	Batsford	1974		208	•	•	E	
The Car Sports Book	Anon	Young World	1968		141	•		E	
Classic Sports Cars	Posthumus	Hamlyn	1980		160	•		E	
Continental Sports Cars	Boddy	Foulis	1951		128	•	•	D	•
Encyclopaedia of European Sports and G.T. Cars 1961-1969	Robson	Haynes/Foulis	1980		471	•	•	F	
German High Performance Cars	Sloniger & von Fersen	Batsford	1965		263	•	•	E	•
Guide to Used Sports Cars Vol.1	Haynes	Haynes	1964		118	•	App	D	•
Vol.2	Haynes	Haynes	1965		150	•	App	D	•
History of Sports Cars	Georgano	Nelson	1970		320	•		D	•
History of the World's High Performance Cars	Hough & Frostick	Allen & Unwin	1967		189	•	•	D	•
History of the World's Sports Cars	Hough	Allen & Unwin	1961		223	•	•	E	•
Italian High Performance Cars	Pritchard & Davey	Allen & Unwin	1967		374	•	•	D	•
Jaguar Sports Cars	Skilleter	Haynes/Foulis	1976		360	•	•	F	
Jaguar 'E' Type — A Collector's Guide	Skilleter	M.R.P	1979		128	•	App	F	
Jaguar Sports Cars 1957-60	Various	Brooklands	ND		100	•		F	•
Jaguar 'E' Type 1961-66	Various	Brooklands	ND		100	•		F	•
Jaguar 'E' Type 1966-71	Various	Brooklands	ND		100	•		F	•

Title	Author	Publisher	1st Ed'n	Later Ed'ns	Pages	Illus	Index	Rate	Text
Jaguar 'E' Type 1971-75	Various	Brooklands	ND		100			F	•
Ken Purdy's Book of Automobiles	Purdy	Cassell	1972		364	•		E	
Specialist Sports Cars	Filby	David & Charles	1974		112	•	•	E	
Speed From the Sports Car	Motor World	Motor World	1950		190	•		E	
Sports Car. (The) Its Design and Performance	Campbell	Chapman & Hall	1954	1954 /5/6/9	285	•	•	E	•
Sports Car (The)	Campbell	Bentley	1959		285	•	•	F	•
Sports Car. (The) Its Development and Design	Stanford	Batsford	1957	1959	224	•	•	D	•
Sports Car Engine (The) Tuning and Modification	Campbell	Chapman & Hall	1963		322	•	•	E	
Sports Car Engine Factors in Performance	Calculus	Motor World	1949	1950	111	•	App	E	
Sports Car Bodywork	Locke	Batsford	1954	1960	120	•	•	D	•
Sports Car Pocket Book (The)	Boddy	Batsford	1961		254	•		E	•
Sports Cars	Cade	Foyles	1962		90	•	•	E	
Sports Cars	Seager				157	•		E	
Sports and Classic Cars	Borgeson & Jaderquist		1955		466	•		D	•
Sports Cars in Action	Bond		1954		252	•		E	
Sports Cars of the World	Stein	Scribners	1952		173	•		E	
Sports Cars on Road and Track	Hutton	Hamlyn	1973		96	•	•	E	
Sports Cars Today	Walkerley	Barker	1962		120	•	App	E	
Sports Cars 1907-1927	Nicholson	Blandford	1970		163	•	•	E	
Sports Cars 1928-1939	Nicholson	Blandford	1969		182	•	•	E	
Sports Cars. The Book of	Markmann & Sherwin	Muller	1960		321	•		E	•

Title	Author	Publisher	1st Ed'n	Later Ed'ns	Pages	Illus	Index	Rate	Text

Section E 3

Veteran, Edwardian and Vintage cars

Title	Author	Publisher	1st Ed'n	Later Ed'ns	Pages	Illus	Index	Rate	Text
Age of Motoring (The)	Dumont, Barker & Tubbs	Lausanne	1965		205	•		D	
Amateur Motorist (The)	Pemberton	Hutchinson	1907	1909	328	•	•	B	•
American Automobiles (Early)	Clymer	McGraw & Hill	1950		213	•	•	D	
An Era of Motoring — Vehicles of a Past Age	Montagu	Macmillan	1973		96	•			
Antique Automobile (The)	Nixon	Cassell	1956		235	•	•	D	•
Any Color so Long as it's Black	Roberts	David & Charles	1976		144	•	•	E	
Autocars	Farman	Whittaker	1896	several	249	•	•	B	•
Automobile (The) Vol.1	Hasluck	Cassell		1905	451	•		C	•
Vol.2	Hasluck	Cassell		1905	413	•	App	C	•
Vol.3	Hasluck	Cassell		1906	415	•	•	C	•
Automobile (The)	Hasluck	Cassell		1903 (3rd Ed)	832	•	•	C	
Automobiles of Yesteryear	Bergere	Dodd/Mead	1962		160	•	•	E	
Automobile Show 1903	SMMT	Stephens	1973		123	•		E	
Batsford Book of Veteran Cars	Bird	Batsford	1962		70	•	•	E	
Batsford Book of Vintage Cars	Tubbs & Barron	Batsford	1962		70	•	•	E	
Batsford Guide to Vintage Cars	Clutton, Bird & Harding	Batsford	1959	1976	224	•		E	
Book of the Light Car	Brown	Chapman & Hall	1926		155	•	•	C	•
Book of the Motor Car (The)	Sloss	Appleton	1905		372	•	•	A	•
Book of the Motor Car Vol.1	Kennedy	Caxton	ND 1920s		212			E	•

Title	Author	Publisher	1st Ed'n	Later Ed'ns	Pages	Illus	Index	Rate	Text
Vol.2	Kennedy	Caxton	ND 1920s		213			E	•
Vol.3	Kennedy	Caxton	ND 1920s		221			E	•
Vol.4	Kennedy	Caxton	ND 1920s		221			D	•
Book of Motors	Aston	Spon	ND 1920s		138	•	•	C	
Book of the Veteran Car (The)	Drackett	Pelham	1973		143	•	•	F	
British Cars 1896-1914	Matthews	Allan	ND		64	•		E	
Cars & Motorcycles 3 Vols	Montagu & Bourdon	New Era	1929		1264	•	•	C	
Cars of the Early Twenties	Burness	Chilton	1968		270	•	•	E	
Carriages Without Horses Shall Go	Sennett	Whittaker	1896		131	•		A	
Complete Motorist (The)	Young	Methuen	1904	many to 1973	352	•	•	C/E	•
Dawn of Motoring (The)	Murchison	Murray	1942		67	•		D	
Early Cars	Sedgwick	Weidenfeld & Nicholson	1962		96	•		E	
Early Days	Lomax & Norris	Cockshoot	1948		47	•		D	
Early Motor Cars 1904-1915 (1st Series)	Oliver	Evelyn	1959		54	•		E	
Early Motor Cars. The Vintage Years 1919-30	Oliver	Evelyn	1961		56	•		E	
Edwardian Cars	Carter	Foulis	1955		245	•	App	D	•
European Cars 1886-1914	Nicholson	Allen	1963		72	•		D	
Facts Concerning Elementary Locomotion	Maceroni	Effingham/Wilson	1833		40			A	•
Facts Concerning Elementary Locomotion	Maceroni	Effingham/Wilson		1834	131			A	
Father's First Car	Tracey	Routledge & Paul	1966		85	•		E	

The Constant Search

Title	Author	Publisher	1st Ed'n	Later Ed'ns	Pages	Illus	Index	Rate	Text
First Hundred Road Motors (The)	Kidner	Oakwood	1950		57	•		D	•
French Vintage Cars	Bolster	Autosport/Batsford	1964		204	•		D	•
From Veteran to Vintage	Karslake & Pomeroy	Temple Press	1956		353	•	•	D	•
Get a Horse	Mussleman	Lipincott	1950		304	•		D	
Happy Motorist (The)	Young	Grant Richards	1906		230			C	
Henry's Wonderful Model 'T'	Clymer	Bonanza	ND 1960s		219	•		E	
Horseless Carriage (The)	Salomons	Kent & Sussex Courier	1895					A	
Horseless Carriage (The)	Rolt	Constable	1950	1954	204	•	•	D	•
Horseless Carriage Days	Maxim	Harper	1937		175	•		C	•
Horseless Road Locomotion 2 Vols	Sennett	Whittaker	1900					A	
Horseless Vehicles, Automobiles and Motor Cycles	Hiscox	Sampson/Low/Marston	1900		459	•	•	B	•
Invention of the Automobile	Nixon	Country Life	1936		143	•		D	•
Light Motor Cars and Voiturettes	Knight	Iliffe	1902	1970	119			B	
Mechanical Road Carriages	Beaumont	Trounce/Cantor	1895-6		46	•			
Mechanical Road Carriages	Beaumont	Trounce/Cantor	1904		52	•		A	
Modest Man's Motor (The)	Matson	Lawrence/Bullen	1903		158	•		B	•
Montagu Motor Book (The)	Sherrin	Car Illustrated	ND 1910s		286	•		C	•
Motor (The)	Armstrong	Paul	1912		374	•	•	C	•
Motor Book. An Anthology 1895-1914	Nicholson	Methuen	1962		317	•	•	E	
Motor Book (The)	Mecredy	Bodley Head	1903		147	•	•	C	
Motor Car 1765-1914 (The)	Bird	Batsford	1960		256	•	•	E	
Motor Cars or Power Carriages For Common Roads	Tayler	Crosby & Lockwood	1897		200	•	•	B	•

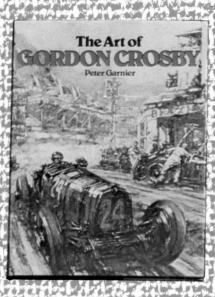

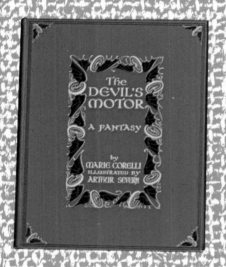

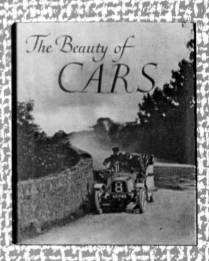

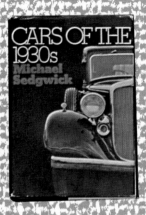

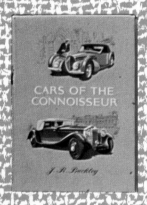

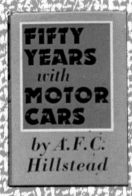

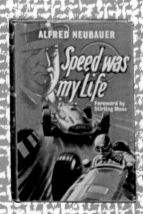

Colour Plate 2

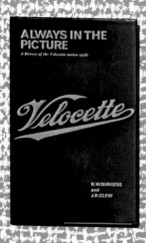

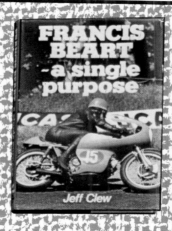

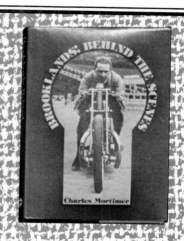

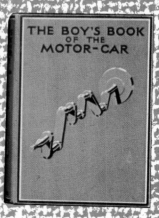

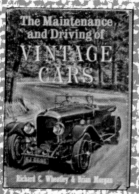

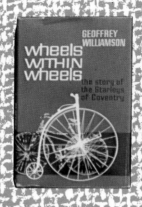

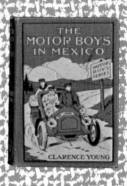

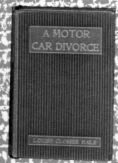

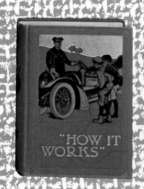

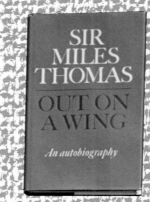

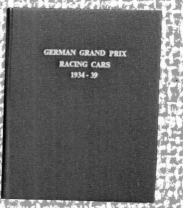

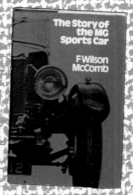

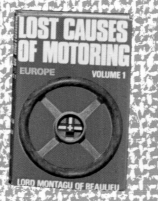

Colour Plate 5

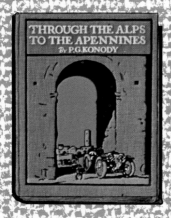

THROUGH THE ALPS
TO THE APENNINES
By P.G. KONODY

THE PASSES OF THE
PYRENEES
C. L. FREESTON, F.R.G.S.

A·PRACTICAL·GUIDE·TO
THE·MOUNTAIN·ROADS·OF
THE·FRANCO·SPANISH·FRONTIER

WRITTEN & ILLUS-
TRATED IN COLOUR BY
GORDON HOME

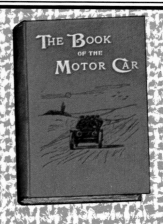

THE BOOK
OF THE
MOTOR CAR

THREE
THOUSAND
MILES
IN A MOTOR CAR

HUGH ROCHFORT MAXSTED

THREE MEN
IN A
MOTOR CAR

WINTHROP E. SCARRITT

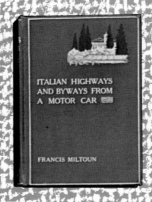

ITALIAN HIGHWAYS
AND BYWAYS FROM
A MOTOR CAR

FRANCIS MILTOUN

CANYONS, CANS
AND CARAVANS
F. H. E. HASELL

THREE MEN
IN A
MOTOR CAR

HUGH ROCHFORT MAXSTED

A CATECHISM
OF THE
MOTOR CAR
JOHN HENRY KNIGHT

PRICE 3/6 NET

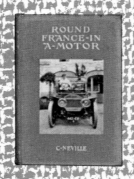

ROUND
FRANCE·IN
·A·MOTOR

C·NEVILLE

MOTORING

R.P. HEARNE

AT THE WHEEL
ASHORE &
AFLOAT

FULL
THROTTLE

HENRY "TIM" BIRKIN

THE
ENZO FERRARI MEMOIRS

By Enzo Ferrari

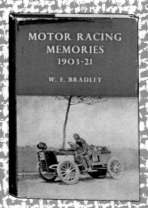

MOTOR RACING
MEMORIES
1903-21

W. F. BRADLEY

Colour Plate 6

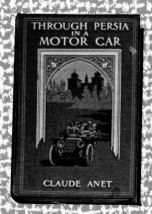

THROUGH PERSIA
IN A
MOTOR CAR

CLAUDE ANET

En Route

Roy Trevor.

ROUND THE WORLD

IN A
MOTOR·CAR

By
Antonio
Scarfoglio

MOROCCO
From a Motor

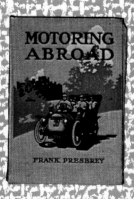

MOTORING
ABROAD

FRANK PRESBREY

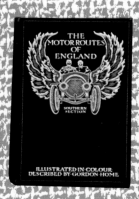

THE
MOTOR ROUTES
OF ENGLAND

SOUTHERN
SECTION

ILLUSTRATED IN COLOUR
DESCRIBED BY·GORDON·HOME

A MOTOR FLIGHT
through
ALGERIA and TUNISIA

EMMA BURBANK AYER

Poor Me
The Diary
of a
Motor Car

VERA FRIEDLANDER

EUROPE
from a
MOTOR CAR

RUSSELL RICHARDSON

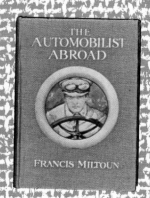

THE
AUTOMOBILIST
ABROAD

FRANCIS MILTOUN

ROUND THE WORLD
IN A BABY AUSTIN
By HECTOR MACQUARRIE

THE
SOUTH-BOUND CAR

OWEN LLEWELLYN
AND
L. RAVEN-HILL

THROUGH
WESTERN CANADA
IN A
CARAVAN

DRIVE
ROUND
THE
WORLD

J-C BAUDOT
& J. SEGUELA

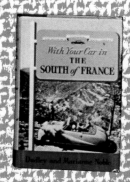

With Your Car in
THE
SOUTH of FRANCE

Dudley and Marianne Noble

ACROSS AFRICA
IN A LORRY
W. B. REDMAYNE

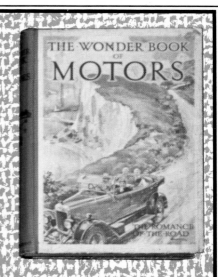

Title	Author	Publisher	1st Ed'n	Later Ed'ns	Pages	Illus	Index	Rate	Text
Motor Cars and Other Motor Driven Vehicles	Walker	Pearson	1920		127	•	•	C	•
Motor Cars and the Application of Mechanical Power to Road Vehicles	Rhys Jenkins	Fisher/Unwin	1902		371	•	•	C	•
Motor Cars and Their Story	Talbot	Cassell	1912		368	•	•	C	•
Motor Car. (The) Its Nature, Use and Management	Thompson	Warne	1902		108	•	•	C	•
Motor Cars of the Golden Past	Purdy & Burnside	Heinemann	1966		216	•		D	
Motor Cars or Power Carriages for Common Roads	Wallis Tayler	Crosby & Lockwood	1897		200	•		A	
Motoring	Berriman	Methuen	1914		312	•	•	C	•
Motoring	Hearne	Routledge	ND		152	•		E	
Motors and Motor Driving	Harmsworth & others	Longmans & Green	1902	1903/4	521	•	•	C	•
Motors and Motoring	Spooner	Jack	1916		326	•	•	D	
Motor Vehicles in a Nutshell	Moore	Eagle Star	1923	& others	331	•		D	
Motor Vehicles and Motors	Beaumont	Constable	1900		636	•	•	C	
New Method of Propelling Locomotive Machines (Compressed Air)	Mann	Taylor	1830		56			A	•
New Motoring (The)	Berry	Hodder & Stoughton	1919		283	•		C	
New System of Inland Conveyance for Goods and Passengers (Compressed Air)	Meohurst	Bretell	1827		38	•		A	•
Notes on Motor Carriages	Knight	Hazell Watson & Viney	1896		84	•		A	•
Old Car Book (The)	Bentley	Fawcett	1953		144	•		D	
Old Cars The World Over	Nagle	Arco	1958		344	•	•	E	
Period Cars	Rogliatti	Hamlyn	1973		318	•		D	
Petrol Motors and Motor Cars	Hyler White	Longmans & Green	1904		187	•	•	B	

The Constant Search

Title	Author	Publisher	1st Ed'n	Later Ed'ns	Pages	Illus	Index	Rate	Text
Petroleum Handbook (The)	Shell	Shell	1948		658	•		E	
Petroleum Motor Cars	Lockert	Sampson Low/ Marston	1898		218	•		B	
Power Locomotion on the Highway. (A Guide To)	Jenkins	Cate	1896		72			A	•
Propulsion of Carriages on Common Roads, other than by Animal Power	Gore	'In London'	1893					A	•
Rene Cutforth Reporting	Cutforth	Arco	1955		195	•		D	
Romance Amongst Cars	Nixon	Foulis	1937		338	•		D	
Romance of Motoring (The)	Bridges & Tiltman	Harrap	1933		292	•	•	D	
Romance of the Motor Car (The)	Jackson	Boy's Own Paper	ND		287	•	•	D	
Self Propelled Vehicles	Homans	Audel	1902	1904/ 6/8	652	•	•	B	•
Silver Lady (The)	Minchin	Foulis	1961		180	•		D	•
Splendid Book of Motors (The)	Jackson	Sampson Low/ Marston	1930s		224	•		D	
Those Wonderful Old Automobiles	Clymer	McGraw Hill	1953		214	•	•	D	
Trailblazers (The)	Nicholson				178	•	•	E	
Trials of Motor Vehicles For Heavy Traffic	Self Propelled Traffic Ass'n.	Winstanley/Watkins	1898 /9	1901	126			A	
Veteran and Edwardian Motor Cars	Moncrieff	Batsford	1955	1956	256	•	•	D	•
Veteran and Vintage Cars	Gibson	Nelson	1970		57	•	•	E	
Veteran and Vintage Cars. The Story of	Posthumus	Phoebus	1977		128	•		E	
Veteran and Vintage Cars	Roberts	Hamlyn	1963		159	•		E	
Veteran and Vintage Cars in Colour	Sedgwick	Batsford	1971		144	•		E	
Veteran and Vintage Cars of Australia	Grant	Reed	1972		108	•	•	E	

Title	Author	Publisher	1st Ed'n	Later Ed'ns	Pages	Illus	Index	Rate	Text
Veteran Car. The Book of the	Drackett	Pelham	1973		144	•	•	E	
Veteran Car Owner's Manual	Carter	Paul	1962		191	•	•	D	•
Veteran Cars	Drackett	Foyles	1961		91	•	•	E	
Veteran Cars. The Boy's Book of	Carter	Burke	1959		144	•	App	E	
Veteran Cars of the World 1890-1915	'Anon'	World	1967		124	•		E	
Veteran Motor Car Pocket Book	Bird & Hutton Stott	Batsford	1963		256	•		E	•
Veterans of the Road	Nagle	Arco	1959		239	•	•	F	
Veteran and Edwardian Cars. Your Book Of	Coleman	Faber & Faber	1971		62	•		E	
Veteran to Vintage Cars	Lloyd	Macdonald	1960		192	•	•	E	
Veteran Years of New Zealand Motoring (The)	MacLean/Joyce	Reed	1971		230	•	•	E	
Victorian and Edwardian Cycling and Motoring	Demaus	Batsford	1977		60	•		E	
Vintage Car Casebook (The)	Hull & Arnold Foster	Batsford	1976		192	•	•	E	
Vintage Car Collector. Adventures of A	Radcliff	Bonanza	1972		192	•		E	
Vintage Cars	Drackett	Foyles	1962		92	•	•	E	
Vintage Cars	Posthumus	Hamlyn	1973		96	•	•	E	
Vintage Car. 1919-1930 (The)	Nicholson	Batsford	1966		390	•	•	D	•
Vintage Cars of the World 1916-1939									
Vintage Cars. Your Book of	Coleman	Faber & Faber	1968		62	•	•	E	
Vintage Motor Car (The)	Clutton & Stanford	Batsford	1954		240	•	•	D	•
Vintage Motor Car Pocket Book (The)	Clutton, Bird & Harding	Batsford	1959		255	•		E	•
Whatever Became of the Baby Austin?	Underwood	Heritage	1965		44	•		D	

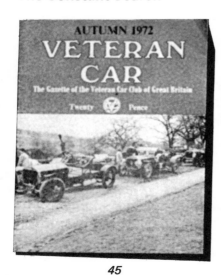

45

46

47

48

49

50

51

52

53

Title	Author	Publisher	1st Ed'n	Later Ed'ns	Pages	Illus	Index	Rate	Text
Woman and Her Car	Henslowe	Gentlewoman	1918		75	•		C	•
Woman and the Car	Levitt	Bodley Head	1909	1970	126	•	•	C	
Woman and the Motor Car	Aria	Appleton	1906		333	•	App	C	•
World on Wheels (The)	Stratton	Stratton	1878		489	•	•	B	

Section E 4

Cars 1931 to 1939

Title	Author	Publisher	1st Ed'n	Later Ed'ns	Pages	Illus	Index	Rate	Text
American Cars of the 1930s	Warne	Olyslager	1971		80	•		E	
Book of Motors	Camm	Collins	c1931		256	•		D	•
British Cars of the Early 1930s	Vanderveen	Warne	1973		80	•	•	E	
British Light Cars 1930 to 1939	Hudson	Haynes/Foulis	1976		336	•		E	
Cars of the Early Thirties	Burness	Chilton	1970		275	•	•	E	
Cars of the 1930s	Sedgwick	Batsford	1970		384	•	•	D	
Motor Cars Today	Harrison		1939		207	•	•	D	
Motoring in the 30s	Robson	Stephens	1979		216	•	•	F	

Section E 5

Cars 1940 onwards

Title	Author	Publisher	1st Ed'n	Later Ed'ns	Pages	Illus	Index	Rate	Text
Book of the Motor Car	Naldrett	Naldrett	1952		192	•		E	
British Cars of 1949	Chambers	P.C. Publications	1949		67	•		E	
British Cars of 1950	Chambers	P.C. Publications	1950		61	•	•	E	
British Cars 1951	Chambers	P.C. Publications	1951		57	•	•	F	
British Cars of 1953	Chambers	P.C. Publications	1953		67	•		F	

The Constant Search

Title	Author	Publisher	1st Ed'n	Later Ed'ns	Pages	Illus	Index	Rate	Text
British Cars of the 1960s	Nye	Nelson	1970		185	•		F	
British Motor Cars 1950-51	Lukins	Ronald	1951		128	•		F	
British Motor Cars 1952	Speed	Foulis	1952		172	•	•	F	
British Cars of the Late 1950s 1955-59	Voller/Vanderveen	Olyslager	1975		60 appx	•	•	F	
Motor Cars Today	Westbury	Barker	1962		124	•	•	F	
Motor Vehicles of Today	Williamson	Elek	1948		232	•	•	E	

Section E 6

Cars — Thoroughbred and Classic

Title	Author	Publisher	1st Ed'n	Later Ed'ns	Pages	Illus	Index	Rate	Text
Age of Cars (The)	Twite	Hamlyn	1974		96	•	•	E	
Automobile Book (The)	Stein	Hamlyn	ND 1960s		317	•		E	•
Automobile Treasures	Nicholson	Allan	1963		120	•		E	•
Batsford Book of Classic Cars	Buckley	Batsford	1964		70	•		E	•
Batsford Guide to British Cars									•
Beauty of Cars (The)	Ullyett	Parrish	1962		128	•		D	•
Bodies Beautiful	McLellan	David & Charles	1975		192	•	•	F	•
Cars of the Connoisseur	Buckley	Batsford	1960		272	•	•	D	•
Cars of the World	Scheel	Methuen	1962		215	•	•	E	•
Great Cars (The)	Stein	Hamlyn	c1960		251	•		E	•
Great Cars	New English Library	New English Library	1971		128	•		E	
Famous Motor Cars of the World	Walkerley	Muller	1964		144	•	•	E	
History of the World's Classic Cars	Hough/Frostick	Allen & Unwin	1963		190	•		D	•
Kings of the Road	Purdy	Hutchinson	1955		216	•	•	E	

Title	Author	Publisher	1st Ed'n	Later Ed'ns	Pages	Illus	Index	Rate	Text
Post War British Thoroughbreds. Their Purchase & Restoration	Hudson	Haynes/Foulis	1975		334	•	•	F	•
Sports and Classic Cars	Borgeson/Jaderquist	Bonanza	1955		466	•		D	•
Style Auto	Bellia	Style Auto	ND 1960s		150	•		E	
Thoroughbred Motor Car (The)	Moncrieff	Batsford	1963		279	•	•	D	•
Upper Crust (The)	Bolster	Follett	1976		200	•	•	E	•
World's Fastest Cars (The)	Horsley	Trend	1955		128	•		E	

Section E 7

Cars — design, manufacture, development, tuning, maintenance and restoration, including coachbuilding

Title	Author	Publisher	1st Ed'n	Later Ed'ns	Pages	Illus	Index	Rate	Text
American Automobile (The)	Rae	Chicago	1965		265	•	•	E	•
American Automobile Manufacturers	Rae	Viking	1974		223	•	•	D	•
Automobile Body Design. The Complete Book of	Beattie	Haynes/Foulis	1977		143	•	•	F	•
Automobile Chassis Design	Averns	Iliffe	1948		238	•	•	D	
Automobile Design. Great Designers and Their Work	Barker/Harding	David & Charles	1970		374	•	•	D	•
Automobile Efficiency	Helme	Trader	1951		116	•	•	D	
Automobile Engine Testing and Tuning	Munday	Newnes	1956		264	•		E	
Automobile Engine Testing and Tuning	Irving	Temple Press	1962		214	•		E	
Automobile Tyres	Setright	Chapman & Hall	1972		195	•	•	D	•
Automotive Chassis (The)	Heldt	Heldt		1948	599	•	•	D	
Body Construction and Design	Giles	Iliffe	1971		269	•	•	E	

The Constant Search

Title	Author	Publisher	1st Ed'n	Later Ed'ns	Pages	Illus	Index	Rate	Text
Book of the Motor Car (The) Vol.1	Kennedy	Caxton	1913		212	•		E	
Vol.2	Kennedy	Caxton	1913		213	•		E	
Vol.3	Kennedy	Caxton	1913		221	•		E	
Vol.4	Kennedy	Caxton	Later		221	•	•	D	
Bosch Book of the Motor Car	Day	Collins	1975		256	•	•	D	
British Leyland Minis	Marshall/Fraser	Foulis	1965	1968/73	266	•	•	E	
Car Body Renovation	McLintock	Foulis	ND		96	•		D	
Car Conversions for Power and Speed	Williams	David & Charles	1971		224	•		E	
Car. (The) Engine and Structure	Bacon	Macmillan/Cleaver	1968		322	•	•	E	
Car Makers (The)	Turner	Eyre & Spottiswoode	1963		260	•		E	
Chrome Dreams. Automobile Styling Since 1893	Wilson	Chilton	1976		310	•	•	F	
Collection of Interesting Cars (A)	Sears	Sears	ND		46	•		C	•
Custom Body Era (The)	Pfau	Barnes	1970		232	•	•	D	
Designing and Building a Sports Car	Lockwood	Foulis	1960		169	•		E	
Development of Road Motors 1898-1945	Kidner	Oakwood						C	
Economics of Carburetting and Manifolding	Brewer	Crosby & Lockwood	1926		176	•	•	D	
Elements of Motor Vehicle Design	Donkin	Oxford	1926		277	•	•	D	
Esquire's American Automobiles and their Makers	Wilkie	Muller	1963		191	•	•	D	
Everyone's Guide to Car Maintenance	Crawley	Haynes	1978		88	•	•	F	
Exhaust and Intake Systems. Scientific Design of	Smith	Foulis	1962		212	•		E	

Title	Author	Publisher	1st Ed'n	Later Ed'ns	Pages	Illus	Index	Rate	Text
From Chariot to Car	Priest	Barker (Coachbuilders)	1930		74	•		C	•
From Engines to Autos	Diesel, Goldbeck & Schildberger	Regnery	1960		302	•	•	D	
Gas Flow in the Internal Combustion Engine	Annand/Roe	Foulis	1974		217	•	•	E	
Gasoline Automobile (The) Vol.1	Heldt	Iliffe	1911	1912/15				D	
Vol.2	Heldt	Iliffe		1919/20 Total				D	
Vol.3	Heldt	Iliffe		1930	1500	•	•	D	
Gasoline, Petrol and Oil Engines	Clerk		1909		124	•		D	
Guide to Component Cars	Haynes	Haynes	ND 1950s		96	•		E	
History of the Art of Coachbuilding	Thrupp							B	•
History of Coachbuilding	Oliver	Cassell	1962		216	•	•	D	•
How Motor Cars Run	Elton	Longmans & Green	1939		79	•		D	
Internal Combustion Engine (The)	Wimpers	Constable	1915		319	•	•	C	
Internal Combustion Engines Illustrated			1950		384	•	•	D	
Internal Combustion Engineering	Kersey	Blackie	1940		487	•		D	
Maintenance and Driving of Vintage Cars	Wheatley & Morgan	Batsford	1964		168	•	•	E	•
Making of a Motor Car (The)	Ware	Moorland	1976		112	•		F	
Manual of Driving and Maintenance for Mechanical Vehicles 1937	Anon	HMSO	1937		612	•	•	E	
Mechanicals (The)	Rolt	Heinemann	1967		163	•	•	D	
Mechanism of the Car	Judge	Chapman & Hall	1925		175	•	•	D	
Modern Gasoline Automobile (The)	Page	Hodder & Stoughton	1912	1913-19	1032	•	•	D	

The Constant Search

Title	Author	Publisher	1st Ed'n	Later Ed'ns	Pages	Illus	Index	Rate	Text
Modified Motoring	Sprinzel	M.R.P	1959		122	•		E	
More Mini Tuning	Trickey	Speed Sport	1968	1970	125	•		E	
Motor Body Building	Terry & Hall	Spon	1914		243	•	•	C	•
Motor Body Building	Shepherd		1923		264	•		C	•
Motor Bodies and Chassis	Butler	Harpers	1912		328	•	•	C	•
Motor Bodywork	Butler	Howell	1924		492	•		C	•
Motor Car and Coach Painting	Oliver	Howell	1924		244	•	•	C	•
Motor Car Construction	Brewer	Crosby & Lockwood	1912		242	•	•	C	
Motor Car Maintenance 4 Vols	Various	Newnes	1932		1172	•	•	E	
5 Vols	Various	Newnes	1931		1452	•	•	E	
Motor Car Principles	Whitman	Appleton	1907	1909	318		•	C	
Motor Cars Today (5 Vols)	Rutter	Virtue	ND		1864	•	•	D	
Motorist's Home Repair Book (The)	Hartley	Souvenir	1961		123	•		E	
Motor Service Digest		Motor Commerce		1950	387	•	•	F	
Motor Vehicle (The)	Newton & Steeds	Iliffe	1929		684	•	•	E	
Motor Vehicle Calculations and Science	Champion & Arnold	Arnold	1954	1955-9	202	•	•	D	
Motor Vehicles and their Engines	Fraser & Jones	Crosby & Lockwood	1924		374	•	•	C	
1930 London Motor Show	Dalton	Dalton & Watson	1970		318	•		E	
Owner Driver's Handbook (The)	Brown	Ward Lock	1925		288	•	•	D	
Performance Conversion Equipment	Smith	Foulis	1960		142	•	•	E	
Petrol and Oil Engines		Temple Press	ND		176	•	•	E	
Petrol Engine (The)	Brown	Car Illustrated	1907		103	•		C	
Pininfarina — Master Coachbuilder	Frostick	Dalton & Watson	1977		190	•		E	

Title	Author	Publisher	1st Ed'n	Later Ed'ns	Pages	Illus	Index	Rate	Text
Practical Automobile Engineering		Odhams		1959	512	•		E	
Practical House, Wagon and Automobile Painter (The)	White	Shrewsbury	1902		157	•		C	•
Practical Motor Body Building	Terry	Spon	1921		340	•	•	C	
Principles of Ignition (The)	Morgan	Pitman	1944		130	•		D	
Private and Commercial Body Building	Butler	Pitman	1932		248	•	•	C	
Restoration and Preservation of Vintage and Classic Cars (The)	Wood	Haynes/Foulis	1977		297	•	•	E	
Restoration of Vintage & Thoroughbred Cars (The)	Wheatley & Morgan	Batsford	1957		192	•		E	•
Some Unusual Engines	Setright	Mechanical Eng.	1975		138	•		E	
Sports Car Bodywork	Locke	Batsford	1954	1960	120	•	•	D	
Steering Problems		Automotive Products	1951		28	•		D	•
Subtleties of Steering		Automotive Products	1954		27	•		D	•
Suspension Efficiencies	Woodhead	Woodhead	1946		52	•		D	•
Technical Facts of the Vintage Bentley	BDC	BDC	1955		248	•		D	•
Testing of Internal Combustion Engines	Young & Pryer	English University	1936	1938-45	200	•	•	D	
Tuning for Speed and Economy	Smith	Foulis	ND		160	•	•	E	
Unsafe at Any Speed	Nader	Grossman	1965		200	•	•	E	
Wankel Rotary Engine (The)	Dark	Indiana Univ.	1974		145	•	•	E	
W.O. Bentley — Engineer	Bastow	Haynes/Foulis	1978		366	•	•	F	•

Section E 8

Steam cars, diesel and electric

Title	Author	Publisher	1st Ed'n	Later Ed'ns	Pages	Illus	Index	Rate	Text
Diesel	Wilson	Van Nostrand	1966		181	•		D	

The Constant Search

Title	Author	Publisher	1st Ed'n	Later Ed'ns	Pages	Illus	Index	Rate	Text
Diesel Engine (The)	Wills & Wallis Taylor	Crosby & Lockwood	1915		304	•	•	C	
Diesel Fuels and Lubricants	Esso	Esso	1960		134	•	•	D	
Early Mechanical Carriages	Rhys Jenkins	Antiquity	1896	1902					
Economy of Steam Power	Young	Atchley	1860		417	•		A	
English and American Steam Carriages and Traction Engines	Fletcher	Longmans	1904					A	
High Speed Diesel Engines	Heldt	Iliffe	1932	1936	438	•	•	C	
Modern Diesel (The)		Iliffe	1932		142	•		D	
Modern High Speed Oil Engines 3 Vols	Chapman	Caxton	1949	1950	685	•	•	D	
My Days with the Diesel	Cummins	Chilton	1967		190	•		E	
Old Time Steam Cars	Bentley	Fawcett	1953	1971	141	•		E	
On Steam Carriages	Yarrow	Trans. Soc. Engineers	1863					A	
Steam Power on Roads	Maceroni	'In London'	1835					A	
Steam Locomotion on Common Roads. Reminiscences of	Bramall	Brit. Assoc.						A	
Steam Locomotion on Common Roads. History and Development of	Fletcher	Spon	1891		306	•		A	
Steam on Common Roads	Young	Atchley	1860		417	•	App	A	•
Steam Cars 1770-1970	Montagu & Bird	Cassell	1971		250	•	•	E	
Steam Carriages on Turnpike Roads	Gurney	Baldwin & Cradock	1832		48	•		A	
Steam Carriages on Common Roads	Hancock	Weale	1838		104	•		A	
Steam Lorry 1896-1939 (The)	Kidner	Oakwood						C	
Steam Traction Engines, Wagons and Rollers	Johnson				180	•		A	

172

54

55

56

57

58

59

60

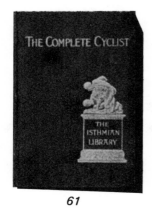

61

62

63

64

Title	Author	Publisher	1st Ed'n	Later Ed'ns	Pages	Illus	Index	Rate	Text
Treatise on Elementary Locomotion by means of Steam Carriages on Common Roads	Gordon	Stevart	1832	1834/6	192	•		A	

Section E 9

Marque histories, see under 'Histories' Section G 2

Section E 10

Driving — including annuals, yearbooks, dictionaries, glossaries and encyclopedias. Books other than under Sections E 1 to E 9

Title	Author	Publisher	1st Ed'n	Later Ed'ns	Pages	Illus	Index	Rate	Text
All About Motoring	Twelvetrees	Hodder & Stoughton	1924		255			D	•
American Automobiles. Encyclopedia of	Georgano	Ebury	1968		222	•	•	D	•
American Automobile. Encyclopedia of the	Ludwigsen & Burgess Wise	Orbis	1977		192	•		D	
Driving. Art and Technique of	Moss & Carlsson	Heinemann	1965		191	•		E	
Art of Driving (The)	Montagu	Car Illustrated	1906	1907	57	•		D	
Art of Driving (The)	'Times'	'Times'	c1928		106	•		E	
At the Wheel	Davison	Industrial Transport	1931		138	•		D	
Austin Healey Year Book 1978	Clarke	Brooklands	1978		100	•		F	
Austin Healey Year Book 1979-80	Clarke	Brooklands	1980		100	•		F	
Autocar Automobile Dictionary	Krausz	Iliffe	1907		122			C	

Title	Author	Publisher	1st Ed'n	Later Ed'ns	Pages	Illus	Index	Rate	Text
Automobile Connoisseur	Vyse	Speed Sports	1969[1]					E	
Automobile Quarterly	Scott Bailey	Automobile Quarterly	1962[2]					E	
Automobilia	Worthington Williams	Batsford/RAC	1979		192	•	•	F	
Automobile Review/ Automobile Year Vol. 1 1953-54	Guichard	Lausanne	1953		223	•		B	•
2 1954-55	Guichard	Lausanne	1954		195	•		B	
3 1955-56	Guichard	Lausanne	1955		262	•		D	
4 1956-57	Guichard	Lausanne	1956		207	•		D	
5 1957-58	Guichard	Lausanne	1957		224	•		D	
6 1958-59	Guichard	Lausanne	1958		234	•		D	
7 1959-60	Guichard	Lausanne	1959		231	•		D	
8 1960-61	Guichard	Lausanne	1960		219	•		D	
9 1961-62	Guichard	Lausanne	1961		213	•		D	
10 1962-63	Guichard	Lausanne	1962		231	•		D	
11 1963-64	Guichard	Lausanne	1963		231	•		D	
12 1964-65	Guichard	Lausanne	1964		223	•		D	
13 1965-66	Molter	Lausanne	1965		224	•		D	
14 1966-67	Wagner	Lausanne	1966		280	•		D	
15 1967-68	Wagner	Lausanne	1967		267	•		D	
16 1968-69	Armstrong	Lausanne	1968		258	•		D	
17 1969-70	Armstrong	Lausanne	1969		254	•		C	
18 1970-71	Armstrong	Lausanne	1970		272	•		D	
19 1971-72	Armstrong	Lausanne	1971		252	•		E	

1 Four volumes per year, in May, June, September and December. Each volume with up to 100 pages. Illustrated. Scarcity Rating — each volume E

2 Quarterly volumes, each illustrated and with up to 450 pages. Scarcity Rating — each volume E

The Constant Search

Title	Author	Publisher	1st Ed'n	Later Ed'ns	Pages	Illus	Index	Rate	Text
20 1972-73	Rosinksi	Lausanne	1972		248	•		E	
21 1973-74	Rosinski	Lausanne	1973		256	•		E	
22 1974-75	Armstrong	Lausanne	1974		232	•		E	
23 1975-76	Armstrong	Lausanne	1975		239	•		E	
24 1976-77	Rosinski	Lausanne	1976		236	•		E	
25 1977-78	Armstrong	Lausanne	1977		229	•		E	
26 1978-79	Armstrong	Lausanne	1978		248	•		E	
27 1979-80	Piccard	Lausanne	1979		263	•		F	
28 1980-81								F	
Best Motoring Stories	Welcome	Faber & Faber	1959		213	•		E	
Book of Cars (The)	Oliver	Macdonald	1968		127	•		E	
Bright Wheels Rolling	Melton & Purdy	Industrial Transport	1954		188	•		E	
Business Motor Handbook (The)	Watson	Cassell	1914		148	•	•	D	
Car Driving as an Art	Davis	Iliffe	1952		182	•	•	E	
Car Facts and Feats	Harding	Guinness	1971		256	•		F	
The 'Car' Road Book and Guide	Montagu	Car Illustrated	1914		655	•		C	
Car Tools — How to Choose and Use	Humphries	Haynes	1974		139	•	•	F	
Cars and How to Drive Them Part 1	Various	Car Illustrated	1903		126	•		C	
Part 2	Various	Car Illustrated	1905		123	•		C	
Cars. The Book of	Oliver	Macdonald	1968		168	•		E	
Cars, Cars, Cars	Davis	Hamlyn	1967		140	•	•	D	•
Cars in Colour	Sedgwick	Batsford	1968		174	•		E	
Complete Book of Motor Cars, Railways, Ships and Aeroplanes	Various	Odhams	ND 1930s		383	•	•	D	•

Title	Author	Publisher	1st Ed'n	Later Ed'ns	Pages	Illus	Index	Rate	Text
Complete Catalogue of British Cars (The)	Culshaw & Horobin	Macmillan	1978		511	•	•	F	
Complete Encyclopedia of Motor Cars 1885-1968 (The)	Georgano	Ebury	1969	1973	639	•	•	D	•
Control of Vehicles During Braking and Cornering	'Anon'	I.Mech.E	1963		118	•		D	
Cyclopedia of Automobile Engineering 6 Vols	Various	American Tech.Soc	1913		1654	•		D	
Cyclopedia of Passenger Transport in Britain 4 Vols			1913					C	
Dictionary of Motoring (The)	Mecredy	Mecredy/Percy	1904		375	•		C	
Dyke's Automobile and Gasoline Engine Encyclopedia	Dyke	Gillam	1911	Yearly to 1920	940	•		C	
Dumpy Book of Motors and Road Transport	Sampson	Sampson Low	1957		315	•		E	
Encyclopedia of the American Automobile	Ludvigsen & Burgess Wise	Orbis	1974	1975 /6/7	188	•	•	D	
Encyclopedia of Motoring (The) 1905	Car Illustrated	Car Illustrated	1905		346	•	•	C	
Encyclopedia of Motoring (The)	Mecredy	Iliffe		1908	272	•		C	
Era of Motoring (An)	Montagu				96	•			
Golden Picture Book of Motors (The)	Ward Lock	Ward Lock	ND 1950s		68	•		D	
Guinness Book of Car Facts and Feats	Harding	Guinness	1971		256	•	•	E	•
Half Safe	Carlin	Deutsch	1955		279	•		F	
Horseless Carriages	Lausanne	Stephens	1968		NN	•		E	
How It Works	Williams	Nelson	ND 1920s		483	•	•	D	
How to Draw Cars	Wooton	Studio	1955		64	•		E	
How to Drive a Car	'Anon'	Temple Press	ND 1920s		149	•		D	

The Constant Search

Title	Author	Publisher	1st Ed'n	Later Ed'ns	Pages	Illus	Index	Rate	Text
Illustrated Motor Cars of the World	Olyslager	Collins	1967		225	•	•	E	
In the Age of Motoring	Dumont	Stephens	1971		83	•		E	
Jaguar Driver's Year Book 1978	Clarke	Brooklands	1978		NN	•		F	
Jaguar Driver's Year Book 1979-1980	Clarke	Brooklands	1980		NN	•		F	
Ladybird Book of Motor Cars (The)	Carey	Wills & Hepworth	1960		51	•	•	F	
Law for the Private Motorist (The)	Evans & Dannreuther	Pitman	1936		195			D	•
Law of Motor Vehicles (The)	Bristow	CMUA	1931		304		•	D	•
Laws Relating to Public Carriages 1910	Roberts	HMSO	1910		495			C	•
Man and Motor — The 20th Century Love Affair	Jewell	Hodder & Stoughton	ND		203	•		E	
Man and Motor Cars	Black	Secker & Warburg	1966		373	•		D	
Miracle on Four Wheels (A)	Seiffert	Macdonald	1965		218	•	•	E	
Modern World Book of Motors	Cade	Sampson Low & Marston	1949		159	•		E	
Motor Driving Made Easy	Davies	Iliffe	ND 1910s		168	•	•	D	
'Motor' Guide to Makes and Models 1946-1956	Culshaw	Temple Press	1959		168			E	•
Motoring and the Mighty	Garratt	Paul	1971		214	•		F	•
Motoring Annual 1933	Henslowe	Joseph	1933		224	•		D	
Motoring Annual 1957	Douglas	Allan	1958		96	•		E	
Motoring Annual 1966					173	•		E	
Motoring By Land, Sea and Air	Gibbard Jackson	Nelson	1927		95	•		D	
Motoring for Women	Prioleau	Bles	1925		120	•		C	
Motoring Handbook	Norman	Bancroft	1969		229		App	E	

Title	Author	Publisher	1st Ed'n	Later Ed'ns	Pages	Illus	Index	Rate	Text
Motorist's Bedside Book (The)	Harding	Batsford	1962	1972	263	•		E	•
Motorist's Dictionary (The)	Webb	Arco	1963		224	•		E	
Motorist's Miscellany (The)	Harding	Batsford	1964		272	•		E	
Motorist's Reference and Year Book 1928		Black	1928		440	•	•	D	
Motorist's Week End Book (The)	Frostick & Harding	Batsford	1960		302	•		E	
Motormania	McKenzie	Cassell	1972		248	•		E	
Motor Reference Yearbook 1960	Tubbs	Temple Press	1960		216	•	App	E	
Motor Specifications and Prices		Stone and Cox	1920	ann'ly	c1000			D	
Motor Trade (The)	Milburn	'Trader'	1950		345	•	•	E	
Motor Yearbook 1905	Anon	Methuen	1905		233	•		C	
Motor Yearbook 1906	Buist	Methuen	1906		320		•	C	

'Motor' Year Books 1949-1957

Title	Author	Publisher	1st Ed'n	Later Ed'ns	Pages	Illus	Index	Rate	Text
	Pomeroy & Walkerley	Temple Press	1949		174	•		C	
	Pomeroy & Walkerley	Temple Press	1950		199	•		E	
	Pomeroy & Walkerley	Temple Press	1951		216	•	App	E	
	Pomeroy & Walkerley	Temple Press	1952		225	•	App	E	
	Pomeroy & Walkerley	Temple Press	1953		212	•	App	E	
	Pomeroy & Walkerley	Temple Press	1954		226	•	App	E	
	Pomeroy & Walkerley	Temple Press	1955		264	•	App	E	
	Pomeroy & Walkerley	Temple Press	1956		252	•	App	E	
	Pomeroy & Walkerley	Temple Press	1957		248	•	App	E	

The Constant Search

Title	Author	Publisher	1st Ed'n	Later Ed'ns	Pages	Illus	Index	Rate	Text
My Favourite Car Stories	Moss	Lutterworth	1960		189	•		D	
Odham's Motor Manual		Odhams·		1964	319	•		F	
Of Men and Motor Cars			1960		208	•		E	
Picnics for Motorists	Leyel	Routledge	1936		118		•	C	•
Practical Motorist's Encyclopaedia	Camm	Newnes	1934	1935-48	375	•		D	
Royal Motoring	McLintock	Foulis	ND		154	•		E	
Royal Road (The)	Allan	Pitman	1946		192	•		F	
Second Motor Book (The)	Nicholson	Methuen	1964		240	•	•	E	
Sixty Miles of Pencil	Reynolds & Clarke	Gentry	1971		126	•		F	
Skilful Driver (The)	Blair	Temple Press	1956	1956	166	•	•	F	
Standard Methods for Testing Petroleum and its Products		Institute of Petroleum	1935		228		•	D	
Successful Car Dealing	Wake	Haynes	ND		104	•		D	•
Three For the Road	Chaloner	Hutchinson	1956		134	•		E	
Turning Wheel (The)	Pound	Doubleday/Doran	1934		517	•		D	
Ward's Automotive Yearbook 1953	Ward's Reports	Ward's Reports	1953		264	•	•	D	
Wonderful World of the Automobile (The)	Purdy	MacGibbon & Key	1961		252	•		E	
World Car Catalogue	D'Angelo	Automobile Club of Italy	1962			•		D	
World Car Catalogue	D'Angelo	Automobile Club of Italy	1963		613	•		D	
World Car Catalogue	D'Angelo	Automobile Club of Italy	1964		564	•		D	
World Car Catalogue	D'Angelo	Automobile Club of Italy	1965		588	•		D	
World Car Catalogue	D'Angelo	Automobile Club of Italy	1966		776	• + Sup		D	

Title	Author	Publisher	1st Ed'n	Later Ed'ns	Pages	Illus	Index	Rate	Text
World Car Catalogue	D'Angelo	Automobile Club of Italy	1967		672	•	+ Sup	D	
World Car Catalogue	D'Angelo	Automobile Club of Italy	1968		672	•		D	
World Car Catalogue	D'Angelo	Automobile Club of Italy	1969		626	•	+ Sup	D	
World Car Catalogue	D'Angelo	Automobile Club of Italy	1970		439	•		D	
World Car Catalogue	D'Angelo	Automobile Club of Italy	1971		439	•		D	
World Car Catalogue	D'Angelo	Automobile Club of Italy	1972		460	•		D	
World Car Catalogue	D'Angelo	Automobile Club of Italy	1973		460	•		D	
World Car Catalogue	D'Angelo	Automobile Club of Italy	1974		439	•		D	
World Car Catalogue	D'Angelo	Automobile Club of Italy	1975		439	•		D	
World Car Catalogue	D'Angelo	Automobile Club of Italy	1976		440	•		E	
World Car Catalogue	D'Angelo	Automobile Club of Italy	1977		440	•		E	
World Car Catalogue	D'Angelo	Automobile Club of Italy	1978		440	•		E	
World Car Catalogue	D'Angelo	Automobile Club of Italy	1979		440	•		E	
World Car Catalogue	D'Angelo	Automobile Club of Italy	1980		440	•		F	

65

66

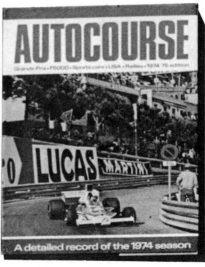

67

68

69

70

71

72

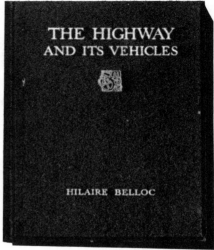

73

Section F

Autobiographies, biographies and personalities

Title	Author	Publisher	1st Ed'n	Later Ed'ns	Pages	Illus	Index	Rate	Text
Alf Francis — Racing Mechanic	Lewis	Foulis	1957	1958/9	326	•	•	D	•
All Arms and Elbows	Ireland	Pelham	1967		189	•	•	D	
All But My Life	Moss	Cassell	1954		239	•		E	
Amateur Racing Driver (The)	Tapper	Foulis	1963		172	•	•	D	•
At the Wheel Ashore and Afloat	Graham White	Foulis	1934		436	•	•	C	
Autobiography	Knowles	Allen & Unwin	1970		163	•	•	E	
Autocar Biography	Owen John	Iliffe	1927		248	•		C	
Barney Oldfield	Nolan	Putnam	1961		250	•	•	D	
Bits and Pieces	Bira	Foulis	1942		192	•		E	•
Blue Wings to Bangkok	Bira	Foulis	1952		184	•		D	•
B.P. Book of the Racing Campbells	Hough	Paul	ND 1960s		127	•	App	F	
Brabazon Story (The)	Brabazon	Heinemann	1956		227	•	•	D	•
Brought Up in England	Chula	Foulis	1943		322	•		D	

The Constant Search

Title	Author	Publisher	1st Ed'n	Later Ed'ns	Pages	Illus	Index	Rate	Text
Bruce McLaren — The Man and His Racing Team	Young	Eyre & Spottiswoode	1971		215	•		E	
Bugatti. Ettore	Bradley	M.R.P	1948		151	•	•	D	•
Bugatti Story (The)	Bugatti	Souvenir	1966		206	•	App	D	
Bugattis. The Amazing	Haslam & Garner Harvey & Conway	Design Council	1979		84	•		E	
Caracciola. Mercedes Grand Prix Ace	Caracciola	Foulis	1955		175	•		D	
Cars in My Life (The)	Bentley	Hutchinson	1961		156	•	•	D	•
Challenge Me the Race	Hawthorn	Kimber	1958		240	•		E	•
Champion Year	Hawthorn	Kimber	1959		239	•		D	•
Climax in Coventry	Hassan	M.R.P	1975		156	•	•	E	•
Crash Cavanagh	Richardson	Parrish	1953		256	•		E	
Designers (The)	Setright	Weidenfeld & Nicholson	1976		199	•	•	D	•
Dick Seaman — Racing Motorist	Chula	Foulis	1941	several	382	•	•	D/E	
Donald Campbell C.B.E	Knowles & Campbell	Allen & Unwin	1969		134	•	•	E	
Donald Campbell	James	Spearman	1968		158	•		D	
Enzo Ferrari Memoirs (The)	Ferrari	Hamilton	1963		164	•	•	C/D	•
L'Epopée Bugatti		L'Action Automobile et Touristique	ND		265	•		D	
Ettore Bugatti	see Bugatti — Ettore								
Fangio — Racing Driver	Merlin	Batsford	1961		215	•	•	D	•
Fangio	Jenkinson	Joseph	1973		146	•		E	•
Fifty Years with Motor Cars	Hillstead	Faber & Faber	1960		224	•	•	D	•
Fifty Years with Speed Kings	McDonald	Paul	1961		176	•	•	E	•
Fifty Years of Travel on Land, Sea, Water and Air	Butler	Fisher & Unwin	1920		421	•	•	C	•
First Class Ticket	Chula	Redman	1958		247	•	•	D	

Title	Author	Publisher	1st Ed'n	Later Ed'ns	Pages	Illus	Index	Rate	Text
Ford — An Unconventional Biography	Herndon	Cassell	1970		408	•	•	D	
Ford — The Times, the Man, the Company	Nevins	Scribners	1954		688	•	•	D	
Forty Years with Ford	Sorensen	Cape	1957		345	•	•	D	•
Foyt	Libby	Hawthorn	1974		218	•	•	E	
From the Cockpit	McLaren	Muller	1964		278	•	•	E	•
Gentlemen, Start Your Engines	Shaw	Bodley Head	1956		320	•	•	D	•
Gerry Marshall — Only Here for the Beer	Walton	Haynes/Foulis	1978		157	•	•	E	
Gilt and the Gingerbread (The)	Montagu	Joseph	1967		232	•	•	D	•
Gottlieb Daimler, Wilhelm Maybach and Karl Benz	Schildberger	Daimler & Benz	ND		109	•		D	
Graham	Hill & Ewart	Paul	1978		174	•		F	
Great Barnato (The)	Jackson	Heinemann	1970		278	•	•	E	•
Grand Prix Driver (The)	Lang	Foulis	1953		143	•	•	D	•
Harry Ferguson — Inventor and Pioneer	Fraser	Murray	1972		294	•	•	D	•
He Lit the Lamp (Professor A.M.Low)	Low	Burke	1958		213	•	•	D	•
Henry Ford	Burlinghame	Hutchinson			184		•	D	
Henry Ford	Caldwell	Bodley Head	1955		206	•	•	D	
Henry Ford	Simmonds	Joseph	1946		290	•		E	
Henry Ford. His Life With Cars	Pritchard	Hulton	ND		32	•		E	
Henry Ford — Engineer	Neyhart	Mifflin	1950		210	•		D	
Hyphen in Rolls Royce (The)	Oldham	Foulis	1967		194	•	•	D	•
Inky Way (The)	Williamson	Chapman & Hall	1931		396	•	•	E	
I Did it My Way	Cotton	Harrap	1970		192	•	•	D	•

The Constant Search

Title	Author	Publisher	1st Ed'n	Later Ed'ns	Pages	Illus	Index	Rate	Text
Innes Ireland	Ireland	Barker	1961		128	•		E	
In the Track of Speed	Moss	Muller	1957		212	•	•	E	
Jackie Stewart — World Champion	Stewart	Pelham	1970		191	•	•	E	
Jackie Stewart — World Driving Champion	Arco	Arco	1970		159	•		E	
Jim Clark — Portrait of a Great Driver	Gauld	Hamlyn	1968		200	•		E	
Jim Clark at the Wheel	Clark	Barker	1964		208	•		E	
Jim Clark Story (The)	Gavin	Frewin	1967		142	•	App	E	
Jimmy Murphy and the White Duesenberg	Carter	Hamilton	1968		38	•		D	
Jochen Rindt	Pruller	Kimber	1970		207	•		E	
Jody — An Autobiography	Scheckter	Haynes/Foulis	1976		128	•		F	
John Cobb Story (The)	Davis	Foulis	ND		111	•	App	D	
John, Lord Montagu of Beaulieu	Troubridge & Marshall	Macmillan	1930		318	•	•	C	•
Jo Siffert	Deschenaux	Kimber	1972		207	•		E	
Juan Manuel Fangio	Molter	Foulis	1956		182	•	•	D	
Kaye Don — The Man	Day	Hutchinson	ND 1930s		288	•		B	•
Last Season. (McLaren)	Beeching	Haessmer	1972		230	•	•	E	
Lanchester, F.W. (The) Life of an Engineer	Kingsford	Arnold	1960		246	•	App	D	
Life of Harry Ferguson (The)	Wymer	Phoenix House	1961		103	•	•	D	•
Life at the Limit	Hill	Kimber	1969		255	•		E	
Life of Lord Nuffield	Andrews & Brunner	Blackwell	1956		356	•	•	D	•
Life of Sir Henry Royce	Pemberton	Selwyn & Blount	ND		280	•	•	C	•
Life of Sir Henry Segrave	Campbell & Day	Hutchinson	ND 1930s		284	•		D	•
Life of Ted Horn	Catlin	Clymer	1949		223	•		D	

Title	Author	Publisher	1st Ed'n	Later Ed'ns	Pages	Illus	Index	Rate	Text
Like Father, Like Son	Drackett	Clifton	1969		117	•	•	E	
Lionel Martin — A Biography	Demaus	Transport Bookman	1980		150	•	•	F	•
Lord Austin — The Man	Lambert & Wyatt	Sidgwick & Jackson	1968		187	•	•	E	•
Louis Renault	Rhodes	Cassell	1969		235	•	•	D	•
Lucky All My Life (Biography of Harry Weslake)	Clew	Haynes	1979		176	•	•	F	
Lure of Speed	Segrave	Hutchinson	1928	1932	288	•		C/D	•
Malcolm Campbell	Lady Campbell	Hutchinson	1951		232	•	•	D	•
Memories and Machines	Ricardo	Constable	1968		264	•	•	D	•
McLaren, The Man, The Cars and the Team	Young	Bond/Parkhurst	1971		272	•	•	E	
An MG Experience	Jacobs	Transport Bookman	1976		188	•	•	E	
Milestones in a Motoring Life	Noble	Queen Anne	1969		252	•	•	E	•
Mind Over Motor	Charnock	Foulis	ND		160	•		D	•
More Equal than Others	Montagu	Joseph	1970		222	•	•	E	•
Motoring for Pleasure	Strathcarron	Paul	1963		175	•		E	
Motoring is My Business	Bolster	Autosport	1958		180	•	•	D	•
Motoring Memories in Peace and War	Harris	St Catherines	1928		91	•		C	•
Motoring Montagus (The)	Montagu	Cassell	1959		144	•	•	E	
Motoring My Way	Sedgwick	Batsford	1976		190	•	•	E	
Motor Racing	Davis	Iliffe	1932	several	305	•	App	C	•
Moving Forward	Ford	Heinemann	1931		310	•		D	
Mr Lionel	Harper	Cassell	1970		161	•		E	
My Father, Mr Mercedes	Jellinek	Foulis	1961		319	•		E	
My Greatest Adventure	Campbell	Thornton Butterworth	1931		260	•		D	
My Life and My Cars	Bentley	Hutchinson	1967		239	•	•	D	•

The Constant Search

Title	Author	Publisher	1st Ed'n	Later Ed'ns	Pages	Illus	Index	Rate	Text
My Life and Work	Ford & Crowther	Heinemann	1922	1922 /3/4	281		•	D	
My Life on Wheels	Wiggin	Baker	1963	1964	142	•		E	•
My Motoring Reminiscences	Edge	Foulis	ND		271	•		C	
My Motor Milestones	Von Laurentz	Jenkins	1909		226	•	•	B	•
My Philosophy in Industry	Ford & Faurote	Coward & McCann	1929		107			D	•
My Thirty Years of Speed	Campbell	Hutchinson	ND		270	•	•	D	
My Twenty Years of Racing	Fangio	Temple Press	1961		224	•	•	E	•
My Years with General Motors	Sloan	Doubleday	1964		472	•	•	E	•
Napier.R. Life of	Napier	Blackwood	1904					B	
New Henry Ford (The)	Benson	Funk/Wagnells	1923		360	•		D	
Nine Lives Plus	Bruce	Pelham	1977		192	•	•	F	
Nuffield Story (The)	Jackson	Muller	1964		254	•	•	E	
Nuvolari	Capelli							D	
Nuvolari	Lurani	Cassell	1959		223	•	•	D	•
Out on a Wing	Thomas	Joseph	1964		406	•		E	•
Parry Thomas	Tours	Batsford	1959		176	•	•	D	•
Passion for Cars (A)	Gibbs	David & Charles	1974		202	•	•	F	
Peterson. Ronnie	Henry & Peterson	Haynes/Foulis	1975		200	•		F	
Porsche. We at	Bentley	Haynes/Foulis	1976		288	•	•	F	
Porsche. The Man and His Cars	Meisl	Haynes/Foulis	1961		223	•	•	D	
Pursuit of Victory	Kling	Bodley Head	1956		192	•		D	•
Racing Driver's World (A)	Caracciola	Cassell	1962		232	•		D	
Racing Motorist (A)	Davis	Iliffe	1949		219	•	•	D	•
Racing Round the World	Lurani	Foulis	ND		220	•		D	•
Renault	St Loup	Bodley Head	1957		316	•		E	•

Title	Author	Publisher	1st Ed'n	Later Ed'ns	Pages	Illus	Index	Rate	Text
Renault. Louis	Rhodes	Cassell	1969		235	•	•	D	
Rickenbacker	Rickenbacker	Hutchinson	1968		316	•	•	D	
Risk Life, Risk Limb	Evans	Pelham	1968		128	•		E	
Roberta Cowell's Story	Cowell	Heinemann	1954		153	•		E	
Rolls. Charles and the Hendre	Jenkins	Monmouth Hist & Educat Tr'st	1974		24			C	
Rolls. The Hon.C.S.	Meynall	Newnes	1955		48	•		C	
Rolls. The Hon.C.S.	Axton	Monmouth Hist & Educat Tr'st	1977		32	•		C	
Rolls. Man of Speed	Meynell	Bodley Head	1953	1961	159	•	•	E	•
Rolls. C.S. Pioneer Aviator	Bruse	Monmouth Hist & Educat Tr'st	1978		48	•		C	
Rolls and Royce Story (The)	Morgan	Collins	1971		46	•		C	
Rolls Royce Men	Rowland	Lutterworth	1969		130	•		C	
Rolls of Rolls-Royce	Montagu	Cassell	1966	1967	250	•	•	D	•
Royce. Fredrick Henry	Smith	Longmans Green	1945	1946/8	34	•		C	
Royce. Sir Henry. The Life of	Pemberton	Selwyn & Blount	ND		280	•	•	C	•
Rudolph Caracciola	Meisl	Foulis	1955		175	•	•	D	
Safety Last	Eyston	Vincent	1975		158	•		E	
Searching for Pirate Treasure in the Cocos Islands	Campbell	Stokes	1931		279	•		D	
Seven Year Twitch	Chambers	Foulis	1963		225	•		E	
Silver Ghosts and Silver Dawn	Rowbotham	Constable	1970		290	•	•	C	•
Sir Henry Segrave	Posthumus	Batsford	1961		227	•	•	D	
Speed on Wheels	Campbell	Low	1949		214	•	•	D	
Speed. Authentic Life of Sir Malcolm Campbell	Day	Hutchinson	1931		288	•	•	D	
Speed Was My Life	Neubauer	Barrie/Rockliffe	1958		207	•	•	D	•

The Constant Search

Title	Author	Publisher	1st Ed'n	Later Ed'ns	Pages	Illus	Index	Rate	Text
Split Seconds	Mays	Foulis	1951		306	•		D	•
Stirling Moss	Burke		1962		110	•		E	
Stirling Moss	Raymond	M.R.P	1953		199	•	•	E	
Story So Far (The)	Moss	Kimber	1967		216	•		E	
Ten Years of Motors and Motor Racing	Jarrott	Grant Richards	1906	1912 1928	297	•	•	C	•
Ten Years of Motors and Motor Racing	Jarrott	Foulis		1956	297	•	•	D	
They Call Me Mister 500	Granatelli	Regnery	1969		341	•		D	
Those Bentley Days	Hillstead	Faber & Faber	1953		196	•	•	D	•
Today and Tomorrow	Ford	Heinemann	1926		281	•		D	
Touch Wood	Hamilton	Barrie & Rockliff	1960		229	•	•	D	•
Turn at the Wheel (A)	Moss	Kimber	1961		239	•		E	
Twain Have Met (The)	Chula	Foulis	1956	1957	299	•	•	E	
Two Brave Brothers	Morriss	Clifton	ND		221	•		C	•
Wall Smacker	De Paolo	Thompson	1935		271	•		D	
Wheel Patter	Colley	Talbot	1951		175	•		D	•
Wheels to Fortune	Leasor	Bodley Head	1954		160	•	•	D	•
When the Flag Drops	Brabham	Kimber	1971		240	•		E	
William Morris — Viscount Nuffield	Overy	Europa	1976		151	•	•	E	
W.O. — Autobiography of W.O.Bentley	Bentley	Hutchinson	1958	1961	213	•	•	D	•
Works Driver	Taruffi	Temple Press	1964		222	•	•	D	
World on Wheels (The)	Duncan	Duncan	ND 1920s		1200	•		C	•

74

75

76

77

78

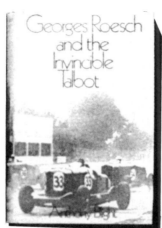

79

80

81

82

83

84

Section G

Histories (however titled)

Title	Author	Publisher	1st Ed'n	Later Ed'ns	Pages	Illus	Index	Rate	Text
Section G 1									
Motoring									
American Car since 1775 (The)	Automobile Quarterly	Bailey	1971		504	•		D	
Cars. The Story of	'Anon'	Oldbourne	1961		92	•		E	
Early History of Motoring (The)	Johnson	Burrow	ND		80	•		C	•
Early History of the Motor Car 1769-1897	Kidner	Oakwood	1946		50	•		D	
Forty Years of Motoring	Young	Paul	1960		190	•		F	
From Steam Carts to Mini Cars	Snellgrove	Longmans	1961		128	•	•	E	•
History and Development of Light Cars	Caunter	HMSO	1957		120	•	•	E	•
History and Development of Road Transport	Paterson	Pitman	1927		118	•		D	

Title	Author	Publisher	1st Ed'n	Later Ed'ns	Pages	Illus	Index	Rate	Text
History of Coachbuilding	Oliver	Cassell	1962		216	•	•	D	
History of English Carriages and Motor Cars	Smith		1896					C	
History of Inland Transport and Communication in England	Pratt	Paul/ Trench/ Trubner	1912		532	•		C	•
History of Motorised Vehicles 1769-1946	Kidner	Clymer	c1950		160	•		D	
History of Motors and Motoring Vol.1	Frostick	Haynes/Foulis	1975		230	•		D	
Vol.2	Frostick	Haynes/Foulis	1976		227	•		D	
History of Motor Racing (A)	Boddy	Orbis	1977	1979/80	332	•	•	E	
History of Sports Cars	Georgano	Rainbird	1970		320	•	•	D	
History of the Art of Coachbuilding	Thrupp							B	
History of the London Taxicab	Georgano	David & Charles	1972		180	•	•	E	•
History of the Motor Car	Ray	Pergammon	1966		119	•	•	E	
History of the Racing Car — Man and Machine	Lurani	Crowell	1972		319	•	•	D	•
History of Ten Years of Automobilism 1896-1906	Montagu	Car Illustrated	1906		124	•		C	•
History of Transport (A)	Georgano	Dent	1972		311	•	•	D	
History of the World's Classic Cars	Hough & Frostick	Allen & Unwin	1963		190	•		D	
History of the World's High Performance Cars	Hough & Frostick	Allen & Unwin	1967		189	•	•	D	
History of the World's Racing Cars	Hough & Frostick	Allen & Unwin	1965		190	•		E	
History of the World's Sports Cars	Hough	Allen & Unwin	1961		223	•	•	E	
History on the Road	Anderson	Hamlyn	1958		61	•		F	

The Constant Search

Title	Author	Publisher	1st Ed'n	Later Ed'ns	Pages	Illus	Index	Rate	Text
Illustrated History of Transport	Ridley	Heinemann	1969		185	•	•	D	
Indianapolis Race History	Clymer	Clymer	1946		318	•		D	
Light Car (The) A Technical History	Caunter	HMSO	1970		191	•	•	E	
Land Transport. Mechanical Road Vehicles Part 1	Forward	HMSO	1926	1948	91	•		E	
Part 2	Forward	HMSO	1936		89	•	•	E	
London Motor Show 1930 (The)	Dalton	Dalton Watson	1970		318	•		E	
Lost Causes of Motoring	Montagu	Cassell	1960		224	•	•	D	•
Lost Causes of Motoring Vol. 1 Europe	Montagu	Cassell	1969		258	•	•	E	•
Lost Causes of Motoring Vol. 2 Europe	Montagu	Cassell	1971		322	•	•	E	•
Memories of Men and Motor Cars	Davis	Seeley/Service	1965		273	•	•	E	•
Men, Money and Motors	MacManus & Beasley	Harpers	1930		284			D	
Mixed Blessing. The Motor Car in Britain	Buchanan	Hill	1958		221	•	•	E	
Motorcade	Hammond	Bell	1969		248	•	•	E	
Motor Car (The)	Brabazon							C	
Motor Car. (The) A History and Souvenir	Hooper	Keller	1908		NN	•	•	C	•
Motor Car (The). and its Story	Gibson	Seeley	1927		185	•	•	D	
Motor Car Lover's Companion (The)	Various	Allen & Unwin	1965		292	•		E	
Motoring Cavalcade	Bentley	Odhams	1953		143	•	•	E	•
Motoring for the Million	Henslowe	Hutchinson	1922		78	•		D	•

Title	Author	Publisher	1st Ed'n	Later Ed'ns	Pages	Illus	Index	Rate	Text
Motoring History	Rolt	Studio Vista	1964		158	•	•	E	•
Motoring Today and Tomorrow	Cottenham	Methuen	1928		155	•		D	•
Motoring Through the Years								D	
Motoring Without Fears	Cottenham	Methuen	1928		102	•		D	•
Pageant of Transport Throughout the Ages (The)	Boulton	Sampson & Low	ND 1930s		238	•	•	D	
Passenger Cars 1863-1904	Nicholson	Blandford	1970		156	•		E	
Passenger Cars 1905-1912	Nicholson	Blandford	1971		162	•	•	E	
Passenger Transport in Britain. Story of	Joyce	Allan	1967		208	•	•	E	
Picture History of Motoring (A)	Rolt	Hulton	1957		160	•	•	D	
Picture History of the Automobile (A)	Roberts	Ward Lock	1973		144	•		E	
Picture History of the Motor Car (A)	Olyslager	Olyslager*				•		E	
Practical History of the Motor Car		IPC	ND		71	•		E	
Private Motor Car Collections of Great Britain	Hugo	Dalton Watson	1973		207	•	•	E	•
Record of Motor Racing (A)	Rose	M.R.P		1949	325	•		C	•
Romance of Transport (The)	Hawks	Harrap	1931		332	•	•	D	
Shape of the Motor Car (The)	Everett	Hutchinson	ND 1950s		166	•	•	E	
Story of Cars (The)	Roberts & Wood	Collins	1975		61	•	•	F	
Story of the Wheel	Boumphrey	Black	1932		96	•	•	D	•
Transport Museums	Simmons	Allen & Unwin	1970		300	•	•	E	•
Treasury of the Automobile	Stein	Ridge	1961		248	•		E	•
Wheel (The)	Sommerfield	Nicholson & Watson	1938		248	•		D	

In 20 Parts

The Constant Search

Title	Author	Publisher	1st Ed'n	Later Ed'ns	Pages	Illus	Index	Rate	Text
Who, Me? 40 Years of Automobile History	Singabough	Arnold	1940		377	•		D	
Who's Who in the Motor Trade	'Anon'	Motor Commerce	1934		167	•		E	
Who's Who in the Motor Industry	Temple Press	Temple Press	1961		607	•	•	E	
World's Automobiles 1862-1962 (The)	Doyle & Georgano	Temple Press	1932 44/57	1959 /63	180			D	•
World's Automobiles 1880-1955 (The)	Doyle	Temple Press	1931	1944 /57	175			D	•
World's Automobiles 1881-1931 (The)	Doyle	Temple Press	1931		112			D	•
World's Motor Museums (The)	Nicholson	Dent	1970		142	•		E	•

Section G 2

Histories. Marque

Title	Author	Publisher	1st Ed'n	Later Ed'ns	Pages	Illus	Index	Rate	Text
AC Cars	Watkins	David & Charles	1976		160	•		E	
AC Cars. History of		Fullerton & Lloyd	1952		100		•	D	
AC Cobra 1962-1969	Various	Brooklands	ND		100	•		F	
AC	Watkins	Haynes/Foulis	1976		159	•		D	
Alfa Romeo	Hull & Lurani	Haynes/Foulis	1975		157	•		E	
Alfa Romeo	Hull & Slater	Cassell	1964		511	•	•	C	
Alfa Romeo Milano	Frostick	Dalton Watson	1974		234	•	App	E	
Alfa Romeo Story (The)	Wherry	Chilton	1969		270	•		D	
Allard	Kinsella	Haynes/Foulis	1977		199	•	•	F	
Allard	Lush	M.R.P	1977		207	•	App	E	
Alvis Car (The)	Day	Day	1965		170	•	App	D	
Annals of Mercedes Benz Motor Vehicles and Engines		Mercedes Benz	ND		223	•	•	C	

Title	Author	Publisher	1st Ed'n	Later Ed'ns	Pages	Illus	Index	Rate	Text
Another Vintage Bentley Book	Various	Brooklands	ND		60	•		F	
Armstrong Siddeley Cars 1945-1960	Various	Brooklands	ND		100	•		F	
Aston Martin — Story of a Sports Car	Coram	M.R.P	1957		348	•	•	C	
Aston Martin 1914-1940	Hunter	Transport Bookman	1976		192	•		E	
Aston Martin 1963-1972	Gershon	Oxford Illus. Press	1975		136	•		E	
Austin Healey (The) Story of the Big Healeys	Healey	Gentry	1977		256	•	•	E	
Austin Healey (The)	Healey & Wisdom	Cassell	1960		128	•		D	
Austin Healey '100' 1952-1959	Various	Brooklands	ND		100	•		F	
Austin Healey '3000' 1959-1967	Various	Brooklands	ND		100	•		F	
Austin 1905-1952	Wyatt	David & Charles	1981		298	•	•	F	
Austin Racing History	Harrison	M.R.P	1949		56	•		E	
Austin 7 in the '30s	Various	Brooklands	ND		100	•		F	
Austin Seven Cars 1930-1935	Various	Brooklands	ND		60	•		F	
Austin Seven (The)	Wyatt	Macdonald	1968		191	•	•	E	
Austin Seven (The)	Wyatt	David & Charles		1972	215	•	•	E	
Austin '10' 1932-1939	Various	Brooklands	ND		100	•		F	
Bentley. Another Vintage Book	Various	Brooklands	ND		60	•		F	
Bentley. All the Pre-War — as New	Sedgwick	Bentley Driver's Club	1976		131			D	
Bentleys at Le Mans	Benjafield	M.R.P	1948		48	•		C	
Bentley Bedside Book (The)	Young	B.D.C	1961		261	•		D	
Bentley. The Book of the	Ulyett	Parrish	1965		120	•		D	
Bentley Boys. The Other	Nagle	Harrap	1964		224	•	•	D	
Bentley Cars 1919-29	Various	Brooklands	ND		60	•		F	

The Constant Search

Title	Author	Publisher	1st Ed'n	Later Ed'ns	Pages	Illus	Index	Rate	Text
Bentley Cars 1929-34	Various	Brooklands	ND		60	•		F	
Bentley Cars 1934-39	Various	Brooklands	ND		100	•		F	
Bentley Cars 1940-45	Various	Brooklands	ND		102	•		F	
Bentley Cars 1945-50	Clarke	Brooklands	ND		66	•		F	
Bentleys. Twenty Years of Crewe	Sedgwick	B.D.C	1973		52	•		D	
Bentley. 50 Years of the Marque	Green	Dalton Watson	1969	1973/74	295	•	•	F	
Bentley. The 4½ litre	Berthon & Stainer							D	
Bentley Golden Jubilee Book	Anon	B.D.C	1969		160	•		D	
Bentley in the Thirties	Various	Brooklands	ND		62	•		F	
Bentley Motor Cars 1921-1970 A Bibliography	Paterson							D	
Bentley. A Racing History of 1921-1931	Berthon	Bodley Head	1956		143	•		C	
Bentley. The 6½ litre	Berthon	Profile Publications	1966		11	•		E	
Bentley. The 3 litre	Berthon	Profile Publications	1966		11	•		E	
Bentley. The 3½ and 4¼ litre	Oliver	Profile Publications	1966		11	•		E	
Bentley. A Vintage Book	Various	Brooklands	ND		60	•		F	
Best Car in the World. Story of the	Rolls-Royce	Rolls-Royce	1977		18	•		E	
Best Wheel Forward	Gregoire	Thames & Hudson	1954		194	•		E	•
Beyond Expectations	Hopfinger	Foulis	1954		176	•	•	E	•
BMW. The Bavarian Motor Works	Frostick	Dalton Watson	1976		207	•		E	
Book of the Phantoms	Ullyett	Parrish	1964		140	•		D	
Book of the Silver Ghost	Ullyett	Parrish	1963		NN	•		E	
British Leyland Minis	Marshall & Fraser	Foulis	1965	1968/73	266	•	•	E	
Bugatti Story (The)	Bugatti	Souvenir	1966		206	•	App	D	
Bugatti Story (The)	Boddy	Sports Car Press	1960		115	•		D	

Title	Author	Publisher	1st Ed'n	Later Ed'ns	Pages	Illus	Index	Rate	Text
Bugatti. The Complete Book of	Kestler	Libraria dell Automobile	1980		68	•		F	
Bugatti	Conway	Foulis	1963	1964 /5/8	451	•	•	C	
Bugatti	Barker	Ballantine	1971		160	•		E	
Bugatti	Conway	Foulis		1974	463	•	•	E	
Bugattis. The Amazing	Haslam & Garner Harvey & Conway	Design Council	1979		84	•		E	
Bugatti	Hucke	Auto-und Motorrad Museums	1976		316	•		F	
Bugatti Doubles Arbres	Jarraud	L'Automobiliste	1977		254	•	•	F	
Bugatti Book (The)	Eaglesfield & Hampton	M.R.P	1954	1956 /8/60	374	•	•	C	
Bugatti. Ettore	Bradley	M.R.P	1948		151	•	•	D	
Bugatti. Evolution of a Style	Kestler	Lausanne	1977		141	•		F	
Bugatti Register & Data Book	Conway	B.D.C	1962		108			C	
Bugatti Automobiles et Autorails	Lot	Gyss	1979		225	•	ann'xs	E	
Bugatti — Thoroughbreds from Molsheim	Dumont	E.P.A	1975		519	•		F	
Bugatti. Type 35 (The)	Eaton	Profile Publications	1966		11	•		E	
Bugatti. Type 57 (The)	Conway	Profile Publications	1966		11	•		E	
Bugatti. Grand Prix	Conway	Foulis	1968		224	•	•	D	
Buick Cars 1929-1939	Various	Brooklands	ND		60	•		F	
Bullnose Morris (The)	Jarman & Barraclough	Macdonald	1965		257	•	•	D	
Bullnose and Flatnose Morris (The)	Jarman & Barraclough	David & Charles	1976		277	•	•	F	
Camaro 1966-1970	Various	Brooklands	ND		100	•		F	
Cars that Got Away (The)	Frostick	Cassell	1968		104	•		E	
Case History	Smith	Autosport	1958		278	•	•	E	

85

86

87

88

89

90

91

92

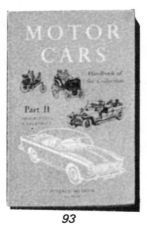

93

94

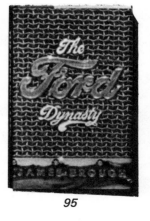

95

Title	Author	Publisher	1st Ed'n	Later Ed'ns	Pages	Illus	Index	Rate	Text
Chain Drive Frazer Nash (The)	Thirlby	Macdonald	1965		208	•	App	D	
Chrysler Cars 1930-39	Various	Brooklands	ND		100	•		F	
Citroen Traction Avant 1934-1957	Various	Brooklands	ND		100	•		F	
Citroen 1919-1939	Various	Brooklands	ND		60	•		F	
Citroen	Broad	Luscombe	1975		144	•	•	D	
Coachbuilt Packard (The)	Pfau	Dalton Watson	1973		224	•		E	
Cobra Story (The)	Shelby	Trident	1966		272	•		D	
Complete Mercedes Story (The)	Nitske	Macmillan	1955		167	•	•	D	
Cord Front Drive (The)	Huntingdon	Motor Books International		1975	224	•		E	
Corvette Cars 1955-64	Various	Brooklands	ND		100	•		F	
Cooper Story (The)	Cooper	M.R.P	1950		25	•		D	
Cooper Cars Year Book 1954	Cooper	Town & Country	1954		64	•		D	
Daimler 1896-1946	Nixon	Foulis	ND		236	•	•	C	
Daimler Tradition (The)	Smith	Transport Bookman	1972	1980	334	•		E	
Datsun 240Z & 260Z 1970-1977	Various	Brooklands	ND		100	•		F	
Delage Series D8 (the)	Buckley	Profile Publications	1966		11	•		E	
Dodge Cars 1924-1938	Various	Brooklands	ND		60	•		F	
Duesenberg	Elbert	Post Books	1951		168	•		D	
English Racing Automobiles Ltd. The History of	Weguelin	White Mouse	1981		288	•	•	F	•
E.R.A. The Story of	Lloyd	M.R.P	1949		46	•		C	
Ferrari Cars 1946-56	Various	Brooklands	ND		60	•		F	
Ferrari Cars 1957-62	Various	Brooklands	ND		100	•		F	
Ferrari Cars 1962-66	Various	Brooklands	ND		100	•		F	

Title	Author	Publisher	1st Ed'n	Later Ed'ns	Pages	Illus	Index	Rate	Text
Ferrari Cars 1966-69	Various	Brooklands	ND		100	•		F	
Ferrari Cars 1969-1973	Various	Brooklands	ND		100	•		F	
Ferrari (The)	Tanner	Foulis	1959		201	•	•	D	
Ferrari (The)	Tanner	Foulis		1960	201	•	•	D	
Ferrari (The)	Tanner	Foulis		1964	316	•	•	D	
Ferrari (The)	Tanner	Foulis		1968	396	•	•	D	
Ferrari (The)	Tanner	Haynes/Foulis		1974	310	•	•	D	
Ferrari	Nye/Tanner	Haynes/Foulis		1979	543	•	•	E	
Ferrari	Setright	Haynes/Foulis	1975	1976	159	•		E	
Ferrari	Rogliatti	Hamlyn	1973		255	•		E	
Ferrari V-12 Sports Car 1946-1956 (The)	Pritchard	Arco	1970		80	•		E	
Fiat	Shimwell	Luscombe	1977		163	•	•	E	
Fiat	Sedgwick	Batsford	1974		352	•	•	E	
Fiat — a 50 Year's Record	Mondadori	Fiat	1950		303	•		D	
Ford Dynasty (The)	Brough	Allen	1978		352	•	•	E	
Ford Mustang 1964-67	Various	Brooklands	ND		100	•		F	
Frazer Nash	Thirlby	Haynes/Foulis	1977		206	•	•	F	
Georges Roesch and the Invincible Talbot	Blight	Grenville	1970		496	•	App	F	
Grand Prix Bugatti	Conway	Foulis	1968		224	•	•	D	
Healey — The Handsome Brute	Harvey	Oxford	1978		239	•	•	E	
Healeys and Austin Healeys	Browning & Needham	Foulis	1970	1973/6	315	•		E	
Hispano Suiza V 12 (The)	Boddy	Profile Publications	1966		11	•		E	
Hudson and Railton Cars 1936-1940	Various	Brooklands	ND		100	•		F	
Illustrated History of the Bentley Car	Bentley	Allen & Unwin	1964		191	•		D	

Title	Author	Publisher	1st Ed'n	Later Ed'ns	Pages	Illus	Index	Rate	Text
Invicta S Type 4.5 litre (The)	Buckley	Profile Publications	1966		11	•		E	
Jaguar Saloon Cars	Skilleter	Haynes/Foulis	1980		602	•	•	E	
Jaguar 'E' Type. A Collector's Guide	Skilleter	M.R.P	1979		128	•	App	E	
Jaguar Sports Cars	Skilleter	Haynes/Foulis	1976		360	•	•	E	
Jaguar Tradition. The	Frostick	Dalton Watson	1973	1975	208	•		E	
Jaguar & S.S. Cars 1931-1937	Various	Brooklands	ND		60	•		F	
Jaguar and S.S. Cars 1937-1947	Various	Brooklands	ND		60	•		F	
Jaguar. A Biography	Montagu	Cassell	1961		273	•	•	D	
Jaguar Cars 1948-1951	Various	Brooklands	ND		60	•		F	
Jaguar Cars 1951-1953	Various	Brooklands	ND		60	•		F	
Jaguar		British Leyland	ND		64	•		C	
Jaguar	Montagu	Haynes/Foulis	1975		159	•		D	
Jaguar Cars 1954-1955	Various	Brooklands	ND		60	•		F	
Jaguar Cars 1955-1957	Various	Brooklands	ND		60	•		F	
Jaguar Cars 1957-1961	Various	Brooklands	ND		100	•		F	
Jaguar Cars 1961-1964	Various	Brooklands	ND		100	•		F	
Jaguar Cars 1964-1968	Various	Brooklands	ND		100	•		F	
Jaguar Sports Cars 1957-1960	Various	Brooklands	ND		100	•		F	
Jaguar 'E' Type 1961-66	Various	Brooklands	ND		100	•		F	
Jaguar 'E' Type 1966-71	Various	Brooklands	ND		100	•		F	
Jaguar 'E' Type 1971-75	Various	Brooklands	ND		100	•		F	
Jensen Healey Story (The)	Browning & Blunsden	M.R.P	1974		160	•	•	E	
Jensen Cars 1946-1967	Various	Brooklands	ND		100	•		F	
Jensen Cars 1967-1969	Various	Brooklands	ND		100	•		F	
Jensen Interceptor 1966-1976	Various	Brooklands	ND		100	•		F	

The Constant Search

Title	Author	Publisher	1st Ed'n	Later Ed'ns	Pages	Illus	Index	Rate	Text
Jensen Cars 1976-1979	Various	Brooklands	ND		100	•		F	
Lamborghini Cars 1964-1970	Various	Brooklands	ND		100	•		F	
Lamborghini Cars 1970-1980	Various	Brooklands	ND		100	•		F	
Lamborghini. History of	Box & Crump	Transport Bookman	1974		169	•		E	
Lanchester Motor Cars	Bird & Hutton Stott	Cassell	1965		240	•	•	D	
Lancia. The Shield and the Flag	Trow	David & Charles	1980		270	•	•	F	
Land Rover 1948-73	Various	Brooklands	ND		60	•		F	
Linea Fiat	Fiat	Fiat	1967		137	•		D	
Lotus Elan 1962-73	Various	Brooklands	ND		100	•		F	
Lotus 49	Hodges	Leventhal	1970		80	•		E	
Lotus — Story of the Marque	Smith	M.R.P	1958	1961	176	•		C	
Lotus. The Story of	Smith	M.R.P	1976		191	•	•	E	
Lotus. The First Ten Years	Smith	M.R.P	1958		144	•		C	
Magic of a Name (The)	Nockolds	Foulis	1938	many to 1966	283	•	•	D/E	
Maintaining the Breed	Thornley	M.R.P	1950	many	92	•		D/E	•
Maserati. A History	Pritchard	David & Charles	1976		399	•	•	E	
Maserati Cars 1965-70	Various	Brooklands	ND		100	•		F	
Maserati	Boschi	Borgo	1965		224	•		D	
Maserati Cars 1970-75	Various	Brooklands	ND		100	•		F	
Maserati — Sports, Racing and G.T. Cars 1926-75	Crump & Box	Haynes/Foulis	1975		299	•		E	
Men and Machines	Wilson & Reader	Weidenfeld & Nicholson	1958		187	•	•	D	
Mercedes Benz Cars 1949-1954	Various	Brooklands	ND		100	•		F	
Mercedes Benz Competition Cars 1950-1957	Various	Brooklands	ND		100	•		F	
Mercedes Benz	Davis	Muller	1956		224	•	•	D	

Title	Author	Publisher	1st Ed'n	Later Ed'ns	Pages	Illus	Index	Rate	Text
Mercedes Benz Cars 1954-1957	Various	Brooklands	ND		100	•		F	
Mercedes Benz Cars 1957-1961	Various	Brooklands	ND		100	•		D	
Mercedes Benz Story (The)	Steinwedel	Chilton	1969		227	•		D	
Mercedes Benz 300SL	Nitske	Motor Books International	1974		164	•		E	
Mercedes Benz Type 600		Mercedes Benz	ND		30	•		C	
Mercedes. The Mighty	Frostick	Dalton Watson	1971		206	•	•	E	
MG Cars in the 30s	Various	Brooklands	ND		102	•		F	
MG Cars 1929-1934	Various	Brooklands	ND		64	•		F	
MG Cars 1935-1940	Various	Brooklands	ND		64	•		F	
MG Cars 1940-1947	Various	Brooklands	ND		80	•		F	
MG Cars 1948-1951	Various	Brooklands	ND		64	•		F	
MG Cars 1952-1954	Various	Brooklands	ND		64	•		F	
MG Cars 1955-1957	Various	Brooklands	ND		64	•		F	
MG Cars 1957-1959	Various	Brooklands	ND		66	•		F	
MG Cars 1959-1962	Various	Brooklands	ND		100	•		F	
MG Midget 1961-1969	Various	Brooklands	ND		100	•		F	
MG MGB 1962-1970	Various	Brooklands	ND		100	•		F	
MG MGB 1970-1980	Various	Brooklands	ND		100	•		F	
MG MGB GT 1965-1980	Various	Brooklands	ND		100	•		F	
MG Story (The)	Wherry	Chilton	1967		205	•		D	
MG The Magic of	Allison	Dalton Watson	1972	1974/6	212	•	•	E	
MG Sports Car. The Story of the	McComb	Dent	1972		206	•	•	D	
MG	McComb	Osprey	1978	1979	300	•	•	E	
Mini Story (The)	Pomeroy	Temple Press	1964		176	•	•	E	

The Constant Search

Title	Author	Publisher	1st Ed'n	Later Ed'ns	Pages	Illus	Index	Rate	Text
Morgan	Bowden	Gentry	1972	1973/4	191	•	•	E	
Morgan Three Wheeler 1930-1952 (The)	Various	Brooklands	ND		60	•		F	
Morgan Cars 1936-60	Various	Brooklands	ND		66	•		F	
Morgan Cars 1960-1970	Various	Brooklands	ND		100	•		F	
More Healeys	Healey	Gentry	1978		224	•	•	E	
More Morgan	Bowden	Gentry	1976		223	•	•	E	
Morgan Cars 1969-1979	Various	Brooklands	ND		100	•		F	
Morris Minor 1948-70	Various	Brooklands	ND		100	•		F	
Motoring Entente	Nickols & Karslake	Cassell	1956		219	•	•	C	•
Nash Metropolitan 1954-1961	Various	Brooklands	ND		60	•		F	
New Ford (The)	Brown	Oxford University	1928	1929	142	•	•	D	
Packard Cars 1920-42	Various	Brooklands	ND		100	•		F	
Packard. The Coachbuilt	Pfau	Dalton Watson	1973		224	•		E	
Pantera Cars 1970-73	Various	Brooklands	ND		60	•		F	
Pantera & Mangusta 1969-74	Various	Brooklands	ND		60	•		F	
Phantoms. The Book of	Ullyett	Parrish	1964		140	•		D	
Pontiac GTO 1964-70	Various	Brooklands	ND		100	•		F	
Porsche Cars 1952-56	Various	Brooklands	ND		60	•		F	
Porsche Cars 1957-60	Various	Brooklands	ND		60	•		F	
Porsche Cars 1960-64	Various	Brooklands	ND		100	•		F	
Porsche Cars 1964-68	Various	Brooklands	ND		100	•		F	
Porsche Cars 1968-72	Various	Brooklands	ND		100	•		F	
Porsche Cars 1972-75	Various	Brooklands	ND		100	•		F	
Porsche Cars in the 60s	Various	Brooklands	ND		100	•		F	
Porsche 914 1969-75	Various	Brooklands	ND		100	•		F	
Porsche 911 Story (The)	Frere	Stephens	1976		187	•	•	E	

Title	Author	Publisher	1st Ed'n	Later Ed'ns	Pages	Illus	Index	Rate	Text
Porsche Book (The)	Boschen & Barth	Stephens	1978		472	•		E	
Porsche. One Hundred Years of	Schrader & Strache	Porsche	1975		216	•		E	
Porsche 911. Collec.No.1 1965-1975	Various	Brooklands	ND		60	•		F	
Porsche Story (The)	Weitmann	Stephens	1967		256	•		E	
Porsche Turbo.Collec.No.1 1975-1980	Various	Brooklands	ND		60	•		F	
Porsches. The Racing	Frere	Stephens	1973		211	•		E	
Quai de Javel — Quai Andre Citroen	Dumont	E.P.A.	1973		NN	•		E	
Racing Coopers (The)	Owen	Cassell	1959		243	•		D	
Racing History of the Bentley Car (The)	Berthon	Bodley Head	1956		143	•		C	
Railton and Hudson Cars 1936-40	Various	Brooklands	ND		100	•		F	
Renault 1898-1966	Richard	Foulis	1966		176	•		D	
Riley	Birmingham	Foulis	1965	1974	248	•	•	D	
Riley Cars 1932-35	Various	Brooklands	ND		66	•		F	
Riley Cars 1936-39	Various	Brooklands	ND		66	•		F	
Riley Cars 1940-45	Various	Brooklands	ND		60	•		F	
Riley Cars 1945-50	Various	Brooklands	ND		60	•		F	
Riley Cars 1950-55	Various	Brooklands	ND		60	•		F	
Rolls & Royce Story (The)	Morgan	Collins	1971		46	•		D	
Rolls-Royce Alpine Compendium	Leefe	Transport Bookman	1913	1973	163	•		E	
Rolls-Royce. The American	Soutter	Mowbray	1976		239	•	•	E	
Rolls-Royce and the Great Victory	Rolls-Royce	Rolls-Royce	1919	1972	267	•		C/D	
Rolls-Royce Armoured Cars and the Great Victory (Reprinted 1972 in Rolls Royce and the Great Victory)	Anon	Rolls-Royce	c1919		76	•		C D	

The Constant Search

Title	Author	Publisher	1st Ed'n	Later Ed'ns	Pages	Illus	Index	Rate	Text
Rolls-Royce and Lockheed — partners in Adversity	Critchley	Lon & Atlantic	1971		19			D	
Rolls-Royce and Bentley Cars — a Brief Guide to	Adams	Adams & Oliver	c1955	3rd 1965	21	•		D	
Rolls-Royce and Bentley Cars 1925-55. A Brief Guide to	Adams	Adams & Oliver		1965	40		•	D	
Rolls-Royce and Bentley Cars 1925-1965. A Brief Guide to	Adams	Adams & Oliver		4th 1972	36	•		D	
Rolls-Royce Cars 1930-1935	Various	Brooklands	ND		60	•		F	
Rolls-Royce Cars 1935-1940	Various	Brooklands	ND		60	•		F	
Rolls-Royce Cars 1940-1950	Various	Brooklands	ND		100	•		F	
Rolls-Royce Catalogue 1910-1911	Wood	E.P	1973		70	•		E	
Rolls-Royce 1906-1939. Coachwork on	Dalton	Dalton Watson	1973		448	•	•	E	
Rolls-Royce Companion (The)	Ullyett	Paul	1969		143	•	•	D	
Rolls-Royce — The Elegance Continues	Dalton	Dalton Watson	1971		264	•		E	
Rolls-Royce. The Engines Were	Harker	Macmillan (N.Y)	1979		202	•	•	E	
Rolls-Royce — Fact and Legend	Schoup	R.R.O.C	1971		46	•		D	
Rolls-Royce. 40/50 hp Ghosts, Phantoms and Spectres	Oldham	Foulis	1974		262	•	•	E	
Rolls-Royce from the Wings	Foxley Norris	Oxford Illus	1976		176	•		D	
Rolls-Royce. Growth of a Firm	Lloyd	Macmillan	1978		164	•	•	E	
Rolls-Royce. The History of the Car	Bennett	Oxford Illus	1974		279	•	•	E	
Rolls-Royce Motor Cars 1903-1907. A History of Vol.1	Morton	Foulis	1964		424	•	•	D	
Rolls-Royce. The Hyphen in	Oldham	Foulis	1967		194	•	•	D	
Rolls-Royce in America	De Campi	Dalton Watson	1975		256	•	•	E	

96

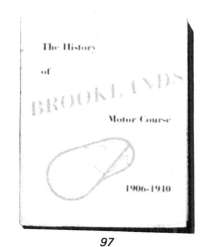

97

98

99

100

101

102

103

104

105

106

The Constant Search

Title	Author	Publisher	1st Ed'n	Later Ed'ns	Pages	Illus	Index	Rate	Text
Rolls-Royce in the Twenties	Various	Brooklands	ND		64	•		F	
Rolls-Royce in the Thirties	Various	Brooklands	ND		66	•		F	
Rolls-Royce Cars in War (Reprinted in Rolls-Royce and the Great Victory 1972)	Anon	Rolls Royce	c1919		76	•		C	
Rolls-Royce and Bentley Periodicals. An Index to	T.C.Clarke	Transport Bookman	ND 1970s		42			E	•
Rolls-Royce — A Living Tradition	Buckley	Rolls-Royce	c1958		33	•		D	
Rolls-Royce — The Living Legend	Post Motor Books	Post Motor Books	1958		383	•	•	D	
Rolls-Royce Memories	Buist	Cambridge University	1926		93	•		C	
Rolls-Royce The Merlin at War	Lloyd	Macmillan	1978		188	•	•	E	
Rolls-Royce Motor Car (The)	Bird & Hallows	Batsford	1964	1966/8 1972/5	320 344	• •	• •	E E	
Rolls-Royce Motor Car. Notes for a Bibliography of the	Schroder	Schroder	1971		19			D	•
Rolls-Royce. The 1905 3 Cylinder	Oliver	Profile Publications	1967		12	•		E	
Rolls-Royce Phantom 1 (The)	Oliver	Profile Publications	1966		12	•		E	
Rolls-Royce Phantom II (The)	Oliver	Profile Publications	1973		24	•		E	
Rolls-Royce Phantom II Continental (The)	Gentile	Dalton Watson	1980		272	•	•	F	
Rolls-Royce Phantoms (The)	Tubbs	Hamilton	1964		64	•		D	
Rolls-Royce — Power of Grace	Allport	Haynes	1963		123	•		D	
Rolls-Royce, Pre-War	Kobayshi	Nigensha	1971	1972	128	•		C	
Rolls on the Rocks	Gray	Compton	1971		89		App	E	
Rolls Royce Silver Shadow (The)	Bolster	Osprey	1979		135	•	•	E	
Rolls-Royce Silver Ghost	Bird	Profile Publications	1967		12	•		E	

Title	Author	Publisher	1st Ed'n	Later Ed'ns	Pages	Illus	Index	Rate	Text
Rolls-Royce. Story of the Best Car in the World	Garnier	IPC/ Autocar Special	1977			•		E	
Rolls-Royce Small Horse Power Engines	Haynes & Grigsby	R.R.E.C	1977		103	•		D	
Rolls-Royce. Those Elegant	Dalton	Dalton Watson	1967 /8	1970/2 1973/8	319	•	•	E	
Rolls-Royce Twenty (The)	Fasal	Fasal	1979		560	•	•	E	
Rolls-Royce. The Years of Endeavour	Lloyd	Macmillan	1978		265	•	•	E	
Rolls-Royce. The Yellow	Pearl	Pocket Books	1965		159	•		D	
Rover Cars	Oliver	Cassell	1971		220	•	•	D	
The Rover	Robson	Stephens	1977		176	•	•	E	
Rover Memories	Hough & Frostick	Allen & Unwin	1966		96	•		D	
Saab — The Innovator	Chatterton	David & Charles	1980		160	•	•	F	
Salmson Story (The)	Draper	David & Charles	1974		167	•	•	E	
Silver Ghost. The Book of the	Ulyett	Parrish	1963		NN	•	•	E	
Singer Sports Cars 1933-1954	Various	Brooklands	ND		100	•		F	
6C Alfa Romeo (The)	Fusi & Slater	Macdonald	1968		187	•		D	
Small Wonder	Nelson	Hutchinson	1967		304	•	•	E	•
Standard Car 1903-1963 (The)	Davy	Sherbourne	1967		143	•	•	D	
Story of Triumph Sports Cars (The)	Robson	M.R.P	1972		189	•		E	
Studebaker Cars 1923-1939	Various	Brooklands	ND		100	•		F	
Sunbeam Alpine and Tiger 1959-1967	Various	Brooklands	ND		100	•		F	
Three Pointed Star	Moncrieff	Cassell	1955		360	•	•	D	•
Thornycroft Activities 1930	Thornycroft	Thornycroft	1930		40	•		C	
Thornycroft Road Transport Golden Jubilee	Twelvetrees	Thornycroft	1946		95	•		D	

The Constant Search

Title	Author	Publisher	1st Ed'n	Later Ed'ns	Pages	Illus	Index	Rate	Text
Three Wheeler (The)	Watts	Morgan Three Wheeler Club	ND		67	•		E	•
Triumph TR2 and TR3 1952-60	Various	Brooklands	ND		100	•		F	
Triumph TR4 and TR5 1961-1969	Various	Brooklands	ND		100	•		F	
Twenty Silver Ghosts	May	McGraw Hill	1971		140	•		D	
Vanwall	Jenkinson & Posthumus	Stephens	1975		176	•	•	E	
Vanwall Story (The)	Klemantaski & Frostick	Hamilton	1958		64	•		D	
Vauxhall Cars	Acres	Pearson	1957	1961	241	•	•	E	
Vauxhall 1857-1946	Darbyshire	Vauxhall	1946		51	•		E	
Vintage Alvis (The)	Hull & Johnson	David & Charles	1967		400	•	•	D	
Volkswagen Cars 1936-1956	Various	Brooklands	ND		100	•		F	
VW Beetle (The)	Fry	David & Charles	1980		208	•	•	F	
Where Have all the Blowers Gone?	Sedgwick	B.D.C	c1975		20			D	•
Why Dennis — and How	Dennis	Dennis	1945		106	•		C	
Wild Wheel (The)	Garrett	Cresset	1952		220	•		E	•
Wolseley	Nixon	Foulis	1949		156	•	App	D	
Zagato	Fagiuoli & Gerosa	Auto Club D'Italia	1969		105	•		D	

Section G 3

Histories — club, industrial, associations and others

Title	Author	Publisher	1st Ed'n	Later Ed'ns	Pages	Illus	Index	Rate	Text
Acceleration. The Simms Story 1891-1964	Simms	Simms	1964		61	•		E	
Automobiles and Motor Cycles in the US National Museum	Oliver	Smithsonian Inst.	1957		157	•	•	E	

Title	Author	Publisher	1st Ed'n	Later Ed'ns	Pages	Illus	Index	Rate	Text
Bouverie Street to Bowling Green Lane	Armstrong	Hodder & Stoughton	1946		224	•	•	E	•
B.P. Our Industry	B.P	B.P	1947	1948/9 1958/9	472	•	•	E	
B.P. Fifty Years in Pictures	B.P	B.P	1959		158	•		E	
BRDC Golden Jubilee Book 1927-1977	BRDC	BRDC	1977		239	•		D	•
BRDC Handbook	BRDC	BRDC	1967		136	•		D	•
BRDC Silver Jubilee Book	BRDC	BRDC	1952		215	•		D	•
BRDC Year Book	BRDC	BRDC	1967		136	•		D	•
Britain's Motor Industry	Castle	Clarke & Cockeran	1950		328	•	•	D	
Brooklands to Goodwood	Walkerley	Foulis	1961		280	•	•	E	•
Calling All Arms	Fairfax	Hutchinson	ND 1940s		159	•		C	•
David Brown's. The Story of a Family Business 1860-1960	Donnelly	Collins	1960		128	•	•	C	•
Eighty Years of Enterprise (Ransome & Rapier)	Lewis	Ransome & Rapier			112	•		E	
Engineers (The)	Nockolds	Shell	1949		107	•		D	
Firestone Story (The)	Lief	McGraw Hill	1951		437	•	•	D	
First Hundred Years of Thomas Allen	Anon	Allen	1954		64	•		E	
Ford at War	Saunders	Ford	1946		93	•		D	
Ford Through European Eyeglasses 1907-47	Duffield	Mercury	1947		210	•		D	
Fuel	Robertson & Herbert				128	•	•	D	
Gang Warily Royal Scottish Automobile Club (History) 1899-1949			1949		80	•		D	
Golden Milestone (50 Years of the AA)	Keir & Morgan	Automobile Association	1955		240	•	•	F	
Hershey — The World's Largest Autojumble and Antique Auto Show	Hershey	Directional Advertising	1971		95	•		D	

The Constant Search

Title	Author	Publisher	1st Ed'n	Later Ed'ns	Pages	Illus	Index	Rate	Text
History of London Transport (Vol.1)	Barker & Robbins	Allen & Unwin	1963		411	•	App	E	
History of Monza Track 1922-1972		Autodromo di Monza	1972		180	•		C	
History of the Institute of Mechanical Engineers 1847-1947	Parsons	I.Mech.E.	1947		299	•	•	E	
History of the Monte Carlo Rally	Frostick	Hamilton	1963		95	•		E	
History of the Pneumatic Tyre	Dunlop	Thom	1921		103	•		D	
History of the Vintage Sports Car Club	Hull	Cassell	1964		208	•	•	D	
Illustrated History of Edison Plant	Whitehead	Edison	1968		50	•		E	
Leyland Motor Corporation 1960s. 70 Years of Progress	Anon	Leyland	1967		55	•		D	
Leyland Papers (The)	Turner	Eyre & Spottiswoode	1971		216	•	•	E	
Lucas. The First 100 Years Vol.1 'King of the Road'	Nockolds	David & Charles	1976		349	•	•	E	
Vol.2 The Successes	Nockolds	David & Charles	1978		342	•	•	E	
Mercedes. Pioneer of an Industry	Ullman	Carroll	ND		64	•		D	
Motor Car Industry in Germany 1939-1945 (The)	Olley & Earl	HMSO	1949		82	•		C	•
Motor Industry (The)	Wyatt	Pitman	c1920		132	•		D	
Motor Industry of Great Britain (The)	SMMT	SMMT	1972		363			E	
Motoring Heritage	Baldwin, Hull & McLellan	Bartholomew	1976		60	•	•	E	
Oil	Tugendhat	Eyre & Spottiswoode	1968		318	•	•	E	
One Hundred Years of Good Company (Ruston & Hornsby)	Newman	Ruston & Hornsby	1957		268	•	•	D	

Title	Author	Publisher	1st Ed'n	Later Ed'ns	Pages	Illus	Index	Rate	Text
Our First Fifty Years 1905-1955	Austin Motor Co.		1955		84	•		E	
Pininfarina. Master Coachbuilder	Frostick	Dalton Watson	1977		190	•		E	
Pioneers of Petrol	Liveing	Witherby	1959		94	•	•	D	
RAC Jubilee Book 1897-1947 (The)	Noble	RAC	1947		200	•		E	•
Reign of Rubber (The)	Geer	Allen & Unwin	1922		344	•	•	C	
Rolls-Royce. 75 Years of Motoring Excellence	Eves	Orbis	1979		208	•	•	E	
Rolls-Royce. 75 Years. A Commemorative Album	Roscoe & Whitelaw	Rolls-Royce	1979		46	•		C	
Simms Story. From 1891 (The)	Nixon	Whitehead & Morris	1955		64	•		E	
SMMT The Story of 1902-1952	Nixon	SMMT	1952		126	•		E	
Story of an English Firm (Jensen & Nicholson) (The)		Jensen & Nicholson	1958		36	•		E	
This Motoring	Cooke	AA	1937		263	•		F	•
This Pilgrimage	Cooke	Cassell	1939		84	•	•	E	•
Vanden Plas. Coachbuilders	Smith	Dalton Watson	1979		302	•		E	
Vital to the Life of the Nation	Noble & Junner	SMMT	1946		155	•		E	•
Waterloo Iron Works	Rolt	David & Charles	1969		240	•	•	E	
Wheels of Fortune	Du Cros	Chapman & Hall	1938		315	•	•	D	•

Section H

Rallies, rallying. Autocross, trials, go karts and karting

Title	Author	Publisher	1st Ed'n	Later Ed'ns	Pages	Illus	Index	Rate	Text
All Hell and Autocross	Carrick	Pelham	1971		160	•	•	E	
Autocross Manual	Noad	Speed Sports	1968		80	•		E	
Castrol Rally Manual	Browning	Stephens	1972		128	•		E	
Destination Monte	Harper	Paul	1964		159	•		E	
Ian Monro's Monte Carlo Rally	Gibson	Brockhampton	1958		128	•		E	
International Rallying	Turner	Foulis	1965		142	•	•	E	
Kart Design and Construction	Burgess	Burgess	ND		155	•		E	
Marathon	Brittan	M.R.P	1969		146	•		E	
Mexico or Bust	Kahn	Harrap	1970		176	•		E	
Monte Carlo or Bust	Dobson	Dobson	1969			•*		E	
Monte Carlo Rally	Lowrey	Foulis	ND		86	•		E	
Monte Carlo Rally. History of	Frostick	Hamilton	1963		95	•		E	
Monte Carlo Rally	Symons	Methuen	1936		286	•		D	

* Cartoons

Title	Author	Publisher	1st Ed'n	Later Ed'ns	Pages	Illus	Index	Rate	Text
More Wheelspin	May	Foulis	1968		192	•		E	
Motor Racing and Motor Rally Directory 1957	Motor Racing	Pearl/Cooper	1957		300	•	•	E	
Nineteen to the Dozen	Green	Dalton Watson	1970		128	•		E	
No Excuses	Van Damm	Putnam	1957		238	•		E	
RAC Rally International. The Story of the	Drackett	Haynes/Foulis	1980		232	•	•	F	
Rallies and Races	Gatsonides & Leonard	Foulis	1950		191	•		E	
Rallies and Trials	Davis	Iliffe	1951		184	•	•	E	
Rally Go Round (The)	Garrett	Paul	1970		140	•	•	E	
Rally Manual	Benstead Smith		1960		184	•		E	
Rally Navigation	Holmes	Haynes/Foulis	1975		159	•	•	F	
Rally of the Forests	Drackett	Pelham	1970		169	•		F	
Rallying '78	Holmes & Bishop	Haynes/Foulis	1978		224	•		F	
Rallying	Turner	Foulis	1960	1963	120	•	•	E	
Rallying. Drive it! The Complete Book of	Turner & Mason	Haynes/Foulis	1978		126	•		F	
Rallying to Monte Carlo	Couper	Allan	1956		196	•		D	•
Rallying with B.P	B.P	Paul	1965		128	•		E	
Safari Fever	Brittan	M.R.P	1972		160	•	•	E	
Tricks of the Rally Game	Palm & Volker	Allan	1972		128	•		E	
Wheelspin	May	Foulis	1945	1946/48	175	•	•	E	
Wheelspin Abroad	May	Foulis	1949		176	•		E	
Why Finish Last	Cowan	Queen Anne	1969		129	•		E	
Works Escorts (The)	Robson	Haynes/Foulis	1977		260	•	•	F	
Works Minis (The)	Browning	Foulis	1971		206	•	•	F	

107

108

109

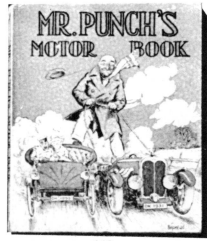

110

111

112

113

114

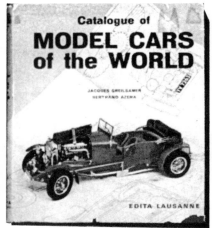

115

Section I

Books other than technical

Section I 1

Children's Books

Title	Author	Publisher	1st Ed'n	Later Ed'ns	Pages	Illus	Index	Rate	Text
Big Book of Motors (The)	Strang	Oxford	1927		128	•		D	•
Boy's Book of Buses of the World (The)	Carter	Burke	1961		143	•		E	
Boy's Book of the Motor Car (The)	Harrison	Oxford University	1926		200	•		D	
Boy's Book of Motor Racing (The)	Castle	Guildford	1954		152	•		E	
Boy's Book of Motors (The)	Aston	Spon	ND 1920s		223	•	•	C	•
Boy's Book of Motor Sport (The)	Grant	Foulis	c1951		160	•		E	
Boy's Book of Racing Cars (The)	Anon	M.R.P	1948		31	•		E	
Boy's Book of Racing and Sports Cars (The)	Marriott	Burke	1962		144	•		E	

The Constant Search

Title	Author	Publisher	1st Ed'n	Later Ed'ns	Pages	Illus	Index	Rate	Text
Boy's Book of Veteran Cars (The)	Carter	Burke	1959		144	•		E	
Boy's Life of Sir Henry Segrave (The)	Campbell & Day	Hutchinson	ND 1930s		284	•		D	•
Great Book of Motors (The)	Jackson	Oxford	1931		128	•		D	•
Modern Boy's Book of Racing Cars	Various	Amalgamated	1930	1938	160	•		D	
Speed Omnibus	Fenwick	Collins	1938	1940/1/ 2/6/7/8	191	•		E	
Stirling Moss' Book of Motor Sport	Moss	Cassell	1955		118	•		E	
Stirling Moss' Second Book of Motor Sport	Boyd	Cassell	1958		120	•		E	
Wonder Book of Motors (The)	Ward Lock	Ward Lock	ND 1920s	many	256	•		D	•

Section I 2

Novels and Fiction

Title	Author	Publisher	1st Ed'n	Later Ed'ns	Pages	Illus	Index	Rate	Text
Alice in Motorland	Wyatt	Car Illustrated	1905		76	•		C	
All Out	Cottenham	Cassell	1932		334			D	•
Black Mercedes (The)	Boshell	Bailey	1974		100			D	
Botor Chaperon (The)	Williamson	Methuen	1913		362	•		D	
Burst Tyres	Edgar	Hamilton	ND 1930s		223	•		D	
Carlotti takes the Wheel	Hawthorn	Children's	1959		169	•		E	•
Car of Destiny (The)	Williamson	Methuen	1906		450	•		D	•
Champion — The Story of a Motor Car	Williamson	Cassell	1907		342	•		D	
Champion	Williamson	Methuen	1913		341	•		D	
Count's Chauffeur (The)	Le Quex	Popular	ND		251			D	

Title	Author	Publisher	1st Ed'n	Later Ed'ns	Pages	Illus	Index	Rate	Text
Dangerous Road	Newton	Dakers	ND		184	•		E	
Death and Four Lovers	Carter	Cassell	1961		332	•		E	
Devil's Motor (The)	Corelli	Hodder & Stoughton	ND		50	•		C	•
Fast Lady (The)	Howard	Howard	1926		254	•		C	
From Paleolith to Motor Car	Lowrison	Whiten	1906		209	•		C	
The Graveyard Rolls	Procter	Harper & Row	1963					D	
Joy of the Road (The)	Young	Methuen	1907		65	•		C	
King of the Speedway	Hunter	Cassell	1927		185	•		D	
Knight on Wheels (A)	Hay	Hodder & Stoughton		1914	317			E	
Knights of the Wheel	Edgar	Harrap	1931		269	•		E	
Lightning Conductor (The)	Williamson	Methuen	1902	many	335	•		D	•
Lightning Conductress (The)	Williamson	Methuen	1916		304	•		D	
Man Who Drove the Car (The)	Pemberton	Eveleigh & Nash	1910		218			D	
Motor Boys in Mexico	Young	Cupples/Leon	ND 1910s		237	•		D	
Motor Boys Overland (The)	Young	Cupples/Leon	1906		237	•		D	
Motor Car Divorce (A)	Hale	Duckworth	1906		319	•		D	
Motoring Tales	Various	Nelson	1943		213	•		E	
Motor Maid (The)	Williamson	Methuen	1909		309	•		D	
My Friend the Chauffeur	Williamson	McClure & Phillips	1905		324	•		D	
'N.7'	Minchin	Stockwell	1930		293			C	
The Princess Passes	Williamson	Methuen	1904	1905	323	•		D	
The Racer	Ruesch	Ballantyne		1955	187			E	•
Salute to the Gods	Campbell	Cassell	1934		314			D	•
Secret of the Silver Car (The)	Martin	Jenkins	1922		286			D	

The Constant Search

Title	Author	Publisher	1st Ed'n	Later Ed'ns	Pages	Illus	Index	Rate	Text
Set in Silver	Williamson	Methuen	1909		445	•		D	
Shriek of Tyres (A)	Rutherford	Crime Club	1958		256	•		E	
Sicilian Circuit	Cottenham	Cassell	1933		357			E	•
Sing Holiday	Chamberlain	Barker	1937		431			C	•
Skid Kennedy — Speed King	Edgar	Hamilton	1936		220			D	
Speed Fever	Lyndon	Nelson	1930		288			C	•
Speed Triumphant	Fisson	Putnam	1951		188	•		E	
Thunder Ahead	Campbell	Cassell	1934		288	•		D	•
Tim Baker — Motor Mechanic	Carter	Chatto & Windus	1957		135			D	
Vintage Timpitters (The)	Wright	Victory	1966		86			D	
Wildcatters (The)	Hine	Sunday School Union	ND		256	•		D	
Wildwode's Garage	Giles	Hutchinson	1930		288			D	

Section I 3

Cartoons, verse and humour

Title	Author	Publisher	1st Ed'n	Later Ed'ns	Pages	Illus	Index	Rate	Text
Auto Fun	Iliffe	Harrap	c1910		70	•		C	
Bees Under My Bonnet	Brockbank	M.R.P	ND		48	•		E	•
Blast Your Horn	Houghton	Paul	1962		126	•		E	
Brockbank Grand Prix	Brockbank	Eyre/Methuen	1973		95	•		E	•
Brockbank Omnibus	Brockbank	Eyre/Methuen	1973		119	•		E	•
Brockbank's Mercedes Benz Miscellany	Brockbank	Not stated	ND		16	•		C	•
Car Canny	Clitheroe & Fenwick	Duckworth	1939		96	•		E	
Car Toons	Sine	Reinhardt	1964	1964	70	•		E	
Casque's Sketch Book	Davis	Iliffe	ND 1930s		60	•		D	•

Title	Author	Publisher	1st Ed'n	Later Ed'ns	Pages	Illus	Index	Rate	Text
Collected Verses of W.H.Charnock (The)	Charnock	Villiers	1959		103	•		D	
Dicing with Death	Lloyd	Daily Mirror	1961		113	•		D	
Dogbite the Tinbasher	Middleton	Morley Cox	ND		143	•		D	
Down the Grid	Mills	Allan	1965		45	•		E	
Down in the Sumps	Charnock	Charnock	1951		39			D	
Drivers Wild	Daniels	Scorpion	1961		68	•		E	
Drivers Wildest	Daniels	Scorpion	1963		66	•		E	
Horseless Savages	Charnock				39	•		D	
How to be a Motorist	Heath Robinson	Hutchinson	c1935		116	•		E	
How to be a Motorist and Stay Happy	Haines & Walker	Muller	1967		128	•		E	
Living with a Car	Spoerl	Muller	1960		250	•		E	
Luck of the Draw (The)	Fougasse	Methuen	1936		138	•		D	•
Monte Carlo or Bust	Dobson	Sphere	1969		157	•		E	
More Bees Under My Bonnet	Collier & Pratt	M.R.P	ND		55	•		E	
More Sketches by Casque	Davis	Iliffe	ND 1930s		63	•		D	•
More Wild Drivers	Daniels	Scorpion	1962		69	•		E	
Most Women Do It	Wilkins & Brockbank	Newnes	1964		151	•		E	•
Motoring Through Punch 1900-1970	Various	Punch	1970		153	•		D	
Motor Racing Sketch Book	Demand	Foulis	ND		151	•		E	
Move Over	Brockbank	Temple Press	1962		65	•		E	•
Mr Punch Awheel	Various	Punch Educational	ND		192	•		E	
Mr Punch Goes Motoring	Various	Punch Educational	ND		240	•		D	
Mr Punch's Motor Book	Various	Methuen	1931		99	•		D	
Over the Line	Brockbank	Temple Press	1955		55	•		E	•
Petrol Fumes	Horder	Jenkins	ND		94	•		D	

The Constant Search

Title	Author	Publisher	1st Ed'n	Later Ed'ns	Pages	Illus	Index	Rate	Text
Recreation Motoring	Marshall	Hodder & Stoughton	1954		191	•		E	
Round the Bend	Brockbank	Temple Press	ND		64	•		E	•
Rubaiyat of a Motor Car	Wells	Harper	1906		58	•		D	
Shell Book of Motoring Humour	Bentley	Joseph	1976		159	•		E	
Sleepless Knights	Sprinzel	M.R.P	1962		123	•		E	
Songs of the Car	Cox	Griffiths	1906		124	•		D	
Stop — or Go	Fougasse	Methuen	1939		50	•		D	•
Up the Straight	Brockbank	Temple Press	1953	1955/ 7/'60	55	•		E	•
You Have Been Warned	Fougasse & McCullough	Methuen	1935		138	•		D	•
You've Got Me Behind the Wheel	Lariar	Hammond, Hammond	1957		NN	•		E	

Section J

Taxis, buses, trams, commercial, military and advertising vehicles

Title	Author	Publisher	1st Ed'n	Later Ed'ns	Pages	Illus	Index	Rate	Text
Advertising and the Motor Car	Frostick	Lund Humphries	1970		159	•		D	•
Bedford Commercial Vehicles	Acres	Pearson	1961		266	•	•	E	
Buses and Trollybuses 1919-1945	Kaye	Blandford	1970		191	•	•	E	
Buses and Trollybuses Since 1945	Kaye	Blandford	1968		184	•	•	E	
Buses in Camera	Booth	Allan	ND		132	•		E	
Buses, Trollys and Trams	Dunbar	Hamlyn	1967		139	•		E	
Cars and Commercial Vehicles. Dumpy Pocket Book of	Orr	Sampson Low	1960		199	•		E	
Commercial Road Vehicles	Cornwell	Batsford	1960		288	•	•	E	
Commercial Vehicles	Gibson	Nelson	ND		62	•		E	
Commercial Vehicles. Observer's Book of	Baldwin	Warne	1974		192	•		E	
Commercial Vehicles of the World	Kuipers	Oakwood	1972		198	•	•	D	

The Constant Search

Title	Author	Publisher	1st Ed'n	Later Ed'ns	Pages	Illus	Index	Rate	Text
Decorated and Advertising Vehicles	Harman	Blandford	ND 1920s		85	•		C	•
Desert Taxi	Marriott	Travel	1953		150	•		F	
Farm Tractor Handbook (The)	Sherwood	Iliffe	ND 1910s		168	•	•	C	•
Fighting Vehicles — World War Two. Observer's Book of	Vanderveen	Warne	1969		340	•	•	E	
Ford Commercial Vehicles	Sanderman	Pearson	1961		280	•	•	E	
Fordson Tractor. The Book of the	Abbey	Pitman	1954		132	•	•	D	
Golden Age of Tramways (The)	Harper	David & Charles	1961	1974	327	•	•	E	
History of the London Taxicab	Georgano	David & Charles	1972		180	•	•	E	•
Kings of the Highway	Tilling	Hutchinson	1957		122	•	App	D	
Know Your Tractor	Shell	Shell	1955		356	•	•	D	
London Buses	Murphy	Foulis	1965		148	•		E	
London's Buses	Sommerfield	St Catherine	1933		103	•		E	
Lorries, Trucks and Vans 1897-1927	Marshall & Bishop	Blandford	1972		154	•		E	
Managing a Transport Business	Barry	Allen & Unwin	1963		210	•	•	E	
Military Transport of World War One	Ellis	Blandford	1970		158	•	•	E	
Modern Motor Cars and Commercial Vehicles (Brown Binding) Vol.1	Judge	Caxton	ND 1920s		277	•	•	E	
Vol.2	Judge	Caxton	ND 1920s		292	•	•	E	
Vol.3	Judge	Caxton	ND 1920s		309	•	•	E	
Vol.4	Judge	Caxton	ND 1920s		306	•	•	E	

116

117

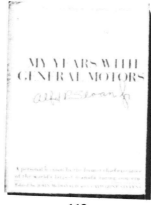

118

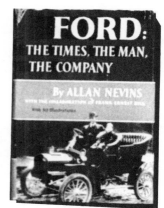

119

120

121

122

123

124

125

126

127

The Constant Search

Title	Author	Publisher	1st Ed'n	Later Ed'ns	Pages	Illus	Index	Rate	Text
Modern Motor Cars and Commercial Vehicles (Green Binding) Vol.1	Judge	Caxton	ND 1930s		273	•	•	E	
Vol.2	Judge	Caxton	ND 1930s		270	•	•	E	
Vol.3	Judge	Caxton	ND 1930s		279	•	•	E	
Vol.4	Judge	Caxton	ND 1930s		278	•	•	E	
Morris Commercial Vehicles	Francis	Pearson	1963		238	•	•	E	
Motor Road Transport for Commercial Purposes	Phillimore	Pitman	1920		212	•		D	
Motor Transports in War	Wyatt	Hodder & Stoughton	1914		192	•		D	•
Motor Truck and Automobile Motors and Mechanism	Russell	Stanton & Van Liet	1918		238	•		D	•
Motor Vehicles and Tractors	Heldt	Heldt	1929		678	•	•	D	
Old Farm Tractors	Wright	David & Charles	1962	1972	77	•	•	E	
Omnibus 1870-1970 (The)	Hibbs	David & Charles	1971		215	•		E	
One Hundred Years of America's Fire Fighting Apparatus	De Costa	Bonanza	1964		112	•		D	
Petrol Cars and Lorries	Heap	Pitman	1922		111	•	•	D	•
Road Passenger Transport	Pilcher	Pitman	1937		383	•	•	D	
Road Transport. History & Development of	Paterson	Pitman	1927		118	•	•	D	
Share My Taxi	Buckland	Joseph	1968		191			E	
Southdown Story (The)	'Anon'	Southdown Motor Services	1965		65	•		E	
Trolly Bus Trails	Joyce	Allan	1963		118	•		E	
Up to Date Road Transport for Commercial Purposes	Phillimore	Pitman	c1920		221	•	•	C	•
Veteran Vintage Series — Commercial Vehicles	Cornwell				63	•		E	

Title	Author	Publisher	1st Ed'n	Later Ed'ns	Pages	Illus	Index	Rate	Text
Vintage Buses and Trams in South Wales	Williams	Williams	1975		203	•		E	
Wonders of Transport	Various	Blackie	1930		286	•		D	
World's Carriers — How to Make Motor Transport Pay	Miller	Carrier	c1920		104	•		D	•
World's Commercial Vehicles 1830-1964	Georgano	Temple Press	1965		122	•		E	•

Section K

Models, model building, model car collecting and racing

Title	Author	Publisher	1st Ed'n	Later Ed'ns	Pages	Illus	Index	Rate	Text
Building a Scale Model Monoposto Alfa Romeo	Posthumus		1946		18			C	
British Diecasts. A Collector's Guide to Toy Cars, Vans and Trucks	Thompson	Haynes/Foulis	1980		160	•		F	
Catalogue of Model Cars of the World	Greilsamer & Azema	Lausanne	1967		297	•		D	•
History of British Dinky Toys 1934-1964	Gibson	M.A.P	1966		152	•		E	
Miniature Car Construction	Posthumus	Percival Marshall	1949		91	•		D	
Model Car Collecting	Jewell	Temple Press	1963		94	•	App	E	
Model Car Manual (The)	Deason	Drysdale	1949		122	•		E	
Model Cars	Orbis	Orbis	1971		64	•		E	
Model Cars of Gerald Wingrove (The)	Wingrove	New Cavendish	1979		110	•	•	F	•
Model Cars of the World	Najima	Hoikusha	1977	1979	124	•		E	
Model Cars. The World of	Williams	Rainbird	1976		208	•		E	
Model Car Rail Racing	Dickson	Model Aeronautical	1957		176	•		E	

Title	Author	Publisher	1st Ed'n	Later Ed'ns	Pages	Illus	Index	Rate	Text
Model Cars. Plastic	Gibson	Model Aeronautical	1962		110	•		E	
Model Commercial Vehicles	Gibson		1971		59	•		E	
Model Veteran and Vintage Cars	Gibson	Viking	1972		57	•	•	E	
Motor Modelling	Hays	Arco	1961		175	•	•	E	
Motor Racing in Miniature	Deason	Harborough	1947		128	•		E	
Racing Cars in Miniature	Hays	Percival Marshall	1951		93	•		E	
Scale Model Cars	Pratley	M.A.P	1956		77	•	App	E	
Simple Electric Car Racing	Smeed	Model Aeronautical	1965		103	•		E	
Slot Car Racing	Drackett	Souvenir	1968		100	•		E	
Toys and Models	Pearce		1947		95	•	•	E	

Section L

Mascots, badges, registration plates, emblems and insignia

Title	Author	Publisher	1st Ed'n	Later Ed'ns	Pages	Illus	Index	Rate	Text
Automobilia	Worthington Williams	Batsford/RAC	1979		192	•	•	E	•
Car Badges of the World	Nicholson	Cassell	1970		173	•		E	
Car Mascots — An Enthusiast's Guide	Sirignano & Sulzberger	Macdonald & Janes	1977		120	•	•	E	•
Car Numbers	Woodall	Garstone	1969		265	•		E	
Car Number Galaxy	Woodall	Woodall	1966		150	•		E	
5000 Cherished Plates	Woodall	Woodall	1972					E	
Hershey. The World's Largest Autojumble and Antique Show	Hershey	Directional Advertising	1971		95	•		D	
Registration Plates of Europe and the World	Parker	Allan	1968		134	•		E	

Section M

Titles other than under A to L. Pictures, prints and photographs

Title	Author	Publisher	1st Ed'n	Later Ed'ns	Pages	Illus	Index	Rate	Text
Art of Gordon Crosby (The)	Garnier	Hamlyn	1978		74	•		E	•
Endless Quest for Speed	Crosby/Davis	Iliffe	ND 1930s					C	•
Klemantaski's Photo Album									
Meteors of Road and Track								C	
Motoraces	Monkhouse	Newnes	1937		120	•		C	
Motor Racing Camera 1894-1916	Georgano	David & Charles	1976		102	•		E	
Motor Racing with Mercedes Benz	Monkhouse	Newnes	1938	& later	167	•		C	
Roadside Camera	Ware	David & Charles	1974		112	•	•	E	
Speed Camera	Tompkins	Foulis	ND		100	•		E	

Section N

Magazines

Section O

Club and marque bulletins, gazettes and journals

Section P

Items other than under Headings N and O

Section Q

Sales literature and commemorative brochures

Title	Author	Publisher	1st Ed'n	Later Ed'ns	Pages	Illus	Index	Rate	Text
About George	McIntyre	MG Car Co.			12	•		C	
Action	Anon	MG Car Co.	1935		16	•		C	
Chequered Career (A)	Linfield & Lester	MG Car Co.	1932		14	•		C	
An Epic of the Double Twelve	Anon	MG Car Co.	1931		6	•		C	
Greatest Achievement of the Year (The)	Anon	MG Car Co.	1939		30	•		C	
Luck of the Game (The)	Kimber	MG Car Co.	1932		20	•		C	
Luck of the Game Again (The)	Lyndon	MG Car Co.	1934		24	•		C	
Mille Miglia	Symons	MG Car Co.	1933		48	•		C	
Octagon. At the Sign of the	Anon	MG Car Co.	1932		32	•		C	
Supremacy	Anon	MG Car Co.	1934	1935	16	•		C	
This is Motoring	Lyndon	MG Car Co.	1935		14	•		C	
What I Think of the MG Car	Anon	MG Car Co.	1934		34	•		C	
Blue Riband of English Motor Racing	Bentley Motors	Bentley	1922		23	•		C	

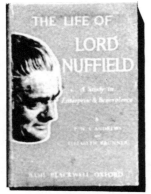

128

129

130

131

132

133

134

135

136

137

138

Title	Author	Publisher	1st Ed'n	Later Ed'ns	Pages	Illus	Index	Rate	Text
Again 1928	Bentley	Bentley	1928		27	•		C	
The Hat Trick	Bentley	Bentley	1929		36	•		C	
Le Mans 1927	Bentley	Bentley	1927		23	•		C	
Plus Four	Bentley	Bentley	1930		40	•		C	
Progress. On Land and Water (The) Golden Arrow and Miss England	Corbett	Fitch	1929		19	•		C	
Sunbeam. Grand Prix de France 1923	Sunbeam	Sunbeam	1923		20	•		C	
203mph! The Supreme Sunbeam	Sunbeam	Sunbeam	1927		24	•		C	
Thorneycroft Activities 1930	Thorneycroft	Thorneycroft	1930		40	•		C	
Thorneycroft Road Transport Golden Jubilee	Twelvetrees	Thorneycroft	1946		95	•		D	
Big Things in the Year (The)	Temple Press	Temple Press	1930		8	•		D	
Book of Brakes (The)	Ferodo	Ferodo	1929		40	•		D	
Chosen by the Men Who Win	Ferodo	Ferodo	1936		32	•		D	
Dunlop Through the Reigns. The Story of	Dunlop	Dunlop	1953		26	•		E	
Season 1938	Ferodo	Ferodo	1938		36	•		D	
Silverstone. Thirty Years 1948-1978	Anon	Anon	1978		4			E	
Some Adventures in 1928	Temple Press	Temple Press	1928		8	•		D	
Brooklands Automobile Racing Club. Souvenir of	Montagu	Car Illustrated	1907	1977	87	•		C/F	

Section R

Service literature — books

Title	Author	Publisher	1st Ed'n	Later Ed'ns	Pages	Illus	Index	Rate	Text
Aston Martin Manual (The)	AMOC	AMOC	1965		404	•		C	
Austin A30. Cassell Book of the	Hawks	Cassell	1958		222	•	•	F	
Austin A30 and 7. Cassell Book of the	Hawks	Cassell	1951	1956	152	•		F	
Austin Seven and Eight. The Book of the	Abbey	Pitman	1935	many	101	•	•	F	
Austin. The Book of the	Abbey	Pitman	1954	1955/6/8	102	•	•	F	
Austin A40 Devon. Cassell Book of the	Hawks	Cassell	1947	1952	160	•		F	
Austin/Morris Mini Cars. Cassell Book of the	Page	Cassell	1962		140	•	•	F	
Austin/Morris Mini Estate Cars and Vans. Cassell Book of the	Page	Cassell	1962		140	•	•	F	
Austin Seven Book (The)	Nicholson, Leather & Mead	Gregg	1927	Eight to 1947	215	•	•	C/D	
Austin Ten. Cassell Book of the	Hawks	Cassell	1939	1947	162	•		F	

Title	Author	Publisher	1st Ed'n	Later Ed'ns	Pages	Illus	Index	Rate	Text
Austin Healey Cars	Davidson	Pearson	1960		188	•	•	D	
Automobile Engineering (6 volumes)		American Technical Soc.	1921		2869	•	•	E	
Automobile Engine Overhaul	Judge	Pitman	1938		226	•	•	E	
Automobile Engines	Judge	Chapman & Hall	1925	many to 1953	474	•	•	D	
Automobile Fault Tracing	Abbey	Pitman	1957		232	•	•	E	
Automobile Repair	Malloy	Newnes	ND 1950s		2246 4 vols	•		E	
BMC 1100s	Marshall & Fraser	Foulis	1966		176	•	•	F	
BMC Minis	Marshall & Fraser	Foulis	1965		172	•	•	F	
Book of the Motor Car	Kennedy	Caxton	1913		212	•		E	
(4 volumes)	Kennedy	Caxton	1913		213	•		E	
	Kennedy	Caxton	1913		221	•		E	
	Kennedy	Caxton	later		221	•	•	D	
Car Care. New Castrol Book of	Chalmers Hunt	Haynes	1974		78	•		F	
Ford Anglia. Cassell Book of the	Hawks	Cassell	1948	many	134	•	•	F	
Ford Book of Competition Motoring (The)	Clark & Brinton	Paul	1965		107	•	•	E	
Ford Book of Electrical Equipment	Nicholson	Temple Press	ND 1920s		148	•	•	C	
Ford Car. The Model T	Page	Hodder & Stoughton	1919		312	•	•	C	
Ford Consul. Cassell Book of the	Hawks	Cassell	1951	1956	154	•	•	F	
Ford 8 Handbook (The)	Jelley	Pitman	1935 /7/9	1941 /6	126	•	•	D/E	
Ford New Anglia. Cassell Book of the	Hawks	Cassell	1953	1958	144	•	•	F	
Ford New Prefect. Cassell Book of the	Hawks	Cassell	1953	1958	144	•	•	F	

The Constant Search

Title	Author	Publisher	1st Ed'n	Later Ed'ns	Pages	Illus	Index	Rate	Text
Ford Popular. Book of the								F	
Ford Prefect. Cassell Book of the	Hawks	Cassell	1938	1953	156	•	•	F	
Ford Popular. The Cassell Book of the	Hawks	Cassell	1953	1959	156	•	•	F	
Ford Ten and Prefect Handbook	Abbey	Pitman	1935/8	1949-1956	104	•	•	D/E	
Ford Tuning Manual (997cc-1558cc)	Haynes	Haynes	1964		120	•		E	
Ford V-8 Handbook	Jelley & Harrison	Pitman	1943		112	•	•	E	
Ford Zephyr/Zodiac. Cassell Book of the		Cassell	1951	1956	154	•	•	F	
Ford Zephyr/Zodiac	Holmes	Odhams	1952		160	•	•	F	
Hillman Minx. Cassell Book of the	Nickols	Cassell	1959		201	•	•	F	
Hillman Minx Handbook	Martin	Pitman	1936	1937				E	
How to keep your Volkswagen alive	Muir	Muir Publications	1969	1979	362	•		D	
Isetta. Cassell Book of the	Anon	Cassell	1959	1960				F	
Jaguar Companion (The)	Ulyett	Paul	1959	1960	148	•	•	D	
Lambretta. Cassell Book of the		Cassell	1953	1959				F	
Lambretta Service and Guide	Lambretta	Lambretta	1954		80	•		F	
Maserati Owner's Handbook	Tanner	Clymer	ND		159	•		D	
Mercedes Benz Companion	Ulyett	Paul	1966		175	•	•	D	
MG Companion	Ulyett	Paul	1960		168	•	•	D	
MG Cars. Tuning and Maintenance of	Smith	Haynes	1952	Seven to 1978	180	•	•	D/E	
Modern Motor Engineer (Blue Binding) Vol.1	Judge	Caxton	1927		234	•	•	E	
Vol.2	Judge	Caxton	1927		228	•	•	E	

Title	Author	Publisher	1st Ed'n	Later Ed'ns	Pages	Illus	Index	Rate	Text
Vol.3	Judge	Caxton	1927		235	•	•	E	
Modern Motor Engineer (Green Binding) Vol.1	Judge	Caxton		1930s	366	•	•	E	
Vol.2	Judge	Caxton		1930s	400	•	•	E	
Vol.3	Judge	Caxton		1930s	363	•	•	E	
Vol.4	Judge	Caxton		1930s	254	•	•	E	
Vol.5 (Wiring Diagrams)	Judge	Caxton		1930s		•		D	
Modern Motor Engineer (Black Binding) Vol.1	Judge	Caxton		1950s	466	•	•	F	
Vol.2	Judge	Caxton		1950s	490	•	•	F	
Vol.3	Judge	Caxton		1950s	487	•	•	F	
Vol.4	Judge	Caxton		1950s	564	•	•	F	
Vol.5 (Wiring Diagrams)	Judge	Caxton		1950s		•		E	
MG Series A and Magnette. Tuning and Maintenance of the	Smith	Foulis	1957		135	•	•	E	
MG Workshop Manual	Blower	M.R.P	1952		584	•		D	
Modern Motor Cars (3 volumes)	Judge	Caxton	ND 1920s		913	•	•	E	
Modern Motors (4 volumes)	Rutter	Virtue	ND 1920s		864	•	•	E	
Morris Cars	Pearson	Pearson	1956 /8	1960 /6	192	•	•	F	
Morris Minor Series 2. Cassell Book of the		Cassell	1959					E	
Morris Ten. The Book of the	Bishop	Pitman	1937	many	81	•	•	E	
Motors of Today (5 volumes)	Rutter	Virtue	c1929		1864	•	•		
Motor Repair and Overhauling (5 volumes)	Anon	Newnes	ND 1930s		2944	•	•	E	
Motor Repair 1964-66. Models	McLintock & Mulcaster	Pergammon	1967		480	•		E	

The Constant Search

Title	Author	Publisher	1st Ed'n	Later Ed'ns	Pages	Illus	Index	Rate	Text
Motor Repair 1966-68 Models	McLintock & Mulcaster	International Learning	1969		479	•		E	
Porsche & V.W. Companion	Ulyett	Paul	1962		163	•	•	D	
Renault Dauphine Cars	Coker	Pearson	1963	1966	160	•	•	E	
Riley Cars	Drake	Pearson	1958		200	•	•	D	
Riley Maintenance Manual 1930-1956	Haddleton	Foulis	1956		390	•	•	C	
Riley Nine. The Book of the	Warren	Pitman	1933		110	•	•	D	
Rolls-Royce Manual 1925-1939 (The)	Haynes	Haynes	1964		86	•		D	
Singer 9. The Book of the	Bishop	Pitman	1938	1946	96	•	•	D	
Standard Car. The Book of the	Abbey	Pitman	1951	1953	96	•	•	E	
Standard Ten. Cassell Book of the		Cassell	1954					E	
Standard Vanguard 1948-53. Cassell Book of the	Hawks	Cassell	1961		247	•	•	E	
Stromberg CD Carburetters	Peers	Haynes	1976		75	•		F	
SU Carburetters	Peers	Haynes	1976		87	•		F	
Triumph Companion (The)	Ulyett	Paul	1962		168	•	•	D	
Triumph Herald and Vitesse	Hartley	Odhams	1964		160	•	•	F	
Triumph TR, TR2, TR3, TR3A, TR4, TR4A					117	•		D	
Useful Hints and Tips for Automobilists	Anon	Iliffe	1905			•	•	C	
Useful Hints for Motorists	Page	Hodder & Stoughton	1920		163	•		D	
Vauxhall. The Book of the	Jelley	Pitman	1935-9	1942	127	•	•	F	
Vauxhall Companion (The)	Ulyett	Paul	1971		160	•	•	E	
Vespa. Cassell Book of the		Cassell	1951	1960				E	
Volkswagen Cars	Broad	Pearson	1960		166	•	•	E	

Title	Author	Publisher	1st Ed'n	Later Ed'ns	Pages	Illus	Index	Rate	Text
VW Beetle Handbook (The)	Konrad & Meisl	Foulis	1970		144	•	•	E	
Weber Carburetters	Legg	Haynes	1979		191	•		F	
Wolseley Cars	Francis	Pearson	1957		191	•	•	E	

Section S

Motorcycling

Section S 1

Road and touring

Title	Author	Publisher	1st Ed'n	Later Ed'ns	Pages	Illus	Index	Rate	Text
Across America by Motor Cycle	Shepherd	Arnold	1922		248	•		C	
Across Europe with Satanella	Sheridan	Duckworth	1925		216	•		C	
Adventures of a Despatch Rider	Watson	Blackman	1925		272	•		C	
Around the World with Motor Cycle and Camera	Range	Clymer	1957		230	•		C	
Bike and Superbike	Woollett	Batsford	1977		64	•		F	
Cossack at Large	Soboleff	Davies	1960		189	•		C	
Daily Mail Motor Cycling Book	Davies	Daily Mail	c1950		64	•		E	
Encyclopedia of Motorcycling	Bishop	Bison/Hamlyn	1980		192	•		F	
Fifty Years of Motorcycles	Posthumus	Phoebus	1978		63	•		F	
First Motorcycles	Posthumus	Phoebus	1977		63	•		F	
From Leipzig to Cabul	Sauer	Hutchinson	ND 1920s		284	•	•	C	

244

Title	Author	Publisher	1st Ed'n	Later Ed'ns	Pages	Illus	Index	Rate	Text
Going Further	Malins	Matthews & Marriot	1931		396	•	•	D	
Historic Motor Cycling	Jones	Modern Magazines	1978		118	•		F	
How to Start Motorcycling	Perriam	M.C.N	1964		78	•		E	
International Motor Cycling Book	Various	Souvenir	1971		128	•		E	
Kaleidoscope of Motor Cycling	Howard	Old Motor	1977		NN	•	•	E	
Motor Cycle Story	Posthumus & Richmond	Phoebus	1979		128	•	•	E	
Motor Cycle Route Book	Anon	Iliffe	ND 1930s		176	•		D	
Motor Cycles	Schilling	Ridge	1975		159	•	•	E	
Land Beyond the Ridge (The)	Battson	Goose	1974		78	•		E	
Ride It! Motor Cycle Touring. The Complete Book of	Craven	Haynes/Foulis	1977		134	•		F	
Motor Cycle World (The)	Schilling	Hamlyn	1974		252	•	•	E	
Motorcycles	Setright	Weidenfeld & Nicholson	1976		159	•	•	E	
Motor Cycling Abroad	Osborne	Temple Press	1956		128	•	•	E	
Motor Cycling in the 1930s	Currie	Hamlyn	1981		144	•	•	F	
My Life on Wheels	Wiggin	Baker	1963	1964	142	•		E	
Nansen Passport	Soboleff	Bell	1936		242	•		C	
Not So Innocent Abroad	Archbold	Jarrold	1957		183	•		D	
One Man Caravan	Fulton	Harrap	1938		271	•		D	
Questions and Answers for Motor Cyclists	Emmott	M.C.N	1963		94	•		E	
Ride in the Sun (A)	Thomas	Hodder & Stoughton	1952						
Superbikes of the Seventies	Nutting	Hamlyn	1978	1979	128	•		E	
Three Wheeling Through Africa	Wilson	Jarrolds	1937		284	•		C	

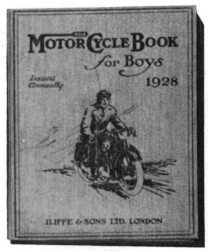

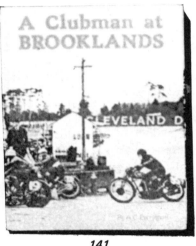

139

140

141

142

143

144

145

146

147

148

149

Title	Author	Publisher	1st Ed'n	Later Ed'ns	Pages	Illus	Index	Rate	Text
Three Lands on Three Wheels	Gordon	Harrap	1932	1934	358	•		D	
Through Algeria and Tunisia	Warren	Cape	1922		160	•		C	
Twist Grip	Setright	Allen & Unwin	1969		149	•		D	
With a Motor Bike in the Bush	Ashley	Blackie	ND 1920s		176	•		D	

Section S 2

Racing

Title	Author	Publisher	1st Ed'n	Later Ed'ns	Pages	Illus	Index	Rate	Text
American Racer	Wright	Megden	1979		255	•	•	D	
Art of Motor Cycle Racing (The)	Hailwood & Walker	Cassell	1963		186	•	•	D	
Barry Sheene's Book of Motor Cycling	Marriott	Stafford & Pemberton	1978		61	•		F	
Barry Sheene — The Story So Far	Beacham	Studio			160	•		F	
Big Bike Racing. Ride It! The Complete Book of	Swift	Haynes/Foulis	1976		152	•		F	
Biker's Guide to Baja	Parkhurst	Parkhurst	1980		98	•		F	
Bikes at Brooklands — In the Pioneer Years	Hartley	Goose	1976		224	•	•	E	
Black Smoke	Irving	Research	1978		127	•		E	
BP Book of Motor Cycle Racing (The)	Walker	Paul	1960		91	•		E	
Briggo	Briggs	Souvenir	1972		190	•		E	
Britain's Racing Motor Cycles	Higgins	Foulis	1952		155	•	•	D	
British Racing Motor Cycles	Clew	Haynes/Foulis	1976		183	•		E	
Brooklands	Wallace	Ballantine	1971		157	•		D	
Brooklands: Bikes in the Twenties	Hartley	Argus	1980		244	•	•	F	

The Constant Search

Title	Author	Publisher	1st Ed'n	Later Ed'ns	Pages	Illus	Index	Rate	Text
Brooklands and Beyond	Mortimer	Goose	1974		240	•	•	E	
Brooklands. A Pictorial History	Georgano	Dalton Watson	1978		112	•		E	
Brooklands: Behind the Scenes	Mortimer	Haynes/Foulis	1980		255	•		F	
Castrol Motorcycle Racing Manual	Miles	Stephens	1973		120	•		E	
Champion's Book of Speedway (The)	Bott	Paul	1970		127	•		E	
A Clubman at Brooklands	Perryman	Haynes/Foulis	1979		127	•	•	E	
Continental Circus	Mellors & Davison	TT Special	1949		159	•	•	D	
Endurance Racing. Ride it! The Complete Book of	Robinson	Haynes/Foulis	1979		159	•		F	
Famous Racing Motor Cycles	Griffith	Temple Press	1961	1963 /5	100	•		E	
Fifty Years of TT History	Higgins & Quantrill	Shell/BP	1956		153	•		D	
Flat Track Racing. Ride It! The Complete Book of	Foster	Haynes/Foulis	1978		153	•		F	
Foreign Racing Motor Cycles	Bacon	Haynes/Foulis	1979		204	•		F	
Francis Beart — A Single Purpose	Clew	Haynes/Foulis	1978		205	•	•	E	
From TT to Tokyo	Robb	Courier Herald	1974		125	•	•	E	
Full Chat	Pope	M.R.P	1952	rep't	80	•		D/E	
Grand Prix Motor Cycle Championships of the World. 1949-1975	Bula	Haynes/Foulis	1975		NN	•		E	
Hailwood	Macauley & Hailwood	Transport Bookman	1968	1978	128	•		E	
Hailwood Story — My Son Mike	Hailwood	M.C.N			66	•		E	
High Efficiency	Anon	Mobiloil	ND 1950s		80	•		E	
High Speed Two Stroke Petrol Engines	Smith	Foulis	1965		430	•		E	

Title	Author	Publisher	1st Ed'n	Later Ed'ns	Pages	Illus	Index	Rate	Text
Historic Racing Motor Cycles	Griffith	Temple Press	1963		87	•		E	
How to See the TT in Comfort	Anon	Mobiloil	1952		22	•		E	
Illustrated History of Speedway (The)	Rogers	Studio	1978		144	•		E	
International Motor Cycle Racing Book (The)	Macauley	Souvenir	1971		128	•		E	
Irish Motor Cycle Races. 1954	Brindley	Brindley	1954		192	•		C	
Irish Motor Cycle Races. 1955	Brindley	Brindley	1955		192	•		C	
Ivan Mauger's World Speedway Book	Various	Pelham	1973		120	•		F	
Johnnie Hoskins' Speedway Walkabout	Hoskins	Studio	1977		208	•		E	
Last of the Great Road Races — Isle of Man TT (The)	Mutch	Transport Bookman	1975		135	•		E	
Manx Grand Prix (The)	Shell	Shell	1963		32	•		E	
Manx Grand Prix. History of the	Shell	Shell	ND		120	•		E	
Manx TT. The Glory of the	Currie	Motor Cycle Weekly	1975		96	•		E	
Mike the Bike Again — The Story of Mike Hailwood's Return	Macauley	Cassell	1980		87	•		E	
Million Miles of Racing (A)	Heath & McGowan	TT Special	1950		208	•		D	
Motocourse 1976-77	Various	Hazleton	1977		200	•	App	E	
Motocourse 1977-78	Various	Hazleton	1978		200	•	App	E	
Motocourse 1978-79	Various	Hazleton	1979		208	•	App	E	
Motocourse 1979-80	Various	Hazleton	1980		190	•	App	E	
Motocourse 1980-81	Various	Hazleton	1981		192	•	App	E	
Motor Cycle Racing	Carrick	Hamlyn	1961		141	•	•	D	
Motor Cycle and Motor Racing. 1951	Gardner	Country & Sporting	1951		48	•		D	

The Constant Search

Title	Author	Publisher	1st Ed'n	Later Ed'ns	Pages	Illus	Index	Rate	Text
Motor Cycle Tuning for Performance	Shipman	H.P	1973		74	•	•	E	
Motor Cycle Year	Various	Edita	1975		188	•		D	
Motor Cycle Year — 1976-77	Various	Edita	1976		204	•		D	
No Time to Lose	Peck	M.R.P	1972		158	•	•	E	
1951 TT Who's Who	Davison	TT Special	1951		64	•	•	D	
Pastmasters of Speed	May	Temple Press	1958		104	•		D	
Phil Read. The Real Story	Read/Wright	Macdonald & Janes	1977		191	•	App	E	
Prince of Speed	Read	Barker	1970	1971	124	•	App	E	
Private Owner	Higgins	Foulis	1948		176	•		D	
Racing All My Life	Minter	Barker	1965		96	•		D	
Racing Motor Cycle (The)	Willoughby	Hamlyn	1980		175	•	•	E	
Racing Motor Cycles	Woollett	Hamlyn	1973		96	•	•	E	
Racing and Tuning Production Motorcycles	Knight	Speed Sports	1970		123	•		E	
Racing Reminiscences	Davison	TT Special	1948		176	•	•	D	
Racing Round the Island	Holliday	David & Charles	1976		212	•	•	E	
Racing Through the Century	Davison	TT Special	1951		176	•	•	D	
Racing Year	Davison	TT Special	1950		232	•		D	
Riding the Dirt	Sandford	Bond/Parkhurst	1972		221	•		E	
Road Racing	Grant	Hamlyn	1979		125	•	•	E	
Roarin' Round the Speedways	Hoskins	McCorquodale	1930		96			C	
Romance of the Speedway	Elder	Warne	1930		184	•		C	
Second Post Vintage Racing Scene (The)	Main-Smith	Main-Smith	1978		64	•		E	
Sheene Machine	Marriott	Pelham	1979		141	•	•	E	
Short Circuits	Davison & Smith	TT Special	1951		152	•		D	
Sidecar Championships	O'Dell & Beacham	Hamlyn	1978		153	•	•	E	

Title	Author	Publisher	1st Ed'n	Later Ed'ns	Pages	Illus	Index	Rate	Text
Sixty Years of Speed	Various	M.C.N	1967		64	•		E	
Speed	Surtees	Barker	1963		168	•		D	
Speed and How to Obtain it	Harwood	Iliffe	1925	4th 1936	156	•		D/E	
Speed from Your Motor Cycle	Motor Cycle	Iliffe	1925	-1947	152	•	•	D	
Speedway. Ride it! The Complete Book of	May	Haynes/Foulis	1976		156	•		E	
Speedway Panorama	Hoare	Haynes/Foulis	1979		167	•		F	
Story of the TT	Davison	TT Special	1947	1948	160	•	•	D	
Story of the Ulster	Davison	TT Special	1949		176	•	•	D	
Taking up Motor Cycle Racing	Bacon	Lodgemark	1964		167	•	•	D	
Thrilling the Million	Stenner	Miles	1934		223	•		C	
Trail Bike Riding. Ride it! The Complete Book of	Melling	Haynes/Foulis	1976		135	•		E	
Triple Crown Plus	Mauger	Pelham	1971	1972	158	•	•	E	
TT — As Geoff Duke Sees It (The)	'Anon'	Castrol				•		D	
TT Races Behind the Scenes	Davison	TT Special	1949		168			D	
TT Races. The	'Anon'	BP	1963		48	•		D	
TT Races 1907-60. History of the	Higgins & Quantrill	BP	1960		175	•		E	
TT Racing	Knight	Speed Sport	1974		90	•		E	
TT Tales	Davison	TT Special	1950		160	•	•	D	
TT. Where to see the	'Anon'	Mobiloil	1954		22	•		D	
TT Thrills									
Tuning for Speed	Irving	Temple Press	1948	many	156	•	•	E	
Ulster Grand Prix (The)	Windrum	Blackstaff	1979		150	•	•	E	
Vintage Years at Brooklands (The)	Bayley	Goose	1968	1972	130	•		C	

The Constant Search

Title	Author	Publisher	1st Ed'n	Later Ed'ns	Pages	Illus	Index	Rate	Text
Wheels to Fortune	Redman		1976		112	•		E	
We Went Racing	Mortimer	E.M.Art	1966		112	•		E	
World Championship Motor Cycle Racing	Woollett	Hamlyn	1980		128	•	•	F	

Section S 3

Motocross, scrambles and trials

Title	Author	Publisher	1st Ed'n	Later Ed'ns	Pages	Illus	Index	Rate	Text
Art of Moto-Cross (The)	Smith & Currie	Cassell	1966	1967	143	•	•	D	
Clean to the Finish	Miller	Main-Smith	1974		72	•		E	
Get Back to Nature — Get Into Trials	Cattone	Fantic Motor	c1980		80	•	•	F	
Greatest of All Trials (The)	Smith	Stevens	1963		88	•	•	D	
How to Ride Observed Trials Just for Fun	Shipman		1973		158	•		E	
How to Select, Ride and Maintain Your Trial Bike	Richmond		1972		160	•		E	
How to Win Motocross	Bailey & Shipman				190	•		E	
Mick Andrews' Book of Trials (The)	Andrews & Beezley	Stephens	1976		224	•		F	
Motocross. The Big Leap	Melling	Hamlyn	1979		156	•	•	F	
Motocross. Ride It! The Complete Book of	Melling	Haynes/Foulis	1975		159	•		E	
Motor Cycle Trials. Ride It! The Complete Book of	Smith	Haynes/Foulis	1975		133	•		E	
Sammy Miller on Trials	Miller	Transport Bookman	1969	1971	112	•		E	
Sammy Miller — The Will to Win	Clew	Haynes/Foulis	1976		165	•		E	
Schoolboy Scrambling	Venables	Oxford Illus	1975	1977/78	92	•		E	
Trials Riding	King	Temple Press	1955	1960	148	•	•	E	

Title	Author	Publisher	1st Ed'n	Later Ed'ns	Pages	Illus	Index	Rate	Text
The Way to Win Motor Cycle Trials	Anon	Miller	1980		132	•		F	

Section S 4

Marque

Title	Author	Publisher	1st Ed'n	Later Ed'ns	Pages	Illus	Index	Rate	Text
AJS. History of a Great Motor Cycle	Grant	Stephens	1969		112	•	•	E	
Always in the Picture (Velocette)	Burgess & Clew	Goose & Haynes/Foulis	1971	1980	253	•	•	D/E	
Bahnstormer. The Story of BMW Motorcycles	Setright	Transport Bookman	1977		190	•		E	
Best of British. Classic Bikes of Yesteryear	Howdle	Stephens	1979		158	•		F	
Best Twin. (The) (Douglas)	Clew	Goose & Haynes/Foulis	1974	1976 1981	224	•	•	D	
BMW Motorcycles Types and Specifications	Haertel								
BMW. The Bavarian Motor Works	Frostick	Dalton Watson	1976		207	•		E	
Bonnie. Development History of the Triumph Bonneville	Nelson	Haynes/Foulis	1979		165	•		F	
BSA Motor Cycles. The Story of	Holliday	Stephens	1978	1979	128	•	•	F	
BSA Twins and Triples	Bacon	Osprey	1980		191	•	App	F	
Built for Speed	Griffith	Temple Press	1962	1973	86	•		D	
Classic Motorcycles 1898-1950 (The)	Louis & Currie	Stephens	1977		128	•		E	
Classic Motorcycles	Willoughby	Hamlyn	1975		176	•		E	
Classic Motorbikes	Puckett & Penny		1979		127	•		F	
Discovering Old Motor Cycles	Crowley	Shire	1973		56	•	•	E	
Don't Trudge It — Rudge It	Reynolds	Haynes/Foulis	1977		175	•	•	E	

The Constant Search

Title	Author	Publisher	1st Ed'n	Later Ed'ns	Pages	Illus	Index	Rate	Text
Douglas Motor Cycle Range 1907-1926	Frost	Frost	c1979		NN	•		E	
Douglas Motor Cycle Range 1927-1939	Frost	Frost	c1979		NN	•		E	
Douglas Mark Series	Frost	Frost	c1978		NN	•		E	
Early Motor Cycles	Page	Post Era	1971		269	•	•	E	
First Post Vintage Scene (The)	Allen	Main-Smith	1976		64	•		E	
First Velocette Scene (The)	Main-Smith	Main-Smith	1977		64	•		E	
First Scott Scene (The)	Shelley	Main-Smith	1977		64	•		E	
First Vincent HRD Scene (The)	Phillips	Main-Smith	1977		64	•		E	
Flyweight Motor Cycles	Perriam	M.C.N	1964		48	•		E	
Giants of Small Heath (The) (BSA)	Ryerson	Haynes/Foulis	1980		190	•	•	F	
Golden Age of the Fours	Hodgdon	Bagnall	1977		164	•		E	
Goldie. The Gold Star BSA	Golland	Haynes/Foulis	1978	1979	79	•	•	F	
Great British Motor Cycles of the Fifties	Currie	Hamlyn	1980		140	•		F	
Harley-Davidson	Hendry	Ballantine	1972		157	•		D	
Historic Motor Cycles	Burgess Wise	Hamlyn	1973		96	•	•	E	
Historic Racing Motor Cycles	Griffith	Temple Press	1963		87	•		E	
Honda Motor Cycles. The Story of	Carrick	Stephens	1976		136	•	•	E	
Illustrated Encyclopedia of Motor Cycles	Tragatsch	Hamlyn	1977		320	•	gloss	E	
Iron Redskin (The)	Sucher	Haynes/Foulis	1977	1978	335	•	•	E	
Kawasaki Motor Cycles. The Story of	Carrick	Stephens	1978		128	•	•	F	
The Keig Collection 1911-1939 3 vols.	Holliday	Main-Smith	1975		104	•	•	F	

150

151

152

153

154

155

156

157

158

The Constant Search

Title	Author	Publisher	1st Ed'n	Later Ed'ns	Pages	Illus	Index	Rate	Text
The Keig Collection 1911-1939 3 vols.	Holliday	Main-Smith	1975		104	•	•	F	
	Holliday	Main-Smith	1975		104	•	•	F	
Lightweight Motor Cycles	Osborne	Temple Press	1951	1955	143	•	•	E	
Matchless	Hartley	Osprey	1981		208	•	•	F	
Modern Motorbikes	Cadell & Spencer	Blandford	1979		153	•		E	
Modern Motor Cycles	Osborne	Pitman	1951		87	•		E	
Morgan Sweeps the Board	Alderson & Rushton	Gentry	1978		249	•	•	E	
Motor Cycle Index	Ball	Autobooks	1964		107			D	
'Motor Cycle' Road Tests	'Anon'	Iliffe	1949	1952	64	•		D	
Motor Cycles and Scooters from 1945	Olyslager	Warne	1976		63	•	•	E	
Motor Cycles, Classics and Thoroughbreds	Patrignani & Colombo	Orbis	1971		64	•		E	
Motor Cycles to 1945	Olyslager	Warne	1975		63	•	•	E	
Motor Cycles in Colour	Thompson	Blandford	1974		191	•		E	
'Motor Cycling' Road Tests	'Anon'	Temple Press	1952		48	•		D	
'Motor Cycling' Sports Road Tests	'Anon'	Temple Press	1959		60	•		D	
My Velocette Days	Moseley	Transport Bookman	1974	1975	120	•		E	
Norton Story (The)	Holliday	Stephens		1976	128	•	App	E	
Norton	Howard	Ballantine	1972		159	•		D	
Norton. The Unapproachable	Holliday	Beaulieu	1979		104	•		F	
Observer's Book of Motor Cycles (The)		Warne	1976		192	•		E	
	Croucher	Warne	1977		192	•	•	E	
	Croucher	Warne	1980		191	•		E	
Pioneer Motor Cycles	Connolly	Main-Smith	1962		52	•		E	
P.C.V — Autobiography of Philip Vincent	Vincent	Vincent	1976		167	•		E	

256

Title	Author	Publisher	1st Ed'n	Later Ed'ns	Pages	Illus	Index	Rate	Text
Road Tests Republished 'The Motor Cycle' Vol.1 1930-1940	Temple Press	Main-Smith	1974		80	•		F	
Vol.2 1955-1960	Temple Press	Main-Smith	1975		80	•		F	
Vol.3 1960-1965	Temple Press	Main-Smith	1975		80	•		F	
Rolls-Royce of Motor Cycles (The)	Clark	Goose	1964		174	•	•	D	
(The) Scott Motorcycle. The Yowling Two Stroke	Clew	Haynes/Foulis	1974		239	•	•	D	
Source Book of Motor Cycles. A	Miller	Ward Lock	1977	1978	128	•	•	E	
Sunbeam Motor Cycle (The)	Champ	Haynes/Foulis	1980		205	•	•	F	
Superbikes of the Seventies	Nutting	Hamlyn	1978	1979	128	•		E	
Suzuki	Clew	Haynes/Foulis	1980		235	•	•	F	
Treasury of Motor Cycles of the World	Clymer	Clymer	ND		238	•		E	
Three Wheeler. The Story of the Morgan	Watts	Morgan Three Wheeler Club	1970		67	•		E	
Triumph Twins and Triples	Bacon	Osprey	1981		192	•		F	
Triumph. It's a	Davies	Haynes/Foulis	1980		237	•		E	
Triumph Motor Cycles — The Story of	Louis & Currie	Stephens	1975		118	•	•	E	
Velocette. A List of Models	Masters	Masters	1974		59	•	•	E	
Velocette 1905-1971	Masters	Transport Bookman	1976		186	•		E	
Velocette. The Story of the	Beresford	TT Special	c1950		136	•		D	
Veteran and Vintage Motor Cycles	Sheldon	Batsford	1961	re-print	208	•	•	D/E	
Villiers 1898-1948	'Anon'	Villiers	1948		50	•		D	
Vincent HRD Gallery	Harper	Vincent							
Vincent. Fifty Years of the Marque	Vincent	Vincent	1977		NN	•		E	
Vincent HRD Story (The)	Harper	Vincent	1975	1979	208	•	•	E	

The Constant Search

Title	Author	Publisher	1st Ed'n	Later Ed'ns	Pages	Illus	Index	Rate	Text
Vintage Motor Cycles Illustrated	Rance	VMCC	1968		45	•		E	
Vintage Years of the Morgan Three Wheeler (The)	Boddy	Grenville	1970		27	•		E	
Vintage Road Test Journals First	Allen	Main-Smith	1973	1979	65	•		F	
Second	Allen	Main-Smith	1974		76	•		F	
Third	Allen	Main-Smith	1975		72	•		F	
Fourth	Allen	Main-Smith	1976		72	•		F	
Fifth	Allen	Main-Smith	1977		72	•		F	
World's Motor Cycles 1894-1963 (The)	Tragatsch	Temple Press	1964		192	•		C	
The World's Motor Cycles. History of the	Hough/Setright	Allen & Unwin		1973	208	•		D	
Yamaha Legend (The)	Macauley								

Section S 5

Sales literature

Section S 6

Service literature

Title	Author	Publisher	1st Ed'n	Later Ed'ns	Pages	Illus	Index	Rate	Text
AJS	Neill	Pearson	1948	1949/52	156	•	•	E	
AJS. The Book of the	Haycraft	Pitman		2nd 1929 10th 1965	182	•	•	C-E	
Ariel	Waller	Pearson	1948	1949	150	•	•	E	
Ariel. The Book of the	Haycraft	Pitman		1935/48	76	•	•	E	

Title	Author	Publisher	1st Ed'n	Later Ed'ns	Pages	Illus	Index	Rate	Text
Ariel Leader and Arrow. The Book of the	Haycraft	Pitman	1964		76	•	•	E	
Auto Cycles and Cycle Motors	'Anon'	Iliffe	1952	1953	140	•	•	E	
Autocycle. How to get the best from your	'Anon'	Iliffe	1949	1950	106	•		E	
BSA 1935-1940	Temple Press	Main-Smith	1974		70	•		F	
BSA	Munro	Pearson	1948	1950/51	94	•	•	E	
BSA The Book of the	Camm	Pitman	1924	many	141	•		C-E	
BSA Bantam. The Book of the	Haycraft	Pitman	1955	1959	122	•	•	E	
250cc BSA. The Book of the	Lupton	Pitman	1963		112	•	•	E	
BSA Twins. The Book of the	Haycraft	Pitman	1960		131	•	•	E	
BSA Sunbeam and Triumph. The Book of the	Thorpe	Pitman	1963	1967	110	•	•	E	
Cyclemotor. The Book of the	Leigh	Pitman	1954		108	•	•	E	
Cyclemotor Manual (The)	'Anon'	Temple Press	1952		107	•	•	E	
Douglas. The Book of the	Heathcote	Pitman	1925	many to 1946	80	•		D/E	
Douglas Vespa. The Book of the	Emmott	Pitman	1957	1958/9	82	•		E	
Francis Barnett	Goddard	Pearson	1957		204	•	•	C	
Gold Star Book (The)	Main-Smith	Main-Smith	1974		138	•		F	
Hints and Tips for Motor Cyclists	'Anon'	Iliffe	1908	many	184	•	•	C-E	
Honda Motor Cycles	Forsdyke	Pearson	1967		192	•	•	E	
Honda. The Book of the	Thorpe	Pitman	1964		104	•	•	E	
Honda Twins. The Book of the	Thorpe	Pitman	1969	1972/3	92	•	•	E	
Improving Two Stroke Engine Performance	Vierdeg	Lodgemark							

The Constant Search

Title	Author	Publisher	1st Ed'n	Later Ed'ns	Pages	Illus	Index	Rate	Text
JAP Engine. The Book of the	Haycraft	Pitman	1939	1942/6	80	•	•	D	
Know Thy Beast	Stevens	Vincent	1972	1977	194	•		E	
Lambretta. Cassell Book of the	'Anon'	Cassell	1953	1959				E	
Lambretta Service and Guide	Lambretta	Lambretta			80	•		E	
Lightweight Autocycles	Mills	Pearson	1957		175	•	•	E	
Lightweight Motorcycles	Osborne	Temple Press	1951	1955	143	•	•	E	
Lightweight Motor Cycle Handbook	Osborne	Temple Press	1951		136	•	•	E	
Matchless	Neill	Pearson	1948		166	•	•	E	
Matchless. The Book of the	Haycraft	Pitman	1950		148	•	•	D	
Matchless Motor Cycles 1939-1955	'Anon'	Temple Press	1958		58	•	•	D	
Modern Auto Cycles	Chadwick	Pitman	1947	1950	72	•	•	E	
Modern Motor Cycle Maintenance	Osborne	Temple Press	1949	1950/7	251	•	•	E	
Modern Motor Cycle Mechanics and Speed Tuning	Nicholson	Nicholson	1942	1945	560	•		E	
Modern Motor Cycles Vol.1	Judge	Caxton	c1933		255	•		C	
Vol.2	Judge	Caxton	c1933		258	•		C	
Vol.3	Judge	Caxton	c1933		263	•	•	C	
Morgan. The Book of the	Walton & Jelley	Pitman		1932	108	•		C	
Morgan 3 Wheeler Handbook. The									
Motorbike Mechanics	Baker	Mirror	1980		127	•		F	
Motor Cycle Care. New Castrol Book of	Clew	Haynes	1975		63	•		E	
Motor Cycle Efficiency	'Anon'	Temple Press	c1920		208	•	•	D	
Motor Cycle Electrical Manual	Tranter	Haynes	1979		128	•	•	F	

Title	Author	Publisher	1st Ed'n	Later Ed'ns	Pages	Illus	Index	Rate	Text
Motor Cycle Engines	'Anon'	Iliffe	1951		64	•		E	
Motorcycle Engineering	Irving	Temple Press		1973	326	•	•	E	
Motor Cycle Mechanic's Yearbook 1980									
Motor Cycles and How to Manage Them	'Anon'	Iliffe	1900	many	346	•		C-E	
Motor Cycle Overhaul	Haycroft	Pitman	1947		115	•	•	E	
Motor Cycle Tuning for Performance	Shipman		1973		174	•		E	
Motor Cycle Manual (The)	Bacon	Newnes Butterworth	1976		180	•	•	E	
Motor Cycle Repair and Upkeep	Molloy	Newnes	1931		675	•	•	C	
Motor Cycles. Maintain Your Own Machine	Bettiol & Willoughby	Chancerel	1976		91	•		E	
Motor Cycling Electrical Manual (The)	Osborne	Temple Press	1953	1960/5	128	•	•	E	
Motor Cycling Manual	'Anon'	Temple Press	1911	many	181	•		D	
Motor Cycling Maintenance Illustrated	Forsdyke	Pearson	1967		80	•	•	E	
Motor Cyclist's Handbook	MacDonald	Pitman	1951		126	•		E	
Motor Cyclist's Workshop	'Anon'	Iliffe	1939 & later		140	•	•	E	
New Imperial. The Book of the	Camm	Pitman		1935	126	•	•	D	
Norton	Franks	Pearson	1948		146	•	•	D	
Norton. The Book of the	Haycraft	Pitman	1935	1942/7	145	•	•	D/E	
Norton Dominator Twins 1955/65. The Book of the	Haycraft	Pitman	1966		120	•	•	E	
Norton Motorcycles 1928-55	'Anon'	Temple Press	1959		58	•	•	D	
Norton Service and Overhaul Manual	Neill	Lodgemark	ND		173	•		E	
Novices Workshop. The	Bradley & Hallows		ND 1950s	1967	112	•	•	E	

The Constant Search

Title	Author	Publisher	1st Ed'n	Later Ed'ns	Pages	Illus	Index	Rate	Text
NSU Quickly. The Book of the	Warring	Pitman	1959	1962/6	112	•	•	E	
P & M. The Book of the	Haycraft	Pitman	1931		139	•		D	
Panther Lightweight Models. The Book of the	Haycraft	Pitman	1937	1939 1948	92	•	•	D	
Panther Heavyweight Models. The Book of the	Haycraft	Pitman	1953		128	•	•	E	
Red Panther. The Book of the	Haycraft	Pitman	1937	1939	83	•		D	
Restoration of Vintage and Thoroughbred Motor Cycles	Clew	Haynes/Foulis	1976	1977 1978	211	•	•	E	
Restoring and Tuning Classic Motor Cycles	Irving	Turnpike	1979		79	•		F	
Rich Mixture	Irving	Vincent	1976	1977	181	•		E	
Royal Enfield	Booker	Pearson	1948	1949	186	•	•	E	
Royal Enfield. The Book of the	Haycraft	Pitman		1935/ 50	167	•	•	D	
Royal Enfield (Crusader singles). The Book of the	Haycraft	Pitman	1966		120	•	•	E	
Rudge. The Book of the	Cade & Anstey	Pitman		1935/8	110	•	•	D	
Rudge Wrinkles	'Anon'	Turntable	1922	rep't 1974	64	•		C-E	
Scooters and Mopeds	Hingston	Iliffe	1958		122	•	•	E	
Sunbeam. The Book of the	Heathcote	Pitman	1933	1951	124	•	•	D-E	
Sunbeam	Munro	Pearson	1954		138	•	•	D	
Sunbeam S7 and S8. The Book of the	Haycraft	Pitman	1954	1955	120	•	•	D	
Suzuki. The Book of the	Thorpe	Pitman	1967		88	•	•	E	
Supercharging Cars and Motorcycles	Brierley	Lodgemark	ND		56	•		E	
Triumph	Masters	Pearson	1949	1950 /1/2	206	•	•	D	
Triumph. The Book of the	Brown	Pitman		1939	130	•	•	D	

Title	Author	Publisher	1st Ed'n	Later Ed'ns	Pages	Illus	Index	Rate	Text
Triumph Twins. The Book of the	Haycraft	Pitman		1939/ 1961	132	•	•	E	
Tracing Motor Cycle Troubles	'Anon'	Temple Press	1911	many	181	•		C-E	
Tracing Troubles: Motor Cycle Faults	'Road Rider'	Iliffe	c1913		NN		•	C	
Two Stroke Carburation and Ignition	Bacon	Lodgemark	ND		48	•		E	
Two Stroke Engine Design and Tuning	Draper	Haynes	1966 /68	1973	127	•	•	E	
Two Stroke Exhaust Systems	Bacon	Lodgemark	c1966		48	•		E	
Two Stroke Motor Cycles	'Anon'	Iliffe	1948		132	•		E	
Two Stroke Ports for Power	Bacon	Lodgemark	ND		52	•		E	
Velocette	Burgess	Pearson	1952		198	•	•	D	
Velocette. All Years of (BMS Service Series)	Hoddinott	Main-Smith	1978		64	•		E	
Velocette. The Book of the	Heathcote	Pitman	1955	1959	116	•	•	D	
Velocette 1925-1952	'Anon'	Temple Press	ND		62	•		F	
Velocette Viper, Venom, Thruxton, 350cc and 500cc singles	Hide	Main-Smith	1978		64	•		F	
Vespa. Second Book of the	Thorpe	Pitman	1964		92	•	•	E	
Vespa. Third Book of the	Thorpe	Pitman	1972		84	•	•	E	
Villiers Engine. The Book of the	Grange	Pitman	1929	many to 1974	97	•	•	C-E	
Villiers Engines. 1935-55	'Anon'	Temple Press	1959		64	•	•	E	
Villiers Engine (The)	Browning	Pearson	1949		140	•	•	D	
Vincent	Richardson	Pearson	1955		215	•	•	D	
Vincent HRD 1947-1955	'Anon'	Temple Press	1960		58	•	•	D	
Workshop Wisdom	'Anon'	Temple Press	1957	1961	81	•	•	E	
Your Autocycle — and How to get the Best From It	'Anon'	Iliffe	1949		106	•	•	E	

Title	Author	Publisher	1st Ed'n	Later Ed'ns	Pages	Illus	Index	Rate	Text

Section S 7

Motorcycling. Novels, fiction and humour

Title	Author	Publisher	1st Ed'n	Later Ed'ns	Pages	Illus	Index	Rate	Text
Dispatch Riders (The)	Westerman	Blackie	ND		288	•		D	
Gawne Crazy	Gawne	TT Special	1952		48	•		D	
Motorcycle Moonshine	Gawne	TT Special			48	•		D	
Motor Scout in Flanders (A)	Gilson	Blackie	c1917		255			D	
Motor Scout	Strang	Hodder & Stoughton	1913		303	•		D	
Racing Wheels	Kenyon	Nelson	1941	1944	228	•		D	

Section S 8

Magazines

Section S 9

Items other than under Sections 1 to 8

Title	Author	Publisher	1st Ed'n	Later Ed'ns	Pages	Illus	Index	Rate	Text
ABC of the Motor Cycle	Jackman	Thompson	1916		222	•		C	
Automobiles and Motor Cycles in the US National Museum	Oliver	Smithsonian	1957		157	•	•	D	
British Motor Cycle Industry. Whatever Happened to the	Hopwood	Haynes/Foulis	1981		315	•	•	F	
Cars and Motor Cycles. 3 volumes	Montagu/Bourdon	New Era	1928	1929	1264	•	•	C	

Title	Author	Publisher	1st Ed'n	Later Ed'ns	Pages	Illus	Index	Rate	Text
Daily Mail Motorcycling Guide	Various	Daily Mail	1951		128	•		E	
	Various	Daily Mail	1952		128	•		E	
	Various	Daily Mail	1953		128	•		E	
	Various	Daily Mail	1954		128	•		E	
	Various	Daily Mail	1955		160	•		E	
	Various	Daily Mail	1956			•		E	
	Various	Daily Mail	1957		104	•		E	
Early Days in the British Motor Cycle Industry	Walford	Industries Association	c1950		74	•		C	
First Military Machine Scene (The)	Allen	Main-Smith	1978		64	•		F	
Further Motor Cycle Reminiscences	'Ixion'	Iliffe	1930s		117	•		D	
Great Motor Cycle Legends	Renstrom	Haessner	1977		128	•		E	
Guinness Book of Motorcycling Facts and Feats	Setright	Guinness	1979		257	•	•	F	
Guinness Guide to Motorcycling	Lacombe	Guinness	1974	1976/7	234	•		E	
How to Organise a Motor Cycle Club	Clymer	Clymer	ND		53	•		E	
Lucky All My Life	Clew	Haynes	1979		176	•	•	E	
Motor Bike	Bygrave & Dowdall	Hamilton	1978		45	•		E	
Motor Cycle Data Book	Williams & Reddihough		1960		207	•		E	
Motor Cycle Cavalcade	Ixion	Iliffe	1950		239	•	•	E	
Motor Cycle Book for Boys	Various	Iliffe	1928		195	•		C	
Motor Cycle News Yearbook 1977-78	Ward	Stephens	1978		138	•		E	
Motor Cycle News Yearbook 1980	Ward	Stephens	1980					E	
Motor Cycle Parade	Holliday	David & Charles	1974		112	•		E	

The Constant Search

Title	Author	Publisher	1st Ed'n	Later Ed'ns	Pages	Illus	Index	Rate	Text
Motor Cycle Pioneers	Partridge	Arco	1977		112	•		E	
Motor Cycle Personalities Past and Present	Sallon	Shell Mex/BP	1957		54	•		D	
Motor Cycle Reminiscences	Ixion	Iliffe	1930		143	•		D	
Motor Cycle Sport	Masters	Pearson	1958		140	•	•	D	
Motor Cycles. History and Development of Part 1	Caunter	HMSO	1955		85	•	•	E	
Part 2	Caunter	HMSO	1958		80	•	•	E	
Motor Cycles — A Technical History	Caunter	HMSO	1970		116	•	•	E	
Motor Cycles, Sidecars and Cyclecars	Page	Hodder & Stoughton	1919		550	•	•	C	
Motorcycling Today	McIntyre	Barker	1963	1964	128	•		D	
'Motor Cycling' Yearbooks	Chamberlain	Temple Press	1951		186	•		D	
	Chamberlain	Temple Press	1952		188	•		D	
	Chamberlain	Temple Press	1953		183	•		D	
	Chamberlain	Temple Press	1954		188	•		D	
	Cook	Temple Press	1955		215	•		D	
	Cook	Temple Press	1956		210	•		D	
	Cook	Temple Press	1957		194	•		D	
'Motor Cycling' Sports Yearbooks	Cook	Temple Press	1958		136	•		D	
	Cook	Temple Press	1959		138	•		D	
	Cook	Temple Press	1960		122	•		D	
	Cook	Temple Press	1961		119	•		D	
Motor Cyclist's Encyclopaedia (The)	Various	Main-Smith	1972		64	•		F	
Motor Cyclist's Handbook	'Phoenix'	Percival Marshall	c1911		264	•		C	

Title	Author	Publisher	1st Ed'n	Later Ed'ns	Pages	Illus	Index	Rate	Text
Motor Cyclist's Handbook	Macdonald	Pitman	1951		126	•		E	
Off Road Motor Cycle Sport	Forsdyke	Hamlyn	1976					E	
On Two Wheels and Four	Brindley	Brindley	1956		240	•		C	
Ransome's Motor Cycling			1908		106	•		C	
White Helmets. (The)	Ladd	Haynes/Foulis	1977		195	•	•	E	
World Motor Cycle Guide	Various	Phoebus	1979		64	•		F	
Yarns of the Speedway	Wingrove & Wilson	Aldine	1930s		144	•		D	

Section T

Cycling — all aspects

Title	Author	Publisher	1st Ed'n	Later Ed'ns	Pages	Illus	Index	Rate	Text
Across France in Wartime	Wray	Dent	1916		181	•		C	
Albanian Back Door	Newman	Jenkins	1936		315	•		D	
Around the World on a Bicycle — San Francisco to Teheran	Stevens	Sampson Low	1887		547	•		B	
Around the World on a Bicycle — Teheran to Yokohama	Stevens	Sampson Low	1888		477	•		B	
Art and Pastime of Cycling (The)	Mecredy & Stoney	Iliffe	1890		238	•		B	
Art of East in Cycling (The)	Hillier	Iliffe & Sturmey	ND		81	•		C	
Awheel to the Arctic Circle	King	Fowler	1940		196	•		E	
Balkans by Bicycle (The)	Hamsher	Witherby	1937		221	•	•	D	
Baltic Roundabout	Newman	Jenkins	1939		283	•	•	D	
Bartleet's Bicycle Book	Bartleet	Burrow	1931		186	•		D	
Blue Danube (The)	Newman	Jenkins	1935		315	•		D	
Bicycle (The)	Spencer	Warne	1870		54	•		B	

Title	Author	Publisher	1st Ed'n	Later Ed'ns	Pages	Illus	Index	Rate	Text
Bicycle for 1874 (The)	Howard	Kent Causton	1874		243		•	B	
Bicycle for 1874 (The)	Howard	Howard	1876		100		•	B	
Bicycle for 1874 (The)	Howard	Bicycle Journal	1877		145		•	B	
Bicycle Repairing	Burr	Spon	1898		215	•	•	B	
Bicycles and Tricycles	Sharp	Longmans	1896		536	•	•	C	
Bicycling for Ladies	Ward	Brentands	1896		187	•		C	
Complete Cyclist (The)	Pemberton, Williams & Sisley	Isthmian	1897		400	•		C	
Complete Cyclist (The)	Moore	Pitman	1935	1962	139	•	•	C-D	
Cycle and Camp	Holding	Ward Lock	1897		232	•		C	
Cycle Racing	Bowden	Temple Press	1958		157	•		E	
Cycle Rides Round London	Harper	Chapman & Hall	1902		288	•		D	
Cycles, Historical Review	Caunter	HMSO	1972		72	•	•	E	
Cycle Building and Repairing	Hasluck	Cassell	1904		160	•	•	C	
Cycles — History and Development of Part 1	Caunter	HMSO	1955		70	•	•	E	
Part 2	Caunter	HMSO	1958		75	•	•	E	
Cycling	Bury, Lacey & Hillier	Longmans Green	1887		459	•	•	B	
Cycling	Griffin	Bell	1890		120	•		B	
Cycling — Its Art and Pastime	Balian	Bishopsgate	1938		132	•		D	
Cycling in the Alps	Freeston	Grant Richards	1900		249	•	•	C	
Cycling for Health	Bowden	Criterion	1913		99			C	
Cycling — Land's End to John O'Groats	Ray	Pelham	1971		154	•	•	E	
Cyclist and the Law	Ruck & Mackrill	Jenkins	1953		170	•	•	E	
Fancy Cycling — Trick Riding for Amateurs	Marks	Sands	1901		115	•		C	

The Constant Search

Title	Author	Publisher	1st Ed'n	Later Ed'ns	Pages	Illus	Index	Rate	Text
Fastest Bicycle Rider in the World (The)	Taylor	Wormley	1928		431	•		D	
Fifty Years of Road Riding	Moxham	Bedford & Reynolds	1936		178	•		D	
Full Tilt	Murphy	Murray	1965	1966	235	•	•	E	
History of the Pickwick Bicycle Club	Crushton	Pickwick Bicycle Club	1905		191	•	•	C	
History of the Pneumatic Tyre (The)	Dunlop	Thom			103	•		C	
Icycles — Christmas Annual	Hillier & Etherington	Etherington	1908		224	•		C	
'Indispensable' Bicyclist's Handbook and Guide to Bicycling (The)	Sturney	Judd	1879		311	•	•	B	
I Saw Spain	Newman	Jenkins	1937		312	•	•	D	
Life and Times of Charley Barden (The)	Swann	Wunlap	1965		125	•		E	
London Cyclist Battalion (The)	Forster	Groom	1932		292	•	•	D	
Modern Cycles	Taylor	Crosby Lockwood	1897		340	•	•	C	
Modern Velocipede (The)	Maddick		1969		60		•	E	
Nauticus on His Hobby Horse	Ridgeway		1880		88			B	
Newnes Every Cyclist's Handbook	Camm	Newnes	1936		199	•	•	D	
Pedalling Poland	Newman	Jenkins	1935		306	•	•	D	
Potterer's Club (The)	Hillier	Gale & Polden			230	•		C	
Raleigh Cycle. Story of the	Bowden	Allen	1975		216	•	•	E	
Ride to Russia	Newman	Jenkins	1938		332	•	•	D	
Road Fortune	Mackenzie	Macmillan	1935		319	•		D	
Round the World on a Cycle	Thorenfeldt	Selwyn & Blount	1926		287	•	•	C	
Romance of the Cyclist's Touring Club	Lightwood	CTC	1928		286	•	•	D	
Round the World on a Wheel	Fraser	Methuen	1899	1904/5 07/16	532	•		C	

Title	Author	Publisher	1st Ed'n	Later Ed'ns	Pages	Illus	Index	Rate	Text
Savoy! Corsica! Tunis!	Newman	Jenkins	1940		282	•	•	D	
Ten Thousand Miles on a Bicycle	Kron	Kron	1887		799	•		B	
Trial by Tandem	McCulloch	Allen & Unwin	1951		236	•		E	
Wheel Within a Wheel (A)		Hutchinson	1885		75	•		B	
Wheels Within Wheels	Williamson	Bles	1966		160	•	•	E	

List of illustrations

The Constant Search

Captions to colour plate illustrations (classification coding in brackets)

Rolls-Royce: The Elegance Continues (G2)
Rolls-Royce and the Great Victory (G2)
Rover Memories (G2)
The Boy's Book of the Motor-Car (I1)
The Maintenance and Driving of Vintage Cars (E7)
The Restoration of Vintage and Thoroughbred Cars (E7)
Rolls of Rolls-Royce (F)
The Cord Front Drive (G2)

Colour plate 4
From Steamcarts to Minicars (G1)
Silver Ghosts and Silver Dawn (F)
A History of the London Taxicab (G1)
Lanchester Motor Cars (G2)
Morgan Sweeps the Board (G2)
The Austin 1905-1952 (G2)
Wheels within Wheels (T)
The Black Mercedes (I2)
Motor-Cars and their Story (E3)
Montlhery (D10)
British Sports Cars (E2)
The Motor Boys in Mexico (I2)
A Motor Car Divorce (I2)
The Man Who Drove the Car (I2)
How it Works (E10)
Around the World on a Bicycle (T)

Colour plate 5
Nuvolari (F)
Juan Manuel Fangio (F)
Out on a Wing (F)
My Life and my Cars (F)
The British Grand Prix 1926-1976 (D1)
The Vintage Sports Car Club (G3)
Automobile Design: Great Designers and their Work (E7)
German Grand Prix Racing Cars (D1)
Alfa Romeo: A History (G2)
Bugatti (G2)
Ferrari (G2)
The Chain-Drive Frazer Nash (G2)
Three Pointed Star (G2)
The Story of the MG Sports Car (G2)
Lost Causes of Motoring: Europe (G1)
The Mercedes Benz Story (G2)

Colour plate 6
Through the Alps to the Appenines (B)
The Passes of the Pyrenees (C)
Along the Rivieras of France and Italy (C)
The Book of the Motor Car (E3)
Three Thousand Miles in a Motor Car (B)
Three Men in a Motor Car (B)
Italian Highways and Byways from a Motor Car (B)
Canyons, Cans and Caravans (B)
Three Men in a Motor Car (B)
A Catechism of the Motor Car (A)
Round France in a Motor (B)
Motoring (E3)
At the Wheel Ashore and Afloat (F)
Full Throttle (D5)
The Enzo Ferrari Memoirs (F)
Motor Racing Memories 1903-21 (D5)

Colour plate 7
Through Persia in a Motor Car (B)
En Route (B)
Round the World in a Motor-Car (B)
Morocco from a Motor (B)
Motoring Abroad (B)
The Motor Routes of England (B)
A Motor Flight Through Algeria and Tunisia (B)
Poor Me: The Diary of a Motor Car (B)
Europe from a Motor Car (B)
The Automobilist Abroad (B)
Round the World in a Baby Austin (B)
The South-Bound Car (B)
Through Western Canada in a Caravan (B)
Drive Round the World (B)
With Your Car in the South of France (B)
Across Africa in a Lorry (B)

Colour plate 8
The Ferrari (G2)
The 1930 London Motor Show (E7)
The Wonder Book of Motors (I1)
The Rolls-Royce 40-50hp (G2)
The Grand Prix Car 1954/66 (D1)
The Coachbuilt Packard (G2)
The Rolls and Royce Story (G2)
The Vintage Years at Brooklands (S2)

Alphabetical index of titles

The Constant Search

The Constant Search

The Constant Search

The Constant Search

The Constant Search

The Constant Search

The Constant Search